Table of Contents

30 YEARS OF INDEPENDENCE IN AFRICA:

the lost decades?

Julia Gallagher

Edited by Peter Anyang' Nyong'o
African Association of Political Science

Citation: African Association of Political Science (AAPS). 1992.
30 Years of Independence in Africa: the Lost Decades?

ISBN: 9966-831-10-X

Published by
ACADEMY SCIENCE PUBLISHERS
P.O. Box 14798
Nairobi, Kenya

Acknowledgements

The African Association of Political Science is grateful to the Swedish Agency for Research and Economic Cooperation with Developing Countries (SAREC), the Ford Foundation, and the McArthur Foundation for the support given to the conference on "Thirty Years of Independence in Africa: Results and Prospects" which was held from May 23 to 25, 1991 in Windhoek, Namibia. The Namibian Government and the Southern Africa Political Economy Series (SAPES) deserve special mention for the hospitality provided for the conference participants and the tremendous work they did to make the conference a success. We would also like to thank Mrs. Winnie Okura and Miss Yasmina Nantalo for inputting all the conference papers, typesetting and indexing and Miss Margaret Anaminyi for proofreading and designing this book.

Preface

The most important aspect of the current debate on Africa's future is the deep awareness on the part of most African scholars that the involvement of the people in the making of their history is important. The political systems that have been imposed on the African people since independence have, by and large, been oppressive and exploitative. The more these systems have been unpopular with the people the more they have used ruthless methods and brute force to keep the people down. The dawn of the second liberation, discussed at length in the essays in this book, attempt to account for the ways in which democracy could be meaningful to the African people. This means that the liberation must embrace problems of underdevelopment and provide opportunities for greater social progress.

As Abdulrahman Babu notes, the struggle for independence (*uhuru*) was not without its shortcomings. The major shortcoming was that the institutions of democracy did not have time to ground themselves in society. There was too much faith in the state taking up the mission of democratic social transformation without necessarily being subjected to democratic transformation itself. As problems of social transformation started to confound the state, non-democratic methods were invoked to deal with the people, and the struggle for freedom was thereby relegated to the background.

If there is any single institution in civil society which has tried to champion the cause of freedom and justice in Africa it is the church. Yet the church has not always acted in unison. There are instances where certain churches and clergymen have identified with the oppressor; there are other instances where they have systematically come to the side of the oppressed.

Bishop Henry Okullu discusses the role of the church in political struggles in East Africa. This is a concise historical account of the relationships between church and state in East Africa, underscoring the need to have a strong institution in civil society which can keep state power in check, thereby ensuring that the people are capable of developing the political agenda which shape processes of social transformation.

It is because development has for long been seen as *the responsibility of the state* that popular initiatives have been thwarted, much to the detriment of Africa's future. This ideology of development needs to be revamped. Development, seen in terms of positive transformation in people's lives at the social, intellectual and moral levels is important. Samir Amin examines various hypotheses that underlie the discussion of development in Africa and comes to the conclusion that little is known about what Africa has achieved in terms of development because the wrong questions are often asked. In order to begin asking the right questions, the ideological cobwebs in our discourses must be cleared first.

It is important to rise to the level of serious discourse on Africa's future notwithstanding what Bourenane identifies as *Afro-Pessimism* which seems to be dominating discussions on Africa. In this respect, Bourenane is probably right: Africa has certain achievements of the post-independence era worth celebrating. In the area of human resources development, some progress has been made. In terms of inter-regional trade a lot goes on which is not quantified or accounted for. Thus, while problems must be identified and dealt with, they should not engulf Africans into a mood of giving up—of saying everything African is always in the negative. No change comes about as a result of giving up; no revolution is made by pessimistic individuals.

Southern Africa provides a case for both hope and despair. Yet Ibbo Mandaza points out that the struggle for democracy, while facing twists and turns at every corner, will not necessarily be put back. The South African state has been riddled with contradictions regarding what path to follow towards democratizing society. The army has tried to sabotage the process by initiating state terrorism and civil disorder. A substantial section of the white elite, using their power base in the Nationalist Party, has tried to coopt the democratic process. The African National Congress, having waged the struggle for so many years underground, may find it difficult to operate as an open political party after being legalized by the state.

Matters are likely to become worse for South Africa as the economic situation deteriorates. Indeed, as Thandika Mkandawire notes, African governments have made worse their economic predicament by being in debt at the wrong time. Recent cases of borrowing in the international financial markets have been to deal with balance of payments crises and not to invest in productive enterprises which could boost the development potential of the continent. Jumanne Wagao gives a catalogue of the various aspects of the crisis, and Ben Turok makes a case for a *democratic coalition against Structural Adjustment Programmes (SAP)*.

If much has to be achieved through Africa's foreign trade, and if this trade has to be linked with domestic programmes of development, then the Lomé Conventions need to be better negotiated. This is the major thrust of Nabudere's essay. In essence, the African peasant has been the sufferer in a long chain of unequal exchange. Founou Tchuigoua gives a detailed analysis of this debate with regard to agriculture and industrialization in Africa. The balance sheet is still more unanswered questions. The more tragic answer comes when underdevelopment dissolves itself into irresolvable political crises and the disintegration of the political community as has happened in Somalia. Eglal Raafat's essay on the Somalia crisis deserves the attention of anybody interested in discussing the lost decades of Africa's independence.

P. Anyang' Nyong'o   *Nairobi, April 1992.*

Chapter 1

THE ONE-PARTY STATE
AND ITS APOLOGISTS:
THE DEMOCRATIC ALTERNATIVE

P. Anyang' Nyong'o

Introduction

The African Association of Political Science is holding this conference at a very critical time. Not only does our conference mark the first anniversary of Namibia's independence. It is also held at a time when important changes are taking place in the Republic of South Africa thanks to many years of unrelenting struggle for liberation by the South African people. Elsewhere in Africa, struggles for a second independence are beginning to bear fruit. We therefore come here not only to celebrate our victories, but also to pause and take stock of the past, present and future of Africa. To build on the past and challenge the future, we must not be pessimistic; at the same time, we must not wallow in euphoria and claim non existent victories.

Nonetheless, there is good news from Africa. The good news is that people are awakening from years of slumber under authoritarian rule to take their future into their own hands; to make their own history as it were. The bad news is that certain regimes which have enjoyed absolute power over "terrorized natives" are reluctant to let go. They are doing all they can to turn back the clock of history. But, as Jaramogi Oginga Odinga, the interim chairman of the emerging opposition National Democratic Party (NDP) said recently regarding the Kenyan situation: "the clock cannot be turned backwards; democratic changes will be home grown."

A Look Back Into History

The advocates of the single-party system in Africa argue that traditional African societies were always akin to the single party system. Contrary to his self-critical statement of 1990, Mwalimu Julius Nyerere, (judging from some statements made at the Jomo Kenyatta International Airport recently), still remains an adamant advocate of this view. While it is true that political parties, *as such*, did not exist in so-called traditional African societies, it also follows *logically* that the concept *political party* cannot be used in analyzing politics in pre-capitalist African societies. People who justify the one-party system on the basis of our cultural heritage have, therefore, been essentially involved in *false* analogies.

With the colonization of African societies, several changes occurred in their structures and social dynamics'. One of these changes involved the introduction of production for the market, superintended by a modern state complete with all its complex institutions of power and authority, and its demands on society to produce the surplus necessary for maintaining its administrative and ideological superstructures.

Obviously, in the case of Africa, there was general *resistance* to the establishment of state structures which engaged in the *political oppression and economic exploitation* of the African peoples. This resistance led to the modification of colonial rule over time, and eventually elements were found in the African societies who supported, and were active agents of, colonial rule. These were elements which were beneficiaries of this rule, and who, of necessity, became its support cushions.

Africans were no longer the culturally homogeneous people ruled by benevolent chiefs who discussed with the elders under a tree for hours and hours until they agreed. Africans were divided into multiple social groups and categories with different interests and different attitudes towards the colonial state. This is why the struggle for independence became so difficult; Africans did not have a united front against the colonial regime. Political parties had to be organized to mobilize the people and develop a strong enough constituency for the independence platform. These political parties represented diverse interests in society, and it is only on one issue that they seemed to agree: getting rid of colonial rule.

It was only *after* independence that the nationalists, *now enjoying state power*, started to convince the people that the single party system would be in their interest. To be brief, these were the arguments advanced to support the single party project:

- the single party would promote *national unity;*
- people's efforts would be directed towards *nation building* and not wasted on politics;
- since the people were generally agreed that the government was to engage itself in *development,* party politics was not necessary;
- whatever differences would emerge, these could be freely discussed under the single party regime as *democracy and human rights would be practised.*

What the Record Shows

The record, however, shows that single party regimes, including Nyerere's in Tanzania, generally failed on all *four* counts. Countries where single parties reigned supreme for most of the post-independence period cannot claim any more *national unity* than in conditions where multi parties have existed. Botswana, a multi-party state since independence and as ethnically homogeneous as Somalia, is a much more prosperous and united nation to-day than Somalia which has degenerated into clan wars due to 20 years of misrule under Siad Barre's single party dictatorship. In terms of *development,* Nyerere's Tanzania performed very poorly, not so much because of the one-party system *per se,* but more because of the rigid ideologies and text book "socialisms" to which single parties in Africa tended to adhere.

No one-party regime in Africa can boast of democratic practice nor of a good record on human rights. Sekou Toure's Guinea had its own Gulag Archipelagos; Mobutu's Zaire excelled in repression as a policy in maintaining a kleptocratic regime in power; Banda's Malawi has been the best run police state in Africa. The list can continue, and the records of single-party regimes will grow worse and worse no matter where we turn in Africa.

The Changes Occurring

Thus the political changes that the African people have been asking for are based on their concrete experiences: years of hopes that were never realized, aspirations that were frustrated, efforts that were misdirected, investments that never paid back. And all this because the African people trusted their governments too much, made them bite what they could not chew, entrusted them with public resources that were not only squandered for personal gain, but—more tragically—left to be chewed by the mice and gnawed by the ants from the anthills of the savannah, through the thickets of the tropical rain forests of the Congo and up the rolling dunes of the Sahara desert.

Democracy is not about what governments do, it is about what the people do to make their governments accomplish people-oriented activities. The people must first of all have power to make their governments do what they want before they can expect these governments to rule democratically. In other words, democracy is not given by the government to the people is possessed by the people in their productive activities, political organizations and ideological orientations before the governments can be compelled to rule democratically because they are people-based, because their powers are derived from popular consent.

In Cameroon, for example, the people forced the Paul Biya regime to accept multi-party politics. But once Paul Biya did this, he started erecting obstacles to the democratization process by refusing the people the chance to discuss what these parties would do to improve life in society, what the new constitution should look like, and what powers should be given to the state in governing society. The people have now gone to the streets to force Biya to recognize their demands, including telling him to quit the presidency. They are succeeding.

The African people are saying that *governments are there to serve them; the people are not there to serve governments.* This is the basic democratic demand that most single-party advocates do not understand. Democratic theory, from ancient Greece to the famous Convention in Philadelphia in 1776, has always been about empowering people to govern themselves. The state, in democratic theory—contrary to what Hegel believed—is always viewed with suspicion by the people. People must have the right to come together and discuss their affairs freely: they must then communicate their ideas to discussion forums involving other organized groups seeking to influence state action. The state must then listen to them and implement their ideas, not breathe down their throats what, from the point of view of the governors, should be taken as non-debatable public policy.

That is what democracy is all about. To be governed and yet to control our governors, as George B. Shaw once put it. To be governed only on condition that those who govern derive their power to do so on a daily plebiscite, a daily empowerment of the state by the people to carry out certain public duties.

Perhaps it is because of this cardinal idea of a daily plebiscite that democratic regimes have such complex systems of laws for accountability and transparency in the performance of public duties. African post-independence regimes, almost systematically, sought to dismantle these complex systems in preference to the rule by one party, and subsequently by one man. Decisions as important as the national budget, and as insignificant as who commands the police post down the road, are almost always made by a small coterie of party officials or a cabal of sycophants who are the constant companions of the head of state.

The corruption in one-party regimes in Africa shows that the African people have been governed but they have not been able to control their governors. The single-party system does not allow effective ways of keeping governments accountable to the people. These governments do not hear the voice of the people since their only channel of communication is *from the state to the people and not the other way around.* This is usually done by state monopoly of communication systems such as state radio and television stations, state newspapers, or newspapers belonging to the ruling party. Where independent newspapers exist, they are quite often subjected to tremendous self-censorship to keep from offending the powers that be by publishing dissenting views.

Monolithism in political organization logically leads to monolithism in ideas, and hence lack of any critical evaluation of public policy.

The new mood in Africa is that this monolithism must be broken. Pluralism must be encouraged in the world of generating ideas as well as in the realm of political organization. Thus while existing one-party regimes are busy blaming advocates of democracy for importing *foreign ideologies* into the continent in the attempts to solve current problems, the latter are preoccupied with explaining their positions to the people at home and abroad regarding the need for far reaching national democratic revolutions. The struggle for democracy is thus *home grown* from the point of view of its advocates, and *foreign imposed* from the point of view of the defenders of the single-party regime.

That is as it should be, for politics is always about contradictory perspectives in public policy; perspectives representing conflicting interests in social relations. The multi-party advocates are looking for qualitative changes that will lead to truly representative and account-able governments. The oligarches in the single-party regimes are looking into ways and means of maintaining their privileges by ra-tionalizing one-party authoritarianism even in the face of its popular rejection.

International Responses

The international environment, ever since the fall of the Berlin wall, has responded to popular pressures for democracy in Africa in several ways. The most reactionary response was that of a group of British Members of Parliament visiting Kenya in early 1990 who concluded that the one-party system is still the best thing for Africa. For them , it was important that people be content with any government they have. In Kenya they had not seen any demonstrations, any tanks on the streets, any soldiers wielding bayonets at the airport. Conclusion: the Kenyan government is a good one and the people are content with what is going on.

As ridiculous as it seems from the point of view of sane political assessment and a social scientist's analysis, this is perhaps typical of many views of Westerners who think that Africans are basically backward and cannot be judged on the basis of any universal matrix. From our point of view, however, human rights are universal; to be ruled by a democratic system is enshrined in the U.N. Charter and the Universal Declaration on Human Rights. All beings, as it were, are born equal and they are endowed by their Creator to enjoy all the basic rights that pertain to them *qua* human beings and not as people of this or that colour, this or that continent, this or that sex, this or that nationality or this or that region.

The second perspective is that of those who think that what goes on in Africa is not important; in any case, if there is a cry for democracy now it is only because changes are occurring in Eastern Europe and the Soviet Union. Thus Africa simply reacts. African people rarely initiate political changes of their own.

The existing repressive regimes in Africa prefer this analysis because it supports their view that changes are being imposed on them from outside. The African people, however, know that there has never been any time since independence when there was no pressure for democracy from below.

In an article entitled *"When Change is Delayed"*, published in Kenya's *Daily Nation* (11 May, 1991), Jonathan Derrick, discussing democratization processes in Cameroon, recently argued that the apparent docility of the Cameroonians under one-party rule was merely skin-deep:

A well educated and politically alert people, they did not accept one-party willingly.

That can be said, as we ourselves observed in many African countries in our book, *Popular Struggles for Democracy in Africa* (London: Zed Books, 1987), of the people of Congo, Zaire, Kenya, Swaziland, Cote d'Ivoire and Mali. The struggle for democracy has been there since independence; the only difference now is that the world conjuncture has changed thus favouring the struggle of the people against the repressive states in Africa. The people must seize this opportunity and accelerate the making of their own history by democratizing their societies to-day and not to-morrow.

The third perspective has been of those who insist on *democracy now*. Interestingly enough, this call has come from diverse quarters: donor agencies, social democrats, conservatives, church groups, popular organizations and international banking institutions. Attempts by certain sectors in Africa to read a *conspiracy theory* in all this has failed since these forces do not seem to have any single common denominator except that they think democracy is good for accountability and what is generally called *good governance*.

This, from the point of view of the popular forces in Africa, is a very good situation. If there is any one thing that has retarded development in Africa during the last thirty years it is *nothing but bad, irresponsible, corrupt and unimaginative government of left, right, military and civilian types*. As Hamlet told Orphelia in Shakespeare's play *Hamlet*, one feels like telling these governments:

"get thee to a nunnery and stop breeding fools into the world."

Only this time we shall tell them:

"get thee to the democratic ballot box, and stop pretending you are governing by the people's mandate."

Progressive Demands

The position of several progressive democratic forces in Africa is that there is no point giving foreign aid and development assistance to governments which are basically corrupt and which have shown very little ability to use public resources for the public good. If it is well known that Presidents divert public funds to swell their bank accounts abroad, what sense is there of giving presidential authoritarian regimes more funds, in the name of *development assistance*, only to transfer these

funds to their bank accounts abroad? Does the West want to continue
to make Africa indebted in this manner?

By its very nature, development assistance should assist develop the
people. The people are asking to be assisted in *participating in making
their own history*. This was the essence of the *African Charter for Popular
Participation in Development* adopted at the international conference on
Popular Participation in the Recovery and Development Process in Africa, in
Arusha, Tanzania, in February 1990. The conference theme was "Putting
the People First."

If the African people are to be put first, and these same people are
crying aloud for democratic government before anything else, why are
certain people in the West listening more to governments than to the
people? The laws of natural justice say that one should not be a judge
in his/her own case. It is interesting that the World Bank, for example,
has not found it fit to call an international assembly of the representatives of the African people to ask them what they think about debt, loans
to their own so-called governments, special drawing rights, etc. When
are the doubting Thomases in the West going to put the African people
first?

Those who want to put the people first must condition aid and
development assistance to democracy and the observation of human
rights in Africa. This is a non-negotiable condition as far as the African
people are concerned. If there is ever to be a New International Economic
and Political Order, it will be an order where the democratization of
global decision-making is complete by including the people in the
periphery at the global centres of decision-making, not through their
governments, but through truly representative institutions. No system
of world government has as yet been thought about which caters for this
urgent democratic goal. The United Nations is far from being satisfactory.

Postscript

This paper was originally read at the Pan-African Conference on
"Thirty Years of Independence in Africa: Results and Prospects"
(Windhoek, 23 May 1991) under the title "The African Awakening" as
my keynote address as the Secretary General of AAPS. I was not
comfortable with the title at all; both Abdulrahman Mohammed Babu
and Ibbo Mandaza asked me, after my keynote address, to think of a
much more appropriate title. I hope the present title expresses more
cogently what is contained in the address.

r

─────────────────────────────Chapter 2

THE STRUGGLE FOR POST-UHURU AFRICA

A.M. Babu

Every political activist in Africa understands the need to study Ghana's struggle for liberation and its political evolution. Ghana's importance to African political practice does not stem from the fact that in 1957 it was the first country in tropical Africa to become independent. The event did, of course, usher in the era of "uhuru" throughout Africa. However, its principal significance derives from Kwame Nkrumah's introducing the theory and practice of mass movements to the African political struggle. Until then, politics was the preserve of the educated elites: lawyers, civil servants, journalists, progressive school teachers, and disgruntled intellectuals. Their politics was limited to demands for equality with the colonialists, better working conditions and privileges for senior civil servants, and for the end of racial discrimination. The bolder ones occasionally would dare to go as far as to mumble inaudibly about the need for "internal self-government".

It was not until Nkrumah parted company with the Danquas and their ilk that Ghana really became "political" with Nkrumah spearheading the formation of a militant political movement with one principal and concrete political demand: self-government now. Nkrumah did not appeal to the British government to grant them their demand, but he made the masses aware of the need to govern themselves. He relied primarily, almost exclusively, on the strength and determination of the Ghanaian people to bring about the desired goal through mass mobilisation and organisation. The people in turn responded to his trust and confidence in them by giving him their whole-hearted support.

In contrast to the "moderates", Nkrumah was castigated as an extremist and his demands were dismissed as "far fetched" and unrealistic. The moderates called for a pragmatic approach, for a reasonable progress, and for a step-by-step evolution to self-government. They did not have self-confidence or confidence in the people. They were in fact so scared of the masses that they attempted to ridicule them. They dubbed Nkrumah's supporters "veranda boys", that is, unemployed lumpens who did not have a decent roof over their heads. They distanced themselves from Nkrumah and his movement, the Convention People's Party (CPP). The colonialists applauded the moderates, whom they described as rational people with whom they "could do business". However, Nkrumah eventually won, the moderates lost, and the rest is history.

During all this double-barrelled struggle, i.e. between the people and the colonialists, on the one hand, and between the so-called extremists and moderates, on the other, the rest of colonised Africa, particularly the British colonies, were watching with keen interest. When victory was achieved in Ghana, every progressive political leader in Africa became an "Nkrumaist". They dressed like Nkrumah, they talked like him, but above all, they employed his method of struggle: reliance on the masses. "Nkrumaism" in Africa became synonymous with a "National Democratic Revolution".

Less than three years after the independence victory in Ghana, British colonialists admitted that the "winds of change" were blowing across Africa and that they would have to surrender political power to the people. In the seven years, between 1957 and 1964, the mass enthusiasm for independence ignited by Nkrumah's method was so great that it spelled the beginning of the end of direct colonialism, not only in Africa but in most of the rest of the colonised world.

Mass Enthusiasm for Production: First Precondition

There is a most important and positive political lesson to be grasped from the Ghanaian experience. A firm and unshakeable reliance on the masses can usher in a mighty and unstoppable historical epoch of earth-shaking significance. Once the masses are aroused to action, the solidarity which necessarily accompanies it propels the oppressed to take the initiative in all fields and begin to act rather than simply to react to others' initiatives. Solidarity, moreover, creates a revolutionary condition for the masses to provide their own leadership for a decisive social change. This process is what Marx called "the formation of a revolutionary mass".

The second, equally important lesson to be grasped, if negatively in the case of the Ghana experience, is that, for the national democratic revolution to be carried to a higher stage, it is essential not only to arouse but also to sustain mass enthusiasm for production throughout the period of the transition from one epoch to the next. This enthusiasm can not be sustained by unfulfilled promises of a rosy future, but only by people experiencing constant improvement in their living conditions, materially, socially and culturally. Thus, to sustain mass enthusiasm for production, an essential priority must be to develop a capacity for the creation and steady expansion of social wealth. In other words, at this stage the most urgent and principal task is to create favourable conditions for the development of the productive forces. Unfortunately for Ghanaians, and to a large extent for Africa, Nkrumah did not create such conditions. Either Nkrumah failed to appreciate the critical role of the development of the productive forces in the revolutionary process or he was unclear about what priorities were essential to the process, given Africa's unique conditions. The penalty for this shortcoming is so grave that both Ghanaians and most of the rest of Africa are paying for it to this day. This omission, moreover, has also helped to nourish and sustain a most vile neo-colonialism at our expense. Therefore, it is to this aspect of the missed opportunity for what could have been a most profound revolutionary experience in Africa that we must now turn our attention, and try to raise as well as answer questions that arise as we proceed with our investigation.

Ghana's anti-colonial revolution was essentially a national democratic one, deriving its support from, and therefore working for the benefit of, the masses. Its nationalism was the nationalism of the oppressed, different from and in conflict with the nationalism of the oppressor, the colonialists. The former is under the leadership of the masses themselves, while the latter is led by, and serves the interests of, the national bourgeoisie. The road which creates social wealth in the former must necessarily be diametrically opposite to that of the latter. The economic viability and the raison d'etre of the colonialists and the national bourgeoisie depends on the exploitation of the colonial people, first in the form of the "primitive accumulation of capital" and then through a world-wide plunder masquerading under the guise of the "world market" or "world trade". That of the masses, on the other hand, can only derive from the diligent labour of its own people. Its viability can only be assured by scientific planning of the national economy based on a careful deployment of the country's socially necessary labour and on an efficient allocation and utilisation of other resources. Any such planning to be effective must begin by analysing the existing concrete economic situation and the structure on which it is based. For instance, in all African countries, imperialist domination has subjected the population to absolute poverty and left the economy in utter shambles, characterised by lopsidedness and extreme backwardness. Consequently the first step towards reconstruction of the national economy must begin by answering the critical question: How do we destroy the economic base established by imperialism in our countries and set in motion the process of transforming the base into one that can lead to the development of an independent national economy?

Destroy the Economy Base of Colonialism: Second Prerequisite

Inevitably, once the question is so posed it becomes clear that an entirely new outlook is essential, one which recognises the need for a complete break with imperialism and its economic hegemony, as a precondition for a viable and self-sustaining development. In other words, the new situation demands that to bring about essential transformation, the national democratic revolution must be superseded. As a vehicle which brought about national independence, it soon outlives its usefulness and it must then give way to a higher form necessitated by the needs of the new situation. In other words, the new situation demands a new type of political and economic approach: the politics and economics of the new democracy. This is what Nkrumah failed to do. The rest of Africa followed Ghana's path, which we now realise has led us down a blind alley.

Lacking any coherent and relevant policy, having firmly remained tied to the old and now obsolete form of "national democratic revolution", national leaders soon began to "grope in the dark", as President Nyerere put it at the time. The imperialists immediately saw the opportunity to take advantage of a confused situation. They immediately stepped in with the support of the US to fill the vacuum "before the Russians took over". They came in to "rescue" their ex-colonies from utter chaos and bringing with them the influence and funds of the World Bank and IMF. Both organizations then put our countries firmly on the track to neo-colonialism and to a more ruthless form of exploitation.

There is no use repeating the details of this exploitation. The worsening poverty of the masses, the humiliations inflicted on our national sovereignty by the IMF and the World Bank, the constant street riots resulting from their "conditionality", the corruption and the lack of democracy that has resulted directly from the need to "contain" the masses, all became part of our daily experiences. What we need to know is: what can we do about the situation? How do we disentangle ourselves from the clutches of neo-colonialism? This is the question to which we must now turn.

The 1980s have seen a massive onslaught on the ideology of socialism both in the advanced capitalist and socialist countries, as well as in the neo-colonies. Ever since the advent of Reagan in the US and of Thatcherism in England, with their declaration of war against socialism, socialists everywhere have been put on the defensive. This era has officially been characterized as the "end of socialism" and the "end of ideology", while conservative theoreticians and writers are daily bombarding us with their advocacy of the "ideology of the market". In the neo-colonies, which have been reduced into dustbins of Western ideological trash, advocates of the "new right" dominate our educational institutions. They are propped up by their foreign backers to take advantage of the confused situation arising from bad politics and muddled economics. Both were initiated by none other than the World Bank and IMF themselves. Thus, in the absence of any coherent and relevant theoretical counter-offensive from the camp of the oppressed, our countries have been turned into fertile fields for reactionary thinking.

This is particularly so in countries which have described their neo-colonial policies as "socialist". In these countries the effects of new-colonial exploitation, compounded by the resultant inefficiency and corruption, have been felt more severely by the people. As a result, the idea of socialism is here inevitably associated with hardship and poverty. It is here also where local and foreign exploiters point their fingers to expose the alleged "failure of socialism". They shamelessly propagate their favourable themes of the benefits derived from the "invisible hand" of the free market, although millions of the oppressed suffer daily and hourly from the vagaries of the world market which is not free at all. The well-meaning leaders of these countries whose "socialism" was mistakenly based on subjective beliefs which equate socialism with charity, are utterly bewildered at seeing their policies proven unworkable, after squandering billions of borrowed dollars on useless projects for which they have nothing to show on the ground. Their only argument in their defence is to plead for more time for their policies to "bear fruit". But the future is borne out of the present, and

if the present which people experience in their daily existence is to be the
mother of that unknown future, then the people are not attracted by it.

Is There an End to Socialism and Its Ideology?

But is socialism outdated and irrelevant? Neither Gorbachev and Deng
Xsiaoping, the great critics of socialism in the Soviet Union and China,
who frankly admit its shortcomings and from whom Western ideologues
base their attacks on Socialism, do not think socialism is outdated or
irrelevant. Even right-wing counter-revolutionaries inside the socialist
countries who have experienced life under a planned economy do not
believe this, although they may have serious criticisms concerning the
violation of human rights and the non-availability of some consumer
goods. In fact, what the socialist leaders say is simply that there is a need
to allow a limited use of the "law of value" (i.e. market mechanism) in
their planned economies to correct some imbalances which would then
accelerate socialist development. This is not a contradiction at all, as
alleged by the anti-socialist forces. It is rather an important socialist
strategy for developing the needed productive forces as quickly as
possible. Only the enemies of socialism insist on saying that socialism
is "irrelevant". However, they have been saying the same thing since
the beginning of scientific socialism in the last Century, and therefore
it is not a new attempt at distorting reality.

Economic planning, being scientific, is essentially a process of trial
and error, but since it involves the livelihood of millions of people, the
duty of socialist leaders is to try and reduce errors to an absolute
minimum. That is why in the drawing up of a national economic plan
and in its implementation, the word caution should be imprinted in the
socialist planner's mind. Taking a cautious approach and resisting
adventurist and hasty decisions in implementation are two prerequisites essential to ensuring the lasting success of a planned economy.

Here I would like to reiterate some aspects of a talk I presented a little
while ago, entitled *"The State and the Crisis in Africa"* given at a Dag
Hammarskjold seminar in Sweden. To understand the structure of our
economies which has to be changed to enable us move forward, it is
necessary to trace their historical evolution and the rationale behind
them. The entire African continent was annexed to the European
capitalist economy by means of colonialism. Hence, these countries
have developed in a specific, historically determined way, with a
definite mode of production which wholly serves external interests by

supplying the production and consumption needs of the colonial powers.

The penetration of external capital in these countries and the subordination of African products to European markets, not only distorted the economic growth of these countries but also it helped to siphon off most of the economic surpluses leaving almost nothing for internal accumulation of capital which is a precondition for an internally integrated and self-sustaining development. To compensate for this massive extraction of surplus (current estimate: $100 million per day from Africa alone), our "trading partners" in the West extend small amounts of aid and credit compared to what they take out. For every dollar sent to Africa as aid or loans, three dollars go out. Currently most African countries are paying more that 60% of their foreign exchange earnings to service foreign debts, at the same time as their balance of trade totally favours these same "trading partners".

Neo-Colonialism-Appendage Economy

The resultant mode of production does not conform to any other mode, capitalist or feudalist. It is an "appendage economy" which has to be studied as such, without complicating it by introducing elements alien to it. Neo-colonialism is the off-shoot of colonial ideologies and economics, conditioned by the needs of the cold war and the reconstruction of European economies devastated by World War II. Africa had to supply cheap raw materials to hasten Europe's recovery. But when that recovery was accomplished in the early 1970s, Africa's economies remained stagnant and its politics deeply rooted in the status quo. The economies developed the peculiar feature of consuming other countries' products with no capacity to accumulate capital internally. The social classes who have evolved with this mode of production have peculiar characteristics, unlike the classes generated by normally developed economies. The "haves" gravitate externally and do not contribute towards internal accumulation of capital. On the contrary, almost invariably they are the agents of extracting out of the country that surplus which eventually filters back from the country's exports.

This colonial mode of production which has resulted in vast unevenness has left the rural areas absolutely stagnant. This stagnation has led to the evolution of theories of rural development, which assumes a dichotomy between urban and rural economies in which the former is said to be "exploiting" the latter. This is not only an erroneous way of looking at the problem of unevenness, but extremely damaging. Throughout the post-colonial period, all third world countries have accepted this dichotomy and have planned their strategies for development accordingly. The price we are paying for this false assumption, perpetrated and encouraged by the World Bank and IMF, is now proving to be unbearable.

Why is the assumption of "urban/rural" dichotomy false? First of all, it is impossible to isolate a part from the whole without creating new and perhaps more serious unevenness and worsening the relationship between these twin sectors. In spite of the many "development strategies" and theories of "rural development", the rural areas have remained stagnant at best, or deteriorating, at worst. Rural youth continue to flock to the urban centres in millions searching for an improvement of their well-being. The urban centres in turn are starving because the rural areas, abandoned by their able-bodied labour force, are not producing enough food to supply the towns, the shanty towns, or the cities. Most African countries which formerly produced food surpluses before the advent of "rural development" theses, are now importing food, thus aggravating their balance of payments problems and deepening the "debt crisis".

Import substitution industrialisation, that is to say, the industrial strategy which begins by producing goods that are normally imported for local consumption, and are as a rule dependent on foreign capital, technology and even raw materials, was another IMF/WB pet theory. This did in fact work in the early "settler colonies": the USA, Canada, Australia, South Africa, Algeria, Zimbabwe (and even Kenya, to a certain extent). Their viability stemmed from a growing internal demand, generated either by a massive influx of new settlers whose consumption habits were based on industrial economies, or from the booming economies kindled by this very influx of skilled manpower and capital. However, such an import substitution industrial strategy has NOT worked in Africa's neo-colonies. The reason is obvious. Whereas in the settler colonies demand has always been expanding, in our economies it has been shrinking due to the massive external exploitation noted above. In other words, whereas the settler economies were based on internal demand, neo-colonies are based on external demand, and therefore import-substitution industries cannot flourish. Moreover, the rural youth continue to flock into the cities, inflating the so-called industrial reserve army, which saturates the labour market and encourages a lowering of wages, and further diminishing internal demand, leading to an even greater industrial decline. (Paradoxically, the policy of lowering wages is encouraged by African governments and insisted by the IMF/WB).

This kind of approach to "development" is not conducive to creating much less expanding social wealth, the creation of which, as we have seen is a precondition for igniting and maintaining mass enthusiasm for production. It intensifies the urban/rural unevenness, it worsens the relationship between the two, and thus blocks the way to future development. Colonial economies did tend to favour cities, especially coastal ones, to facilitate the export of our primary commodities and import goods from metropolitan countries. However, this irrational unevenness cannot be corrected by abandoning the cities, as "rural developers" advocate. On the contrary, it can be achieved only by making maximum utilisation of the existing urban facilities and thus, initially, creating a demand for rural goods as raw material and food, during the early period of rehabilitating the national economy. As the structure of the old colonial economy is gradually changed and the economy begins to be internally integrated, industrialisation will take a new and more dynamic form. Thus, our agriculture will be geared towards serving our industry and our industry in turn geared towards serving agriculture. This strategy will help solve Africa's two most serious economic constraints, namely rural underdevelopment and industrial backwardness. It will stimulate rural economic activity in harmony rather than in conflict with urban economic activity. In other words, it will achieve the desired objective economic complementarity between urban and rural economies which is essential for a self-sustaining development.

Market versus Planned Economies

There are currently deafening noises emanating from the same imperialist moralists who have historically exploited and still continue to exploit the African masses through the "free market". These noises are now bombarding us with their ideology concerning the sanctity of the market economy and the weakness and failure of centrally planned economies. It will, therefore, help us briefly to compare the two. As we know, the development of capitalism and market economies depended on the subjugation of the weak by the strong and on the destruction of the former's economy, culture, and way of life, to conform with and serve the needs of the subjugator. Among non-European peoples, only Japan escaped the direct domination of Europe. The reason for Japan's escape is that its bourgeoisie started its "primitive accumulation of capital" and developed its productive forces concurrently with its European bourgeois counterpart at a time when the latter was still weak, and thus could not bar Japan from entering the scramble for domination and exploitation.

Once the European bourgeoisie, US and Japanese, was consolidated internationally, the road to independent capitalist development was effectively blocked. Only appendage capitalism was possible; that is to say, only an extension of US, European or Japanese economies in poorer countries was possible. Since the end of the First World War not a single country from the third world has developed an independent capitalist economy. The so-called newly industrialising countries, the NICs, which are typical appendage economies, cannot even claim to be independent capitalist economies. They are "national" only in name, but the real powers are either Japanese, US or European capitalists, or the Multinational Corporations. In other words, historical evidence amply supports the assertion that in the modern world, it is no longer possible to develop a viable national economy on the basis of a free-for-all market economy.

If the advanced market economies achieved their highest development by means of plundering the weak in the form of slavery and colonialism, African countries have no colonies to plunder. How, then, can Africa put in motion the process of capital accumulation without exploitation? How can Africa rapidly develop the productive forces without sacrificing the welfare provision?

Internal Accumulation of Capital - First Precondition

The first most important precondition for accumulation in our situation as noted above, is that the people must rely on their own diligent labour on frugality, and on constantly investing in the creation of new social wealth by means of expanded reproduction. This can be achieved in our circumstances by encouraging national unity and the collaboration of oppressed classes guided by the dialectical approach, and by observing the law of unity and struggle of opposites. It is a mistake, for instance, to look for only contradictions and not collaboration of various social groups and classes in society. It is equally wrong to see only struggle and not to see the possibility of the unity of the opposites. This approach, unlike that of the "development" theorists, recognises first of all that balance and imbalance are the two sides of a "contradiction" within which imbalance is absolute and balance is relative. In an imbalance you struggle to achieve balance. Once this is achieved, a new imbalance necessarily follows, and a new struggle for balance is set in motion, and so on, *ad infinitum*. That is why in researching economic problems and their solutions, it is necessary to use balance and imbalance among the productive forces, the relations of production and the superstructure as a guideline.

In a planned economy, the allocation of scarce resources between alternative and competing ends is determined by establishing a proper ratio between accumulation and consumption, and by achieving a balance between production and needs. Whereas in market economies production is regulated by the "law of value", i.e. by competition, by demand and supply, and by the maximisation of profit, (at considerable waste of resources), in a planned economy, production is regulated by the "Law of Planned and Proportionate Development". However, a planned economy in its early stages must utilise the law of value for the purpose of regulating exchange, but its use must be put under strict control in order to avert the chaos of capitalist economies. The current experience in China is instructive. In the last few years the Chinese economy has allowed the utilisation of the law of value in a rather undisciplined and reckless fashion (which the capitalist countries hail as a victory for capitalism, and a defeat for planned economy). The result has been the worst chaos in production and consumption ever experienced in Chinese post-revolution history.

To ensure the enthusiastic support of the masses and to retain their enthusiasm for production, the economy must make sure that the provision of food, clothing, and shelter for the people receives a top priority. In market economies, the provision of these basics is achieved haphazardly and indirectly by obeying the capitalist law of supply and demand, making full use of the principle of "comparative advantage", in other words, by observing the "law of surplus value". In a planned economy, on the other hand, the provision of these basics is the essential first step towards achieving the welfare of the whole society by continuously expanding and perfecting production on the basis of higher technology. This can be attained in a comparatively short historical period, by observing the law of balanced, proportionate development of the productive forces.

For progressive African countries to begin the above process, they must first struggle to change their colonial economic structure. This would enable them to conserve their economic surplus which is now exploited by foreign interests through their dependency on the "world market". This will enable them to divert their *socially necessary labour* now wasted in *useless* production to the production of *useful* goods: food, clothing and shelter. This would entail gradually diverting production for export and concentrate on internal needs. It would entail diverting resources, step by step, away from export branches in favour of techno-logically advanced food production, farming, textile industry, modern construction and engineering industries for the supply of modern housing for the people, and an efficient transport system essential for an internally integrated economy. This revolution shift would require a fairly substantial investment programme. The purpose of such invest-ment would be two fold: first, to reactivate existing industries now operating at very low capacity, if at all; second, to provide for the expansion and replacement of the existing industries and the introduction of new ones, without cutting back necessary social welfare provisions. The state will have to play a leading role throughout this process of reconstruction as it will involve transferring vast sums and resources from export branches to new areas of investments.

Over 90% of Africa's population lives in the rural areas and therefore it is to this area that our planning must initially aim to provide the "motive force for development". On the basis of harmonising the relationship between the rural and urban areas, it is essential that the peasantry must be encouraged to expand production through raised productivity to highest possible levels. This will help to expand both the home market and also the tax base. The major constraint to the expansion of peasant production is the drop in world market process, which is a major disincentive to increased production. Price stability can be attained only when the peasantry ceases to produce for the world market and relies instead on the home market where price stability can be regulated. Unlike the development experience of capitalism (or the experience of Stalin's Soviet Union) where primitive capital accumulation was attained by massive exploitation of the peasantry, a progressive planned economy can achieve accumulation by expanding peasant production, either through cooperatives, through individuals or from family enterprise.

In an economy where industry is linked to agriculture and agricul-ture to industry, peasants and urban workers can raise their incomes simultaneously. Due to the historical back drop of uneven development, the incomes of the urban workers might be slightly higher for a little while. Raising the income of the peasantry would create demand for industrial finished goods which in turn will help industry to develop. Labour-intensive industries such as textiles, dairy, leather, and food processing, on the one hand, and housing and construction industries, on the other could act both as consumers and suppliers of the rural economy. Above all, such industries would create massive employment opportunities for hundreds of thousands of school leavers as well as introducing them to the brave new world of skills and technology. There is no room here to think in terms of rural/urban dichotomies, of "rural development", and such meaningless abstractions, as the sectors must necessarily develop as one, single organism.

One of the most attractive aspects of Tanzania's *Ujamaa*, which was damaged and possibly lost for ever due to the adventurism and vulgar "practicalism" of the political leaders was that, in addition to its obvious economic potential, it could have been politically useful to the urban workers. The concentration of hitherto dispersed peasants in a vast country like Tanzania, could have led to a dynamic rural/urban economic complementarity and could have invalidated the sterile thinking of "rural development" which actually perpetuates rather than eliminates the peasants' notorious social backwardness and retarded development. It would have cemented in real terms a genuine worker/peasant alliance.

In other words, whereas the previous modes of production debased agriculture and destroyed rural life, a scientific and planned approach to development would transform rapidly expand and enrich the rural life, side by side with the expansion and enrichment of urban life. Unlike market economies, a planned economy does not experiment with human life; it takes seriously society's awareness of its historic responsibility. In sustaining and expanding rural/urban economic, social and cultural complementarity, a planned economy utilises the "law of value" to regulate production and exchange commodities of farm produce for industrial goods, between state-owned and privately-owned industries, etc.

However, experience has shown that it is a serious error for the state to monopolize the economy and to ignore other forms of exchange. However, to be productive the former must play a leading role and the latter a supporting role. Planning must concentrate on major products, leaving minor ones to private enterprise. As long as this scientific approach is adhered to strictly, the process towards the *structural change* will be fulfilled with minimum pain or sacrifice. However, the superiority of a planned economy over market economy can be realised only if the democratic rights of the people are not undermined. The state which intervenes in the economic life of the people must do so only to liberate people, rather than to oppress them.

If Nkrumah helped to usher in the era of *Uhuru* in Africa he has also, unfortunately, left behind a tradition of repressive politics; the politics of the *One Party State*. One party states in Africa have not only denied the people much of their political rights, but they have also contributed towards de-politicizing them. This process of depoliticization is so extensive that today Africa has become the playground of military rulers. The masses having no political role accept that of celebrating the overthrow of one military regime and of hailing the incoming one as their new redeemer. Thus, Nkrumah's leadership failed to introduce both economics and politics of new democracy in post-colonial Africa. If Nkurumaism can be described as Africas equivalent of a pre-independence national democratic revolution, its extension to post-colonial Africa nevertheless did not accelerate the move to a new democracy. It only ushered in an era of Uhuru which now we know is only another term for the period of neo-colonialism: economically stagnant, politically undemocratic and repressive. A meaningful struggle for the future in Africa must, therefore, lie in superceding the era of uhuru, in a post-uhuru phase, which must necessarily be the era of new democracy.

We discussed above the economics of New Democracy essential for arousing and sustaining *mass enthusiasm for production*. This, as we have seen, it is a precondition for enabling society to develop its *productive forces*, to increase its social wealth, as fast and as humanly possible. But, as Khrushchev once said, man can not live by bread alone. There must be freedom: freedom of movement, of association, of speech, of choice, of conscience. Above all, there must be freedom from state interference in one's private life, and freedom to develop one's full potential in all fields of human activity. To achieve these basic democratic rights without allowing loopholes for the reintroduction of the old practice of exploitation of 'man by man' or the exploitation of the people by the state, people must ensure that they establish the politics of the new democracy.

The Politics of New Democracy

The one-party-state always assumes that a handful of party bosses in the ruling party's "Central Committee" or a "Politburo" have all the answers to every problem that faces the country. The evolution of this kind of thinking has a very interesting history which we need not go into here, but most of it leaves a very bad taste in the mouth. Some of the most heinous crimes have been committed, and are still being committed, against innocent people on the basis of this undemocratic system. But one interesting aspect of its evolution is itself based on a false assumption. Socialist parties are organised on the principle of *democratic centralism*, which means that all party organs, from the central committee downwards, must observe the principle that once the majority agrees on any subject, the minority must abide by the decision although they may be against it. If they don't accept this condition they are obliged to leave the party, or be expelled. This is all right as far as the party disciplinary codes are concerned. But to raise this principle and practice of "democratic centralism" to the level of the state is not only wrong but very dangerous indeed. The state represents the entire people of all political views. People have the right to disagree with some of its policies or with all of its policies. If they do disagree and say so, what then? You cannot "expel" them as you would from the party which they have joined on their own free will. The one party state either locks them up as "enemies of the people" or they are forced into exile.

The State of New Democracy must be the state of the people, respecting their views and controlled by them. We cannot go into the mechanics of the state in this short essay, but it can only be the state of a united front of various political persuasions or parties. They may differ in their strategy or tactics, but with one common national objective. They must be free to organise their political parties, free to propagate their views, free to form alliances with other political parties within the country and free to contest elections separately. Whichever party would form a broad-based "united front" government in which all parties of patriotic and anti-imperialist credentials would participate.

Another important step is to dismantle the neo-colonial army and in its place build a "people's militia" based on localities and street areas, whose purpose would be exclusively for the defence of the country. There should be a small contingent of professional personnel to supervise militia training and deployment, and to act as the backbone of the militia in the event of the need to resist foreign aggression. The present neo-colonial armies handed down from the colonial rule, arrogant and excessively privileged, are of no use in the era of New Democracy. Almost without exception, the established armies in Africa at present are the biggest drain on the national economy, squandering a large proportion of the country's income on useless and unproductive activities. Their function so far has been either to undermine the citizenry or to overthrow legally established governments by means of coups and counter-coups. Their establishments are the centres of corruption and sources of enriching most of the generals and the colonels who are now among the richest millionaires in Africa, at the expense of the poor and starving masses in their respective countries. None of them have fought any external wars, and those that did, were wars of interference in other countries' internal affairs. No, there is no room for such armies in the Africa of New Democracy.

Of course there will be a lot of problems, but they will be problems of a new kind. They will be problems of establishing and safeguarding democracy. The old forces with vested interest in the old status quo will certainly attempt a last ditch attempt to regain their hold, assisted no doubt by their external backers. But organised masses in special vigilante brigades would be the instrument of mobilising the entire population against the old exploiters. The threat of the old guard, however, should never be allowed to be a pretext for denying the rest of the people their democratic rights. A truly democratic society in the era of New Democracy is the greatest safeguard against any form of internal and external subversion.

In spite of his shortcomings discussed above, Nkrumah will remain a great leader in Africa's history who has set in motion a process of liberation whose first step was the attainment of uhuru. The second step would be the achievement of Nkrumah's greatest goal which is African unity, which also must be the goal of the New Democracy. But if Nkrumah aspired to the attainment of the unity of African states, New Democracy will work to bring about unity of the people of Africa, either by means of state to state cooperation, cooperation of political parties, cultural cooperation, or by any other means. We have seen the limits of attempting to unite the continent at the level of the state. The OAU has turned into a mini-UN, while it has some useful diplomatic functions, so far it has done very little to bring about a united continental government as envisaged by Nkrumah. There is obviously a need for thinking anew about the strategy and tactics needed to unite the continent as it is our only hope of survival in this world of superpowers. This is no longer the epoch of small nation-states; that era has been outdated by the very needs of modern politico-diplomatic organisation and technology. The need to fully utilise the enormous natural and human resources of Africa, now squandered by imperialist interest, is the greatest inducement to bring about a much cherished African unity. The way to begin the next step towards this end is by releasing the spiritual and physical energies of the masses of Africa through the politics and economics of New Democracy. To echo Nkrumah's earliest slogan: *Forward Ever, Backward Never.* That is the spirit of the New Democratic United Africa!

Chapter 3

CHURCH, STATE AND SOCIETY IN EAST AFRICA

Bishop H.Okullu

It gives me great pleasure and honour to be invited by the organizers to address this Conference on "Africa: Thirty Years of Independence". I wish to try to reflect with you upon this subject from the stand point of the role of church and state in the task of human development. I have been asked to do this from the perspective of East Africa, that is primarily Kenya, Uganda and Tanzania. This task is not an easy one because I am only a churchman and should have no business with temporal concerns. In fact, interestingly in our ordinal, i.e the service we Anglicans still use for ordaining persons into priesthood we exhort them:

> "consider how studious you ought to be in the reading and learning of the scriptures... and for this self-same cause, how you ought to forsake and set aside (as much as you may) all worldly cares and studies".......

Some of us have long forgotten this exhortation and we often find ourselves locked in a war on two fronts. Some of our church members tell us that society can only be changed by changing individuals, while on another front we live with constant stern rebukes from politicians that we should not interfere in politics.

First of all, let us try to remember what kind of societies political leaders in East Africa set out to build when we became independent in the sixties.

According to their stated objectives, nations were to be socialist

(African) communities in which peoples' role in society would not depend on the size of their house, or the number of cars, wives and children they had. Human dignity was to be respected and upheld. Every person would have the right to be heard and the freedom to participate in the politics of his country. The new nations would respect the homogeneity and the cultural heritage of existing communities and base the new national life on them. Independent institutions, trade unions, associations of intellectuals, student movements, women's organizations, the church, the press and the rest would be strengthened to become pillars of society. The rights of the minority and opposition parties were to be allowed and protected and, where these did not exist, free discussion between the rulers and the ruled would prevail.

In achieving these goals and objectives religion and the church was considered to be an important factor as is clearly stated in Kenya's Sessional Paper No. 10 on African Socialism.

> Another fundamental force in African Traditional life was a religion which provided a strict moral code for the community. This will be a prominent feature of African Socialism.

The states themselves, were, of course, secular even though religion was to play a major role in society. Kenya, Uganda (before Amin's time) and Tanzania are secular states. Many people including the majority of politicians and civil servants are members of one religion or another. In Kenya, almost every government function begins with prayer. Julius Nyerere once declared that "Tanzania has no religion; the party has no religion; the government has no religion. But almost all Tanzanians are religious people, and the party and the government guarantee each citizen the right to choose his own religion". Thus these states are secular only in the sense that their constitutions do not specifically state that they are based on Christian laws.

Many political leaders have made clear their positions concerning the relationship between church and state. President Moi was reported to have made the following statement when he met the Anglican Bishops at State House, Nairobi, in January, 1981:

> He urged Churches not to relax their efforts in preaching spiritual matters, adding that preaching the Holy Scriptures helped the Government maintain stability. He called on Churches and all able-bodied in society to help those who could not help themselves. He stressed that religion was not a privilege but a right and said

that Churches should regard themselves as a part and parcel of Government.[2]

Mwai Kibaki once Kenya's Vice-President, has been the most outspoken leader in Kenya in his statements concerning the relation between church and state.

Politics and religion are inseparable. To suggest that politics should be left to the politicians and religion to the clergy, is a terrible intellectual arrogance.[3]

Mwai Kibaki believes that it is through the involvement of church leaders in public affairs that Africa can retain its soul. Kibaki emphasizes that Christians should stop thanking the government for the freedom to worship. This was a God-given right which the government has the obligation to protect in the same way it protects other rights.

Before the year 1986, there had never been any open conflict between church and state in Kenya. Kenyatta did not want that kind of confrontation and was himself close to the leadership of Kenya's National Council of Churches.

Kenyatta refused to attach himself to any organized religion. However, he confessed that he believed in God and all his political speeches were full of biblical references. In his public addresses he maintained that no religion or church, in the case of Christian denominations, was superior to the others. This delighted smaller sects which continued to mushroom in Kenya.

In contrast to Kenyatta, President Arap Moi is a churchgoer and a member of the African Inland Church, a strongly evangelical church. He tends to worship in any church of his choice each Sunday, and often addresses the congregation during or after the service.

The irony is that there have been sharp and open conflicts between church and state in Kenya during the time of Moi unlike that of Kenyatta. The explanation is yet to be found. Just ponder the following quotations taken from the February 1990 edition of a Nairobi journal called *Finance*:

"Church and Politics in Kenya: What went wrong? Why the Strife?"

I have found out that some church leaders have been attacking the Government without proper reasons. We cannot tolerate such people. I am now calling for their arrest and later detention to curb their excesses. *Hon. Elijah Mwangale, Minister for Livestock Development.*

Intimidation and threats against Church leaders from January 1, to December 31, of every year, will not shake some of us. *The Rt. Rev. Alexander Kipsang' Muge of the Eldoret Diocese.*

Kenyans want to live in peace so that we can develop our country and we are getting tired of being diverted from the main issues of development by idle and unpatriotic elements whom it can be concluded are being manipulated by the outside forces. *Vice President and Minister for Finance, Prof. George Saitoti.*

People are fed up all over the world with dictator regimes and the recent signs of the times are nothing but an indication that everyone is now ready to stand on his or her own in life or death to win back self respect and freedom. *The Anglican Bishop of Maseno South Diocese, the Rt. Rev. Dr. Henry Okullu.*

We will never allow the Church to run the Government. *Hon. Shariff Nassir, Mombasa Kanu Chairman.*

Some people say we do not have a right to speak. They should know that our right is God given. *The Most Rev. Manasses Kuria, Archbishop of the Church of the Province of Kenya (CPK).*

The Rev. Njoya is a tribalist and before he accuses others of tribalism, he should give Kenyans a breakdown of the tribal background of all PCEA pastors in the country. This will establish beyond any doubt that he is a leader in a tribalistic Church. *Mark Too, Nandi branch Chairman of Kanu.*

Do not fear to speak out when you see things going wrong. If the Church fails to condemn evil, we are then failing in our duties. *The Rt. Rev. George Wanjau, the Moderator of the Presbyterian Church of East Africa (PCEA).*

Never in the history of Kenya has so much misunder-
standing and so much distrust existed between the Church
and the State, concludes the article.

These conflicts escalated in 1986 after a National Pastors' Conference
which passed a resolution opposing a new Kenyan electoral system in
which a system of lining up behind candidates displaced the secret
ballot. The church's leadership opposed the system on grounds that it
would be divisive and dangerous for people in the armed forces,
government administration and in the church to show open partiality
in lining up behind candidates. "Mlolongo", its popular Kiswahili
name, was finally abolished in December 1990.

Let us briefly hear some other voices from other parts of Africa. From
Kaunda of Zambia comes one of the most pointed challenges to the
church, more precisely the clergy, to take seriously their part in nation-
building:

Is not a disproportionate amount of their time and intellectual talent
solely devoted to matters of domestic ecclesiastical concern? Would
it be unkind of me to say that many of the clergy have completely
shut themselves off from the on-going life of our nations?[4]

Kaunda argued that as a humble Christian he was saddened by the
lack of church involvement in discussing great national issues. He
noted,"Both our government and nation need to have kept before them
the moral and spiritual standards against which we should measure
their policies and actions".[5] He also maintained that he expected only
the best that the church could offer, not tired cliches and platitudes
which would be an insult to the intelligence of the people.

Never has the Church had a more wonderful opportunity to be a
relevant and effective spiritual and moral force than it has in these
newly established states where persons are hungry for the truth".[6]

However, when sometime in 1990 the Roman Catholic Bishops
issued a pastoral letter on Peace and Justice issues in Zambia which was
very critical of the human rights record in the country, Kaunda reacted
sharply in contrast to his above challenges. The same catholic bishops
strongly criticized Mugabe for turning the country into a one-party
state. Mugabe retorted by telling the bishops that their church was not

democratic either, although things are different in Zimbabwe now.

Uganda during Amin's period was a special case exemplified by the murder of Archbishop Janani Luwum in 1977.

Nyerere has been widely viewed as Africa's guru and an original thinker on these issues. His address to the Maryknoll Sisters' Conference in New York, on 16 October, 1970, lays down very plainly what he perceived to be the role of the church in nation-building. Nyerere is firmly persuaded that it is the duty of the church to help men and women to rebel against everything which enslaves and dehumanizes them:

> But most of all, the Church must be obviously and openly fighting all those institutions and power groups which contribute to the existence and maintenance of the physical and spiritual slums - regardless of the consequences to itself or its members.[9]

If the Church kept silent on established evils, it would be identifying itself and the Christian religion with injustice. The reputation of Catholicism and the total Christian body was only redeemed by those individual servants of the Church who spoke out, even if that meant personal sacrifice.

Nyerere never had a quarrel with church leaders. He freely lectured churches on their role in society, although they almost all endorsed the Arusha Declaration, declaring that it was in accordance with Christian spirit and teaching on human society. While there may be some matters in which we are not in agreement, but they are right in principle.

Now, let us turn our attention to the role which church and state should play in the development of the human person in the future. As we have noticed, many government functions, including political rallies, are opened with prayer. President Moi would be appalled if he addressed a meeting without first being led in prayer. The Kenya National Anthem is a prayer to 'God of all creation.....' Both the Tanzanian and Zambian anthems are also prayers to God to bless Africa. 'Oh Uganda may God uphold thee', begins Uganda's anthem. Almost every other African national anthem also includes the name of God. In the whole of Eastern Africa, the Churches have produced a joint Christian Religious Educational Syllabus for all primary and secondary schools. This is the first joint Catholic/Protestant syllabus widely used anywhere. The University of Nairobi has a department of Religious Studies and Philosophy. These same governments also employ and pay chaplains to serve in the armed forces.

Generally, exhortations from various statements concerning the church tend to view its role in terms of helping government leaders to maintain peace and stability . The church in Africa, they imply, exists for nothing else apart from serving the state. In this regard we should remember that, for a statesman, the overriding moral dictate is the survival of the state. As Stanley Hoffman notes:

> Theirs is the burden of putting burdens on everyone else. Any moral statecraft has to be an ethnic of consequences, in the sense of being concerned for the foreseeable effects. It means that the good in politics is not separable from its realization.[10]

The politician thus tries to preserve the state by any means, including lying, deceiving, killing and doing evil. He believes that it is his moral imperative to do so. To him this is not an immoral code of behaviour, whereas to a Christian, it is.

Secondly, the missionary church was regarded by many as part and parcel of colonial governments in Africa. Mozambique is one of the best examples of this.

African national leaders unconsciously sound as though they have replaced the colonial government and have therefore assumed the leadership of every institution, including the church. Mobutu complains of the Catholic Church sticking it out even when all other major institutions had given in to him.

Thirdly, there is a totalitarian view of statehood in Africa. All social institutions, the church included, must be subjected to the supremacy of the state. In Kenya, the massive women's organization known as Maendeleo ya Wanawake has been affiliated to the ruling party, the Kenya African National Union (KANU). There was some thought of doing the same with the Central Organization of Trade Unions (COTU). But now, the party leaders are instead accusing leaders of COTU of working with foreigners to destabilise the country. There was a startling report in the Kenyan press in 1990 that the party wanted the Kenya Law Society affiliated to it. Kenya Law Society, the churches and the press are the three institutions still struggling to stay independent. The current wave of totalitarianism in Africa has in fact been responsible for destroying the so-called ruling parties, even nationhood itself, and also resulted in empire building in many countries.

A last point to remember is that national leaders should not be allowed to set the agenda for churches. It is the duty and responsibility of the church to clarify its own understanding of its mission, and to state it strongly, clearly, and repeatedly in public so that everyone may understand. Far too often the agenda and tone in the task of nation-building has come from political leaders alone. The church must move back to the centre of life, think of the African people in all matters, and state its case clearly. If the trumpet does not give a clear sound, no one will go to war. It should be as in the case of Prophet Amos, 'the lion has roared who will not fear?' (Amos 3:8)

As has been mentioned earlier, there are Christians who would prefer to adopt a Calvinistic view that because God is Lord of all, there ought to be a theocratic system of government. Whenever they are faced with a problem in society they cry: 'make laws to ban it, or allow it'.

They would prefer to establish a Christendom, a 'holy' nation, in which Christian ethics are enforced by state law. This view regards the separation of religious conviction from social and political life as sheer hypocrisy. This would seem to be a commendable idea until we realize that in a society with several religions, such a step would infringe upon the liberties of other people. A second group of Christians is the separatist, sectarian type who believe that all of those who are not for us are against us, so we share no part with them. To convert society, every individual must experience the inner conversion. For this group, religion and politics do not mix. Social issues and religious matters have to be kept separate. Emphasis is put upon living a life of individual holiness as the only means of meeting God's challenge to society. This is the predominant attitude in East Africa. This also has been the main approach to social issues by some of the major evangelical churches in the U.S.A.

Politicians fall generally into the same categories. There are those who want the church to adopt a more active role in society like Nyerere and Kaunda, providing it does not make any public statements critical of the political party or the national leaders. For instance, President Moi recently made a strong appeal to Kenyan Churches to approach his government quietly and not through the Press. Another category of leaders regards the Church as a praying department of the government to give divine support to official, political and economic schemes, while keeping away from politics, not only publicly, but also privately. They also believe that politics is the sole prerogative of those people called politicians.

We must recognize that there is yet another category of people, found mainly among intellectuals, for whom faith has no meaning. The numbers are still small but steadily growing. They too, denying spirituality, hold the view that religion and politics are absolutely irrelevant to each other.

The authentic Christian view is nevertheless one which affirms the reality and necessity of the world of politics, but demythologizes and relativizes its importance. The life of faith, hope and love cannot be established by political powers.

What then do we mean by different roles for church and state? Or by a contrasting statement that 'the Church is part and parcel of the government?' The answer is that the separation is institutional only, but at value level, the two are bound together in the realm of ethics by owing their origin to God. Both are established for the service of God and individuals. The recognition of the separation of church and state at the institutional level must be seasoned by an equally vigorous recognition of the integrated view of life at a deeper level. Here we must work out a unified ethical perspective which gives us a vision of the unity of the whole. There is a reason for this, namely that God is the Lord of the Church or individuals. Our religious ethics must speak of interpersonal love as well as social justice, if they are to keep a true balance. A theology which speaks only of social concerns, and neglects a deep personal faith in the risen Lord is equally lopsided. In this view of the integrated whole lies the oneness of church and state, and it provides the church with its mandate for being involved in politics.

In practical terms, separation for the church means guaranteed freedom from interference with doctrine or ritual. State officials cannot and should not exert pressure on the appointment of church leaders, and politicians should not intrude on the inner life of the church. Secondly, such freedom means that the church can and should have its own financial resources and be free to determine the use of its resources. Thirdly, each national church must be free to have contact with other churches. The universal nature of the church is essential for its world mission and must be recognized and maintained, although each church has a responsibility to relate and be relevant to its own particular culture and political situation.

There is no blue print or ideal situation which is universally applicable to all places. There are areas in which generalizations can be made with some degree of safety, but ultimately, although there are differences which may not be permanent, each situation calls for a fresh approach by the church in its particular context.

To the state, the separation means that there is no interference by the church, and that government decisions are reached through government processes. The government is responsible to its citizens or the elector-

ate, not to ecclesiastical authorities. Churches and all their leaders have
the right of all citizens and other institutions in the nation to exert
influence on the government, but no one church or a church council has
legal authority over government. Bishop John Talor explains:

> Both Church and State are the servants of God and responsible to
> Him. Neither is responsible to the other. The Church is not to be
> regarded as a department of the State, and the State should never be
> dominated by the Church. But both can, if they will, support one
> another in their complementary tasks.[11]

Although the church is never part of the state, to express the strong
African sense of social and civil functions of religion, it is very proper
for it to hold prayers at public and civic rallies, for example, during the
opening of a new session of Parliament.

Looking at various parts of the world, one can see that even in the
USA or Great Britain where there is an explicit statement on the subject,
the church/state relationship is still evolving, with people's understanding of the functions and nature of the two continuing to change.
For this reason, all positions, whether one speaks of radical separation,
as in America, or establishment, as in Britain or Sweden, must be
critically re-examined, particularly given the church's constantly renewed understanding of the gospel. What does this new revelation
mean to the church's understanding of its relation to the state in modern
society? These are the questions we must ask.

The relationship of church and state should be dynamic rather than
legalistic or static. Everywhere the Christian community is part of
larger communities. The overriding question which Christians must
examine critically, is the nature of the gospel and the Church's call to
witness in society. This determines what the relationship of the church
to the state is going to be, what kind of witness the church wishes to have
in society, and what services it seeks to render.

The first and primary duty of the church's witness is the proclamation
of the word of God. This witness is distinct and indispensable. This is
traditionally known as evangelism, which is the telling of the story of
God in Christ, fulfilling the commission of the Lord 'to go into the world
and preach the Gospel', with the aim of making disciples. The telling
of this story in the power of the Holy Spirit is an inescapable mandate
for the church. It must not be viewed, however, as separate from the
other forms of the Church's ministry, but as an integral part of its total
mission in society. Secondly, part of that total witness is for Christians

to be a community - a living, sharing, and serving community. This kind of witness is visible and effective where churches are truly open to the poor, the despised, and the differently disabled for whom our modern societies have little care.

The Church, as a worshipping community, will certainly have some minimum requirements for survival. These are the opportunity for worship, eucharistic and other forms of fellowship, instruction, and education. There are those who argue that to live wholly for the world the church needs to deinstitutionalise, but in our opinion its existence as an organic loving community is itself a form of witness in society. Against this background of our understanding of the nature of the church's witness and service, we must place our understanding of the nature of human society.

The combination of modern statehood with the nation has given new authority and functions to the state to regulate life in society and to plan for the welfare of its people as well as to engage in medical, education, industrial, agricultural and other national projects. This is particularly so in the developing world, which has developed a vast way of parastatal functions which in other nations are not directly governmental. These include university education, agricultural marketing, and certain aspects of banking. The state now assumes responsibility for its citizens in almost every department. This is so at least nationally, though in fact many social services are supplemented by voluntary agencies.

Much as this national approach to the fight against poverty, disease and illiteracy is appreciated, there is always the danger of state absolutism and the idolization of leaders in Africa has in fact become demonic. At this point and time churches in Africa and indeed other living faiths face an enormous task of calling upon their governments to democratize. Without sufficient political reforms our future could be very disastrous. Christian responsibility demands that we take the modern state seriously. We have to recognize its status as an agency for political, social, economic and indeed religious and cultural reforms. But we must reject dictatorship and emperor worship.

The mechanisms controlled by the state can become either positive forces for social reform or agencies for evil repression in society. It is therefore the duty of the Church to prepare its members for responsible and effective participation in nation-building.

The Church is the Church only when it exists for others. The Church must share in the secular problems of ordinary human life, not dominating, but helpful and serving.[12]

At this point, I wish to turn to the specific question of how churches contribute to the task of redirecting the development strategies in Africa. For the church to be able to contribute effectively towards alternative development strategies, the main area of focus must be clearly defined and identified.

It is commonly understood that the rural sector is the area on which development should be focused because that is where we find the largest number of poor people, and if one is poor, one is not developed. This conception is not altogether wrong except that it does not describe the problems of the rural poor in totality. It should be understood that poverty in itself does not constitute the problem. The forces that perpetuate poverty are the real problems. These forces may be political, economic, technological or social and are most often found together.

The Editorial of an ECA publication, *Rural Progress*, sums up the problem, thus:

> The disadvantaged segment of the rural population which is left behind in the rural areas, can hardly be expected to make the economic base of rural development more productive. Similarly, they cannot be expected to be a vocal lobby to make the ruling authorities accountable to them and establish a dialogue with them in deciding, inter-alia, priorities of resource allocation - especially internal, price policies and fiscal measures. They become passive and loyal "law abiding citizens". The consequence is the gradual erosion of the principles of accountability. Distorted priorities dictate resource allocation, and this largely explains the under development of Africa's rural sector today.

This statement truly underscores the premise on which any meaningful development strategy must be based. This is the plight of the rural folk, rendered powerless, and marginalized from the entire development process. Without the participation of rural people there can be no equitable distribution of national wealth and consequently no meaningful development.

The Church, therefore, has a duty to address this problem by ensuring that political leaders are accountable while at the same time educating the community on their right to such accountability. This prophetic duty is unfortunately misunderstood by politicians to mean opposition or incitement.

Education of the community should not end at the question of rights alone. Education should be a means of enabling the people to think and do things for themselves. This kind of education is often called development education. Many donors now believe that for any development programme to succeed, education must be built into such a programme.

It is often said that "lack of resources, technology, infrastructure and inappropriate policies largely account for the prevalence of rural poverty in Africa". I believe that lack of education and community organization do account for the prevalence of rural underdevelopment because when a person is poor in mind and spirit nothing else can make him rich. Enrichment of the mind and spirit is the first step towards the development of the total person.

Such enrichment can only be achieved through knowledge. It is only when one knows what to do, how to do it, and when he or she has to do it, that one is considered knowledgeable. It is only when the person has become knowledgeable that he knows how to utilize resources, technology, infrastructure and appropriate policies.

In many African countries, development implementors often discover that to put education first, presents great difficulties. It is said, and rightly so, that "a hungry man has no ears". Given the present and worsening food situation in Africa one wonders which has to come first; food or knowledge?

African countries have come from a situation of self sufficiency, from being food exporters to being dependent on food imports. Self-sufficiency in food production must be placed at the top of any list in the search for alternative strategies.

We must find ways of blending aspects of food production and development education if we are to get a word into the people's ears. In the past many development programmes have created dependence on handouts, quite contrary to what was intended.

In spite of the fact that smallholder rural agriculture produces 80% of the food and provides employment for the majority of the rural population, past policies have often ignored this fact. The result has been a lack of incentives for the small farmer and consequently the acceleration of rural - urban migration.

Many small scale credit schemes do not cater for the smallholder agriculture subsector. It is claimed due to past experience that this is a high risk area. The problem stems from the fact that the small loans usually given out by NGO's are not guaranteed and, therefore, the chances of default are greater. This then puts the smallholder into even deeper trouble.

It is a great relief that many donors and .financial institutions are beginning to come up with loan guarantee schemes. It is also a great relief that African governments are favouring food subsidies for the poor consumer while raising the prices of agricultural produce. It is doubtful whether these measures actually help the rural poor, although they may add to the overall economic burden of African countries.

The third area which should be considered is that of Public Health. Sick people do not make good participants in development. In this area, churches have been at the forefront of having established numerous mission health centres even before integrated rural development programmes came into being.

In many developing countries health is tied to other programmes such as water, sanitation, and income generating activities. These programmes are considered to be necessary compliments of any successful health programme.

For such programmes to be truly successful they must be community based. The community must learn to organize and manage their own projects. This fact is becoming increasingly accepted by major international donor and service agencies which previously favoured large scale projects. They have now realized that development must start at the grassroots level.

The church has a unique structure which, if effectively utilized, can contribute enormously to development in Africa. Due to this unique structure the church can easily reach the entire rural population. The church network can be used to mobilize and educate people, given the trust and goodwill people have in its institutions. It is not usually possible for bureaucracy-burdened government institutions to reach down to the grassroots level, but the church being a simple, people-based institution is already there.

Searching for appropriate strategies and the type of institutions through which development can easily be promoted is a vital issue. Institutions such as churches and other local NGO's can encourage the full participation of the people. Churches are, however, the most desirable of all institutions mainly because they cannot be politicized. Politicisation of peoples' organizations stifles development by making those institutions answerable to political masters, whose development philosophy may not necessarily be people oriented. Self-interest on the part of politicians which they interpret to mean "what the people want" brings about false development. It is in fact a type of development which is not sustainable; it is not based on what the people really want but on the perpetuation of political authority. When the political initiator goes, so do his projects.

Let me finish by quoting Jesus Christ:

"I came that they may have life and have it abundantly". (John 10:10)

References

1. Kenya Sessional Paper No. 10. p.41
2. *Daily Nation*, Nairobi, 22 January, 1981
3. *African Press Service*, 25 May, 1981
4. Kenneth D. Kaunda, *A Humanist in Africa*, p.100
5. Ibid, p.101
6. Ibid.
7. Hastings Adrian, *A History of African Christianity*, Cambridge University Press, 1979, pp.187
8. Ibid 188
9. Julius K. Nyerere, *Man and Development.* p.91
10. Stanley Hoffman, *Duties Beyond Borders*, Syracuse University Press, Syracuse, 1981, pp.22/28
11. John V, *Christianity and Politics in Africa*,p.42
12. Dietrich Bonhoeffer, *Letters and Papers*,p. 382
13. Ngindu Mushete, in *Christianity in Independent Africa*, p.238
14. Ibid; p.238
15. Ibid, p.235 (quoted by Mushete from Mobutu's speech)

──────────────────────────────── Chapter 4

IDEOLOGY AND DEVELOPMENT
IN SUB-SAHARAN AFRICA

Samir Amin

If the 1960s was characterized by an optimism concerning development in the third world, this is the era of disillusion. The development process is nonexistent, its theory is in crisis, and its ideology is the object of doubt. Everybody agrees on the general failure in Africa. This is a contrast to the case of Asia and Latin America where some analysts emphasize the economic success of newly industrialized countries, concluding that development can only occur through an integration of all world economies. It is in this framework that I would like to consider discussions concerning the relationship between ideology and development in Africa and in the third world in general. According to these debates, I will put forth the following hypotheses:

> *Hypothesis 1: The main reason for the failure of Sub-Sahara Africa to develop is that the region has not had an agricultural revolution which would, in turn, propell the process of industrialization.*

Africa has not experienced an agrarian revolution characterized by sustained agricultural growth and by an increase in food production per capita per rural household. Yet this is the necessary condition for industrialization, urbanization and social development. In parts of Africa, production and productivity per rural household is either stagnating or declining. Under these conditions, rural out migration is not the result of the over-population from agricultural growth but is instead a desperate move by people attempting to escape rural hunger. This genre of out migration leads to massive urbanization, without any hope that industry will take charge of the influx or sustain it.

The basic condition for effective development depends on the intensification of agriculture. It is a challenge that African people must accept which has not yet been assumed. The colonialists never actually considered such an undertaking. It was easier for them to extract their surplus without making significant investments. They did this by forcing African peasants to overwork, sometimes through indirect methods of control. The production per capita produced through overwork, a lack of equipment, modern inputs (but through the destruction of the production support-soil or land-in Africa) and associated with the degradation of the well being of the household was enough to generate an acceptable level of profits. Colonization followed the path of the old slavery tradition: exploitation by looting without consideration for the long term, without regeneration of the work force and the sustainability of the natural support of production.

Independence did not modify this mode of integration into the world capitalist system. The world capitalist system has come as a response to requirements of the new step towards the globalization of international economy of capital (reconstruction of Europe and American hegemony) and not as a response to problems facing the African peasant. The prosperity of the 1960s in the Western countries has initiated a new "extraverti system" euphoria in Africa.

The crisis in the 1970s is the consequence of the combined effects of over-exploitation, and the global crisis which is affecting the capitalist system as a whole. From this perspective, the influx of fix it proposals descending on Africa at an accelerated rate are just the expression of a desperate search for palliative stop gap measures.

These are no more than palliatives because discussions concerning the need to support agriculture are juxtaposed against those which favoured industrialization, now considered to be the cause of failure. However, increasing the level of productivity per farmer, necessitates a certain level of urbanization, while an urbanization without industrialization can only lead to stagnation. Industry (only the industry at the service of agriculture) is essential to agricultural growth, given the latter's dependence on equipment and inputs, which in return offer a potential expanding market for industry. If we reject this choice and choose to be systematically integrated into the world capitalist system, talks on "giving priority to agriculture" become empty. The contradictions between these propositions are obvious: export based industry translates into low salaries and low prices for food production and at the same time international bodies pressure for improved producer prices to get farmers to produce more!

The populist cover-up that some quarters have given to this proposition does not change the meaning despite all discussions concerning "basic needs". Africa in the imperialist vision is first of all a source of mineral resources for the West. Thus, industrialization and agricultural development are not really taken seriously.

Hypothesis 2: The world expansion of capitalism is based on the expression of the global internationalized law of value which implies an unavoidable polarization.

There are two ways of looking at modern social reality. First, we tend to emphasize what we define as "capitalism" at its highest level of abstraction, meaning, the "capital/work" contradiction, and thereby defining the historical limits of capitalist society as the limit imposed by the economy. This inspires a "step" perception of the required evolution with a prescription for retarded (or peripheral) capitalist societies to catch up with the advanced model or face being left behind. Second, we give undue importance to what I call "effectively existing capitalism" i.e.t a system which in its world expansion has generated polarization centres/peripheries which cannot be overcome internally in the context of capitalism.

This vision of the modern world, places the unit of analysis unit at the world level. It is based on a theory of the global internationalization of the law of value in opposition to the prevailing liberal doctrine.

The liberal doctrine is premised on the idea that the development process is synonymous with market expansion and that at world level it is just the product of a permanent adjustment process of national reality to world constraints. The naive version of the doctrine reduces the adjustment to the liberalization of trade and flux of capital. In its "real-politik" version, it assumes that state policies (meaning it does not deny the crucial role) and the objectives of cultural and social changes are the basic parameters determining this adjustment, reached through the combined actions of state intervention and the market dynamics.

The liberal doctrine must be viewed as pure ideology, without scientific foundation, given its assumption that an expansion of the market economy allows for a maximization of growth and balanced distribution. Among other problems with the theory, is the fact that market remains a truncated market, where the idea of the free movement of products, capital, and other labour is still not accepted.

Keeping in mind that my analysis is situated at the world level, the various social classes which make up the world capitalist society find their places in this frame. On the other hand, these societies also have their own internal/national differences. By considering the world system as the central unit of analysis, we take the true measure of a social fact whose reach is decisive in the understanding of deciding stakes in social struggles, meaning that the reserve army of the capital is geographically located in the peripheries of the system. The integration of the fractions of the reserve army in that active army - always partial - is either done locally by "semi-industrialization" which characterized the true current and tomorrow peripheries by an international migration towards the centres. But this option only concerns a small fraction of the world reserve army.

Thus, we understand why history does not support the liberal hypothesis and that polarization is the unvoidable consequence of the truncated market it is proposing. In that way, the submission of national policies to the supreme criteria of universal "competitivity" is a false response to the challenge. In fact, the objective of development implies a sustainable improvement of productivity in all possible areas and a guaranty that the benefit of this improvement will be distributed to promote the progressive integration of the entire population (in other words, a policy which rejects the marginalization caused by the implementation of the absolute rule of international competitivity).

World polarization dominates the scene. The struggle of people who are victims of capitalist expansion occupies the forefront of the arena. The concept of "people" is that of a historical block of the oppressed, including the distinctly established classes and the reserve army .

Hypothesis 3. The forms of polarization are in a state of permanent evolution. The evolution from an international economy to the interpenetration of national economies in the world productive system, which characterizes the current era does not open up itself to the homogenization; of the planet, but to the reinforcement of centres vs peripheries.

The modern economic system of developed capitalist countries has been built up progressively over several centuries. Nationally, this represents the product of a specific combination of social alliances in each country. The result has been the stable establishment of the bourgeoisie hegemony, through which each national state is characterized by a particular political culture.

The national character of dominant social formations of the world system established in this way, has itself shaped the international economy. By international, we mean to suggest that behavior of operators in this system is determined by the structures of national social hegemony of the central partners.

This edifice is now giving way to a new phase of the capitalist evolution. We should not underestimate the fact that this universalization has entered a new phase. The autonomy of national economies is fading partly because of a reduction of barriers to exchange and foreign investments.

Does this genreof evolution offer any hope for third world countries? With universalization could they overcome their historical under-development? Can they catch up with developed western countries?

Without expanding on the details, my conclusion is the following: That unequal development created and continuously reinforced by the capitalist expansion has produced a very diverse world. Consequently, no universal solution - "the market"- can be effective or acceptable. Thus, the significant differences between various world regions implies the adoption of specific politics which cannot be derived solely from market rationality. The imperatives of our era imply the reformulation of the world system on the basis of polycentrism.

It is vital that a true place be given to third world countries and regions within that conception of world polycentrism. Those countries and regions which are able to coordinate their visions must devise their own solutions and not just adjust themselves to the expansion of world capitalism.

Hypothesis 4. World polarization has led to the requirement of human progress. Regarding capitalist evolution, this way is very different from those conceived by the historic socialism including marxism.

In the existing world capitalism system, "antisystemic" forces and movements are those which are against polarization, refuse to submit to its consequences, and engage in an on the ground struggle which is in fact objectively anti-capitalist, and attacks the basic characteristics of capitalist expansion which they strongly reject.

If development able to meet needs of all social classes of the nation appears to be impossible in the periphery of the capitalism system, then the study of types of development is required. That is the meaning of the expression "disconnection".

Disconnection is not a recipe but a choice. Then there must be peoples' projects for which we cannot find an adjective other than socialism. We must assume that the socialism remains a project largely ahead of us and not a reality already built which could just be imitated.

This means of challenging the capitalist order through revolt by its peripheries obliges us to think again about the question of "socialist transition" and the abolition of classes. Whatever nuance we put to it, the Marxist tradition has remained handicapped by the theorical vision of a "workers revolution", based on the development of advanced productive forces. Nevertheless, all revolutions of our time (Russia, China, Vietnam, Cuba, Yugoslavia, etc) which were qualified as socialist (and which in the intention of their actors have assigned themselves this objective) are in reality a series of anti-capitalist or nationalist revolutions carried out in retarded regions which have not led to the development of socialism as envisaged by Marx. Unequal development as a result of capitalist expansion has led to another type of revolution, that of peripheral peoples. This genre of revolution is anti-capitalist rather than socialist. In the future, these national peoples' revolutions will shape up the North/South relations and create in the dynamic basis for the global evolution of our world. The stakes of these struggles which occupy the forefront of modern history can be summarized by the alternative: popular national power or state power.

In a world threatened by barbarous North-South conflicts, a solution of "mutual adjustment" would be most appropriate. However, there is no chance of progress, unless there is a convergence between social movement objectives in each of the three conventional parts of the world (West, East and South). This in turn implies progress towards a universal culture.

Hypothesis 5: The strategic choices of the European community is directly responsible for the failure of development in the sub-Sahara Africa.

In Sub-Saharan Africa, post-independence reconstruction could not go very far, given the divisions between nations and their neo-colonial alliances to Europe through the EEC. The Lome convention is a reflection of Europe's own interests and its international position. Europe covers its trade deficit with the United States and Japan by the surplus it obtains from the Third World and the Eastern bloc countries. It also depends heavily on an immigrant work force mainly from dependant areas (Arab, African, and Antillais), which have been hit by unbalanced capitalist development. This European strategy also includes Latin America and South East Asia.

Hypothesis 6: The ideology of development has found its most radical expression in what I call the "Bandoung era" (1955-1975). This ideology did not mark a divorce form the foundations of the world capitalist systems.

The idea of radical "national" reconstruction was part of the spirit of Bandoung (1955-1975). It was devised to advance a national bourgeois modernization project, objectively part of the new dynamics of the world capitalist expansion (The industrialization of the peripheries), based on internal economic and social reforms (agrarian reform, nationalizations, populism etc). Conflicts with western interests were limited and "non-aligned countries" could mobilize Soviet support to negotiate better terms. This strategy collapsed reflecting the impossibility of this national bourgeois project, and the collapse of the Soviet support. In some areas, this radical nationalism left behind it some achievements, including the beginnings of industrialization and social change. In other cases, mainly South of the Sahara, the extreme fragility of the state also limited the effects of the strategy. Following the Bandung period, there were collective attempts to negotiate better international terms, through the strategy of the "New International Economic Order"(1975). However, western countries, rejected the idea and after 1980 and initiated their own "counter-offensive", exemplified by the World Bank /IMF position on structural adjustment.

Hypothesis 7: After World War II there was an "ideology of multi-dimensional development which is currently in a state of crisis.

The concept of development was strange to bourgeois thinking which totally and blindly accepted colonial exploitation. The ideology of development, dominant from 1945, in its liberal neo-colonial radical, reformist and nationalist form, has legitimated the project of building up bourgeoisie national states along Western lines.

The era of this ideology of development is closed. On one hand, the new universalization of the world capitalism is being reflected by a return to the traditional concept of brutal management (even military) of the world system for the benefit of the dominating centres. On the other hand, the internal crisis of third world societies resulted in the questioning of all concepts relating to the organization of the state and to the content of development. Under these conditions the danger of generalized chaos is real. The only possibility of avoiding this chaos is the formulation of new guide-lines based on acceptance of people centered development and on the reconstruction of the international order. However, we are far from meeting these conditions.

Chapter 5

PROSPECTS FOR AFRICA FOR AN ALTERNATIVE APPROACH TO THE DOMINANT AFRO-PESSIMISM

N. Bourenane

Introduction

To ask the question today as to where Africa is going increasingly seems to resemble a mere fantasy. It demonstrates a lack of understanding of the continent's realities given that the evidence, the analyses and the arguments appear clear and the conclusions irrefutable. Indeed, afro-pessimism has ended up being accepted by everyone as the only realistic attitude.

This attitude, largely supported by the powers that be, by groups opposed to the regimes in power, including experts of international bodies responsible for finance and development, is nevertheless open to scrutiny. It is hardly neutral. It has, for this reason, a precise social function in the current epoque in which a greater and greater number of people, particularly the young, are demanding the right to speak out and to have a share in shaping their future. The social movements which have sprung up in different regions of Africa are becoming more widespread and more intense. They are likely to spread to other regions of the continent in different forms and give rise to upheavals, the meaning and ramification of which may be difficult to predict.

Afro-pessimism plays different roles for different people. For the regimes in power, it justifies the selective economic austerity which is imposed on them and which they put in practice. For the opposition, it justifies their struggle for power, without considering alternative political or socio-economic programmes which are, in most cases, non-existant or even identical to those currently applied by the regimes in power. For the experts, it justifies their dominating interference as "normal" and unavoidable. For all concerned, it provides a framework for reflection, for problem-solving, and for implementation. Nevertheless, a more critical look at the type of information available and the manner in which it is made use of by those concerned would lead us to adopt a less dogmatic and more balanced viewpoint, concerning the achievements of three decades of independence as well the prospects facing Africa on the threshold of the second millenium.

We propose in this context to take a brief look at the position of the continent, starting with a retrospective analysis of the economic and social situation, based on generally agreed upon statistics and evidence. This will provide an opportunity for a critical evaluation of the current analyses which often exclude from their frame of reference any information likely to give rise to doubt as to their coherence and accuracy.

The Approach of the Traditional Framework

What attracts one's attention when one first looks at the writing on Africa is the homogeneity attributed to the continent, whether one is discussing politics, economics, or society. Africa is viewed as one, with the same history, subject to the same constraints, facing the same problems and, consequently, going forward towards the same future. This perspective is not new, it goes back to the colonial period, and was so internalised by African leaders themselves that it led to a stereotypic type of panafricanism, which in fact has retarded regional integration. This monolithic view of Africa continues to survive and endure notwithstanding the increasing complexity of national economies, the relationship between countries, the states themselves, and various social groupings.

In the name of Panafricanism, the powers that be, those in opposition, and the African intelligentsia, have denied the existence of local differences, and have even tried to destroy them. Nevertheless, as the continent regresses the existence of the local has become increasingly obvious. Everywhere there is a tendency for local power structures to reappropriate political and economic decisions taken at the national and international level. This is not only the case in the countryside where traditionalism is said to hold sway, but also in the towns which have become even more important in numerous African countries.

Ethnic, tribal, regional and religious configurations seem today to have an unyielding historical consistency, as well as a cultural, political, social and economic dimension.

The emergence of local power, despite attempts at rendering the society more homogeneous, and the generalised desire to gloss over differences, by any means, including violence, during the past three decades brings us to ask the following questions. What would be the fate, whether today or in the past, of all these populations who have no means of survival of their own, if these frameworks of local solidarity did not exist? Where would we be today in terms of social inequality, poverty, malnutrition, and death, resulting from the many forms of marginalization dictated from on high?

Perhaps the task of reversing this trend of collective alienation should be undertaken, so as to acknowledge the complexity of both collective and individual mechanisms of reproduction and to consider these as the basis of any viable project.

It is from this starting point that we should look into current analyses of Africa and examine their relevance, using an approach which refuses to suggest one and the same solution for the whole continent. We will start therefore by the prevalent Afro-pessimism, the theories which underpin it and the analyses on which it is founded.

The Terms of Reference of the Prevalent Afro-pessimism and its Conclusions
Africa: a Continent Headed towards the Apocalypse

In the beginning of the 1960's, there was hardly anyone who questioned the economic success of Africa, but today the situation has now been reversed. Africa has today reached a state of "development break-down", with both the states and the "people" incapable of breaking this vicious circle of regression and poverty. The policies and economic programmes applied in the last thirty years have been destructive in every respect. From the ecological point of view, the balance of nature has been destroyed. Desertification and drought, accompanied here and there by torrential rains, have upset our fragile ecology, creating a problem of survival for populations reduced to sub-human conditions of existence. From the economic and social stand point, states which gave priority to the urban areas and to the middle class have ended up destroying the social equilibrium, bringing about migration, unhealthy living conditions, and poor or inadequate nutrition. From the political point of view, the powers that be, reluctant to adopt principles of power-sharing, have *tended to overlook any critical evaluation of their performance* while much of the educated labour force has emigrated to escape an environment where corruption and deceit prevail. At the same time, the meagre progress achieved during the first two decades of independence has been wiped out, leaving only a mirage or a day-dream.

Many figures support the above analysis. An infaillible indicator is the rate of growth of GDP. Equivalent to the rate of .population growth (nevertheless very high) in the 1960's (3.3%), the GDP fell to 2.4% in the 1970's and turned in the following decade (-2.2% already in the middle of the 1980's). Simultaneously despite this drop in resources, the recurring expenditures of the state have continued to grow. In relative terms, they have tripled while personal spending has dropped.

In this context, agriculture has continued to evolve and perform erratically while remaining profoundly influenced by various calamities, whether they be climatic or political. It has been adversely affected by various disasters, ranging from locusts to civil wars, all of which has created starving hoards of people, totally dependant on external food aid for their survival. For this reason the sector appears to be moving backwards, with a lower and lower growth rate and one which falls well below that of the population.

Industry appears not to be making any more progress. In fact, we are witnessing a massive and pronounced de-industrialisation, likely to confine the continent to its former role, that of a supplier of raw materials.[1] On this basis, there are many who believe that the 1980's has been a lost decade for Africa.[2]

The above evidence, plus Africa's debt crisis all indicate that the continent is moving backwards into a state of generalised and absolute poverty. At the same time, other regions of the world are moving forward.

According to OECD estimates, if the average income per capita in the West was 7 times that of an African in 1960, it represented 15 times that of an African in 1985. Compared with Latin America or Asia, the disparities are even more alarming, and are proof of a widening gap between production and productivity. The average revenue in Asia was half that of Africa in 1960 while Latin America's was twice that of Africa. In 1985, the trend had reversed itself in favour of Asia (1.25 more) while Latin America earned three times what Africa earned per capita.

According to the World Bank, two thirds of the rural population in Africa is below the poverty line. According to the OECD, the loss of per capita income in Africa was more disastrous in the 1980's than that experienced during the 1930's in Europe and the USA. If one adds to these statistics others pertaining to the financial situation including: the level of the deficit in the trade balance or the balance of payments,[3] the extent of debt and interest on the debt,[4] or again the implications of energy consumption, more than half of which consists of wood fuel (synonymous with massive deforestation), the need for more jobs,[5] or the refugee situation,[6] one can only become pessimistic and predict the total disappearance of this sickly continent which can only survive with support from others, notwithstanding all sorts of aid and assistance, whether it be aid without strings attached or programmes of restructuration and economic reforms. Thus a recent title for an article in a Kenyan daily: "Africa: Cry the Unloved Continent!" One is also forced to conclude that this continent is living beyond its means.

Consequently, pictures provided by the media take the place of analysis and form the basis of decisions taken about investment or disinvestment by foreign companies. In addition, the traditional partners of the continent, when they do not disengage themselves, tend to give preference to "sure" and short-term operations.

In such a context, it is not surprising that different plans and international programmes (i.e. UN-PAARED, SAP, WB, APPER - IMF) have remained a dead letter and have had little effect on the reversal or drying up of direct foreign investment. Nevertheless, the rigid management of African economies by expatriate personnel and the heavy burden this has created has grown. One is almost tempted to say that, with some few exceptions, they have become the masters of major economic decisions.

One must therefore ask oneself what is the continent's future and how can it emerge from the crisis. In a situation where nothing allows us to predict a rise in the value of raw materials exported by the continent, nor a positive development in internal savings, all that we can hope for is to suffer less from the abandon which would inexorably affect a continent which has at most the GNP of the Benelux countries, in other words, of less than ten million.

In such a context, the economic and social fragmentation of African countries seems unavoidable and the collapse of the state obvious. The continent therefore seems likely to degenerate into chaos, under the double impetus of its economic and political marginalisation and the breakdown of a modern organisational structure, given its inability to meet the irreducible needs of a young and rapidly growing population. Africa will not be able to face up to the demand for basic education from a population which has already exceeded 20 million children and which will reach 31 million by the year 2015. This continent will not be able to easily make up its cereals' shortage which stands today at 10 million tons and which will rise to 50 million tons by the year 2000. Africa can expect to face the apocalypse in the present and in the future.

The solutions suggested to limit the effects of this regression or, for the optimists, to reverse the trend in the long run, are well known. They all revolve around the idea of adjusting to the world economy, to the organisational and social models prevailing in Europe and the USA, and to the models of political democracy practised in the same places. The decade of the 1990's has been assigned the catch-word of "democracy" by the seven most industrialised countries in the world. A state like France does not hesitate to link its aid to the exercise of democracy, understood as freedom of political association, coupled with the supremacy of parliament, although this linkage remains largely a matter of verbiage.

If one confines oneself to the most recent period, it would be interesting to query the relationship between adjustment and the social groups taken here as a reference or model. One soon realises that the recommendations proposed and applied on the continent for more than a decade result more from rigid theory than the concrete historical situation in the countries one is seeking to adjust. In fact, in no country have the theories of adjustment really been applied, including in the practice of democracy. The events of the gulf, from this point of view, have been very instructive. They have revealed the very violent anti-democratic and even fascist nature of states who pretended to be in the fore-front of democratic expression.

It is this discrepancy between the actions of the dominant states in the OECD and the recommendations made (in terms of economic deregulation, the raising of all forms of protectionism within national economies which are, however, embryonic and fragile, the adjustment to the world economy, the respect for the sacrosanct principle of the comparative advantage in the short term of devaluation and of privatisation) which obliges us to go back to the proposed solutions and the analyses on which they are based.

The Limits of Afro-Pessimism and the Necessity of Alternative Approaches

The analyses previously referred to, all of which have spoken about the absolute and relative degradation of the economic and social situation in Africa constitute, from a purely methodological point of view, a dangerous short-cut for any attempt at finding solutions to the problems posed, whether these concern food, employment, the creation of a viable economic base, or the strengthening of democratic procedures. The major reason is that they gloss over realities, and fail to examine facts which do not support their conclusions.

In this sense, the first limitation comes, in fact, from the reasoning which considers the continent as a homogeneous whole, with the same characteristics, the same history and the same future.   An analysis, however, by sub-region or even by country would reveal the existence of wide differences in all areas. Whatever criteria used, even countries situated in the same region (i.e. the ECA) cannot easily be grouped together, unless one wishes to incorrectly homogenize them.

But quite apart from this short-cut, there are a number of other deficiencies which make the analyses and the conclusions arrived at questionable. One can only remain perplexed at the ease with which analysts generalise at the country level, based on occasional surveys or drawing on samples which are limited and other unrepresentative. Many examples exist, with discussions of malnutrition or the extent of AIDS ; not even being the worst. In addition to this stumbling block, there is another which is even more serious. This concerns the state of ignorance in which one finds oneself when one carries out an evaluation of productive activities. In fact, the whole field of activity which does not fall directly under the state escapes observation. In certain European countries, (such as Italy) despite being relatively well organised from the statistical point of view, studies calculate the contribution of this sector at about 20% of GDP. What then about a continent where the economic development is often situated outside the formal sector? What is even more serious in Africa is that the idea of a statistical survey is seen at the local level as being linked to the possibility of outside intervention, whether to siphon off resources (a connection made with taxes), to invest or to initiate an external aid project. In all cases, the result will be the same: coming up with less than the actual local resources. If one adds to this the fact that, in their definition, statistics rarely take into account local specificities (the universality of definitions and the search for comparisons impose themselves)[8] one realises the extent of the historical misconceptions which can abound. There is, in fact, no shortage of these.

Thus, theoretically, during the past decade, given the decline of available food stocks in a number of countries on the continent, due to a fall in food production and an increase in imports compared with the rate of population growth, one should find a rise in mortality, particularly infant mortality. In the case of African countries that would be seen in a reversal of the trend concerning the death rate and a fall in life expectancy. Nevertheless, up to now, no country has shown this trend. On the contrary, the previous trends have been accentuated and continue to be observed, which, in terms of population pressure, is very worrying.

This type of example is multiplied in other fields, whether it be in production, in housing, in employment, in education,[9] in the supply of foodstuffs to the population or in the circulation of goods and products. On this topic, it is useful to remember that many populations can and do easily cross frontiers to sell and buy. Thus, it is not rare to see products in short supply in the country of origin available in large quantities at prices which defy competition in neighbouring or even distant countries.

All this shows, in fact, the very complexity of African realities, which cannot be reduced to an over-simplified tableau reproducing figures published here and there, either by states or by specialised international agencies. In fact, official statistics only give a good picture of the performance of those sectors directly linked to the state or those which carry on their activities in conjunction with the public sector. This is to say that, at most, when one talks about crisis and degradation we are referring to sectors whose existence is directly and traditionally linked to the state. Therefore, the extent of the crisis is directly proportional to that experienced in the social and economic areas dominated by the state.

Such an interpretation therefore implies that we cease to adopt an attitude of Afro-pessimism, which refers, after all, mainly to a crisis in areas of national activity dominated by the state or by the foreigners directly linked to it.

This does not mean that African societies and countries are not faced with financial, economic, social, cultural and political problems, which we must scrutinize. It is likely that the structural adjustment programme adopted here and there have had an impact which has differed from one country to another, one social category to another and one place to another. Indeed, the variety of situations and abilities to respond to different social groups affected by the same measures can only result in a variety of different outcomes. In other words, what we have probably observed does not represent an example of homogenization but rather one of diversification.

Such a hypothesis will be easily confirmed by examining the specific reactions of various local communities coming to grips with adjustment, whether they be in towns or in the countryside, in terms of strategies of self-employment and the creation of alternative forms of revenue. When one takes the example of countries like Mali, Cote d'Ivoire, Guinea or Ghana, one sees the extent and variety of the reactions and the general ability to adapt and to adopt alternative strategies based on the family to maintain the level of income-earning or even improve it.

We can thus see that the macro-economic evidence available to us tends, by the very way in which it was gathered, to establish a false premise, since it is a simplified version of reality and since it assumes a one to one relationship between the formal set-up of the central state machinery and society. One could even say that the evidence demonstrates more than any thing the seriousness of the crisis faced by the authorities, who have less and less backing, both at home and abroad.

This brings us to the degree of the state's role in creating the present historical situation. Some are of the opinion that the state should assume total responsibility for the failure of the development experiments in the decades following independence. Not only were the states consumers of revenue, they are also unable to correctly manage the volume of aid and the means put at their disposal. This has necessitated eliminating them from this process and using other systems of management, whether experts from international institutions or NGO's which are directly or indirectly controlled by the lending agencies. Thus, at a time when the complexity of problems requires maximum national energy output, particularly in the management of the state, such efforts are frozen by putting NGO's and experts in their place, in the name of efficiency and democracy.[10]

The above remarks can be elaborated still further. One could put forward the hypothesis that Africa's post-independence regimes have in fact greatly contributed to generally bettering the living conditions of their populations, whether it be in the urban or the rural areas. Whatever country one considers, the level of investment into social and economic infrastructure, and the facilities accorded income generation have contributed both to the emergence of new social classes as well as to the general improvement in the level of training and local access to information. Today, it would be difficult to say that the majority of the rural population has remained on the fringe of society. These people have, in one way or another, come into the market and money economy.

As such, quite apart from its purely economic significance, this transformation has formed the basis for any future democratic process. Both the improvement in the general standard of living of the masses plus their increased awareness has created a climate where people are now demanding a greater share of the common national output, and are against the misuse of national resources. What is happening in countries such as Benin, Congo, Ethiopia, Kenya and Togo all points in this direction.

Ironically, the state which is blamed for having produced the crisis, has in fact played a role in improving the economic and social situation as well as having facilitated the conditions which are now bringing about its own failure, or its lack of backing, as an instrument of power to maintain national, social and political consensus. This applies equally to countries where independence did not lead to violent military action as to the others.[11]

In reality, the criticisms which are directed at the state seem to have another function: that of glossing over the responsibility of the partners of the regimes in power, notably other states and institutions which have played a part in developing and carrying out investments during the past three decades. To safeguard their immediate interests in the short term, these partners in development have tended to reflect the men and the authorities who headed the civil service in the former colonies.

State bureaucrats have had to face financial and managerial difficulties, due to the weakness of their national administrative systems and the influence of foreign operators on the systems of production and commercialisation of the nation output. Hence, they have had little choice but to give in partially or totally to the former colonial powers.

We are not trying here to minimize the role of the State in the multi-faceted crisis affecting the organs of national administration, but to underline the nature of the different players who also bear some responsibility for the current situation.

From this point of view, a look back at the so-called decades of development, will show the extent to which the range of manoeuvrability of the states was reduced, whether it be in choosing which plan of action to adopt, its financing, or its implementation. In fact, from such a perspective, one is tempted to view national states as no more than the extension of external powers, situated in the "former mother countries",

whether it be a question of ministries in charge of international cooperation or firms and enterprises interested in one way or another in having
African markets.[12]

The above perspective suggests that the idea of Afro-pessimism is
rather stereotyped. It simply reproduces existing attitudes rather than
going beyond them. In terms of action, this obviously leads to a
continuation of procedures already in practice, with the addition of a
few euphemisms such as "adjustment with a human face".

Democratization and Alternative Development

Africa has less and less influence internationally and its economic and
political leverage is also regressing. Today the marginalisation of
Africa is a fact. It is however being accompanied by two phenomena
which are dangerous in the long run: the development of economies
based on aid on the one hand and the fragmentation of nations and the
break-ups of regional entities on the other hand.

The first phenomenon signifies a worsening of the present inequalities
between Africa and the rest of the world as well as the marginalization
of its economies. Its focus is on balancing the budget at the expense of
productive investment. In this context, there is little place for development research without which it would be difficult to relaunch
structured economic activities. Thus, if the current tendencies are to
intensify, Africa will become one huge bazaar: a small-scale market for
shoddy goods (of all sorts which are not locally produced) of no utility,
except to firms of the countries from which they come. The development of economies such as those of Senegal, Algeria and Tanzania, is
already evidence enough of the above. This pattern fits in well with the
current international division of labour, whereby Africa is a continent
which supplies raw materials of less and less value for prices directly
controlled by those who buy them. Obviously, nothing will escape this
tendency, neither oil and gas nor precious metals.

The drama of Africa, in comparison with other regions of the world
is that with technological progress and the demand which it induces,
together with the social, cultural, and political conditions of its implementation, the marginal productivity of its work and its capital appear
relatively low, in fact too low to attract potential investors.

However, a second process, the result of a generalization of the first,
is that Africa is being divided up by different imperial powers into
regional entities. The advantage for these powers is more than evident.

Apart from the reduction in the costs involved in the nation-states' machinery of administration and repression, the setting up of intermediary structures avoids the necessity of direct intervention. It ensures the creation of more viable entities so as to contain the menace of our migration to Europe. Europe, just like other geo-economic units, needs to ensure the security of its territory, in the face of the growing disparities between the standards of living in different regions of the world, and the ensuing immigration which it is likely to encourage.

At this point, a look at the process of democratization is in order. If it tends to be founded exclusively on the emergence of a political set-up consisting of a multitude of little parties which lack scope or real social roots, this will mean diverting national energy from the field of the struggle for productive investment in favour of a clientage approach, each party will be preoccupied with enlarging its electoral support, winning power and amassing the funds necessary for its survival at the expense of the national good.

This process will express itself in terms of greater social, economic and cultural differentiation than that which already prevails at the moment in different regions of the continent. It is synonymous with an upsurge of violence, insecurity and instability, all of which generate unfavourable conditions for the increase of national and international savings for the purpose of investment. Thus, the present situation, which is already a crisis of the management systems of the state and certain sectors associated with it, could become worse by being transformed into a multi-faceted and profound crisis with immeasurable consequences.

What then are the alternatives? A simple answer cannot be provided, however, certain hypotheses can be advanced.

The first concerns the academic milieu. It is, in fact, illusory to pretend to make a contribution to the research of alternative solutions when one continues to mechanically reproduce existing knowledge, starting with inadequate categories and conceptual instruments which simplify our realities. The task of reversing the trend of scientific estrangement needs to be undertaken. It is in fact urgent.

The second also concerns intellectuals but to a greater extent the social forces in the making, in particular, the youth who, today, are on centre stage. It is important today to restore the state to its former position as the organ of collective and consensual management, carrying out national and international projects with the aim of avoiding the current fragmentation of social and economic units. Intellectuals should avoid seeing themselves only as advisors to the throne, all the more so since the quality of their knowledge does not allow them to do so.

At this point, we cannot insist too much that democratization should be synonymous with simply "less state". It should mean a greater participation in a project of global economic and social security, through the well-organized creation of systems of management and accountability. To head down the path of privatisation, when no alternative structure exists, is to participate in the liquidation of the historical acquisition of society, including those inherited from the colonial period. That does not only signify a step backwards: it is synonymous with regression, which is much more serious.

The third concerns the procedures to be adopted. Given the complexity of the present situation, and international trends, cooperation and regional integration among neighbouring countries is essential.

Two approaches would be relevant:

The first consists of letting the process be shaped by the forces which today dominate the state and the international economy. This would imply a great rush forward in the direction of privatisation and denationalization (this is synonymous with the buying of national assets by foreigners). The second consists of attempting to indigenize development projects and to implement them. It is this second path which is likely to avoid the apocalypse and to break radically with the prevailing Afro-pessimism.

It presupposes, however, the building up of democratic structures founded on a respect for mutual differences on the rejection of exclusivity, on the integration of the youth, into both national and international institutions. It also involves an effort in the fields of training and education, since democratic attitudes are not inborn; they need to be cultivated and result from a conscious and well-constructed process of training and education.

This is the challenge of the future for all the countries of the continent.

Notes

1. There are numerous articles and published works containing varied figures which do not always agree. Cf. for example the reports of the WB, the OECD, the ECA and writings such as those of Adebayo Adedeji, "The African Challenges in the 1990's" in *The Indian Journal of Social Science*, Vol. 3, no. 2, 1990, Sage Publication Philippe Hugon "What economic future for Africa?" in *Afrique Contemporaine*, no 146

1988, Paris, Jeff Hyne, "Africa in the international system: problems and prospects" (review article) in *Africa: Journal of the international African Institute* 60(3) 1990, London, Joseph Wheeler, "Subsaharan African Thirty Years From Now", *Observateur de l'OCDE*, no 143, November 1986.

2. Cf., for example, Adebayo Adedeji, "The African Challenge in the 1990's" in *The Indian Journal of Social Sciences*, Vol. 3, no. 2 1990. Sage Publication.

3. The deficit in the trade balance has today exceeded $U.S. 5 billion while that of the balance of payments is today more than $U.S. 11 billion.

4. Interest on the debt represents half of exports and the debt will reach $U.S 500 billion by the year 2000.

5. According to U.N. estimates, the active population will exceed 200 million persons in the year 2000.

6. Their number is estimated at more than 10 million persons.

7. See in this connection N. Bourenane, "The Food Crisis in Africa", ACARSTOOD ECA, 1988, "The State and the Promotion of Entrepreneurs in Africa", AAS/1988, "A Socio-economic analysis of hunger and food self-sufficiency in Africa", CODESRIA / UNESCO 1984, "The instruments of economic measure: inappropriate tools in measuring the crisis" in *Revue Politique Aujourd'hui*, 1985, Paris.

8. One example is of weighty significance. It concerns the definition of illiteracy. In a good number of cases, any person incapable of using the former colonial language, now transformed into the official language, was considered illiterate. By the same token, writing and reading one's mother tongue is synonymous with illiteracy. Obviously, in the relationship between knowledge and power, as in the process of indigenization loudly proclaimed by the state, this system of hierarchy is far from neutral.

9. In 1960, the number of illiterates stood at some 124 million. In 1985, it was 162 million. In absolute terms, there was an increase. However, one needs to compare these figures with the population growth. A small calculation would show that a vast effort had been undertaken which had brought about a more than relative improvement. The present generation has fewer illiterates than the earlier ones.

10. In fact, with the programmes of adjustment and the manner of their implementation, the liberty of action of the local representatives is not enhanced but rather reduced. The state, which has less and less

latitude in its conduct and the choice of policies to pursue remains - an irony of history - responsible for the eventual results. Cf. for example, the food strategy of Mali or the evaluations carried out by the PAS.

11. For all these aspects, see N. Bourenane, "The State and the promotion of entrepreneurs" .....op cit.

12. Cf. N. Bourenane "The impact of bi-lateral and multi-lateral aid on African Agriculture" (Ed. CODESRIA).

Chapter 6

THE STATE AND DEMOCRACY IN SOUTHERN AFRICA

Ibbo Mandaza

Introduction: The Problem of Methodology

The current debate in Africa about governance and the one party state is a manifestation of the crisis of the state, democracy, and development. The developments relating to both the growing prominence of the international human rights movement in the course of the last decade, and the culmination of the crisis in Eastern Europe, have contributed to the high profile that the African condition (i.e. the current political and economic crisis) has assumed in 1990. To understand both the nature of the African condition, and the current debate about it, it is necessary to focus on the analysis of the post-colonial state in Africa and its relationship to civil society. Engaged without this holistic approach that encompasses a historical analysis of the continent, the debate on governance and on the one party state in Africa borders on the abstract, reflecting a tendency to view the African situation itself as peculiarly African. In general, the latter perception in particular represents one not so unrelated to the now well-known racist stereotypes: namely, that Africans are incapable of ruling themselves. This is the kind of sentiment illustrated in an article, which appeared recently in a leading Western newspaper, entitled "For Distressed Africa, What About International Colonialism?" Excerpts from the article will suffice:

Sub-Saharan Africa is in a terrible condition. The causes are complex, but the result is that most of sub-Saharan Africa has lost control of its own future. Its governments have become the stipendiaries of the International Monetary Fund and other international lending agencies. Economies have all but collapsed as prices have plunged in the markets for Africa's commodities. Between 1980 and 1987 the value of Africa's cocoa exports fell by 38%, that of coffee exports by 41%, of phosphates by 47%, of lumber wood products by 80%. Investment already has substantially dried up; that happened long before Eastern Europe's liberation. News from Eastern Europe, and the spirit of liberation it set loose in the world, had affected Africa, producing popular challenge to established authority...

But Africa's opposition forces are chaotic and fragmented, usually politically naive, without coherent programs. Opposition leaders often are as much the prisoners of obsolete or irrelevant ideologies as the people who govern. Infact, Africa has been stripped of its elites. Talented and educated people-the ones Africa desperately needs - are driven into emigration or political exile. Some 70,000 middle - and upper-level managers and administrators have abandoned Africa since the beginning of the 1980s.

In the past it has been convenient to blame Africa's problems on colonialism, or present-day "imperialism". Today it is evident that it makes no difference who is to blame....

The Europeans then tried to remake Africa and Africans to their own advantage and in their own image. Whatever the merits of that effort, which is based on a conviction of European superiority, but was not without altruism and sacrifice, it came to an end in the 1950s and 1960s. The moral upheaval produced by the two world wars, and the revolutionary doctrines preached from Moscow and Beijing, destroyed both the Europeans' belief in their right to rule Africa and the Africans' willingness to be ruled....

Today, in fact if not in name, a new colonialism exists. The World Bank, the IMF, the French government and the aid agencies of the other developed countries, together with the private lending institutions, set the terms on which Africa's economies function, or malfunction....

A unique opportunity exists. The Cold War struggle over Africa's ideological orientation is finished. The Soviet Union is ready to cooperate. The United Nations needs a serious role to play in today's world. Africa's post-independence models of state-socialist development and one-party rule are completely discredited. The human needs of Africa are desperate. Disease as well as hunger and chaos threaten its people.

What about a declared, internationalised colonialism for Africa? A

disinterested international interventionism? What about installing
a frankly paternalist international authority in Africa and a conti-
nent-wide development structure and program? The idea may be
outrageous in terms of the political pieties of the last 50 years, but
those pieties helped put Africa where it is today. What is the
alternative to neo-colonialism? Africa's condition demands desperate
measures.[1]

In addition, some African analysts, are also guilty of the tendency to
view the *African condition* as peculiarly African. How often do we hear
these laments, most of which emanate from the most erudite of African
writers: Chinua Achebe's *Things fall Apart*, an eternal indictment of an
Africa apparently unable to govern itself; or Ngugi wa Thiongo's
celebrated critiques of the post-colonial society and likewise, some of
our analyses in this collection.   As usual, the lament is about the
manifestations of deep-seated historical, socio-economic and political
factors. Seldom does the lament provide an insight into the causes of
this African condition; the lament itself hides the causes behind a screen
of apparent helplessness which, as racists would wish to suggest from
their own viewpoint, almost justifies the call for a recolonisation of
Africa. Surely, the duty of the analyst is to seek to explain rather than
describe and thereby to contribute toward the resolution of the problem.

If there is anything peculiar about the African condition, it is the
extent to which it is an outcome of both the character and conjuncture
of the colonisation of the continent and its incorporation into the
international capitalist system. This accounts in part for the tendency
among many analysts to generalise about the African condition and
therefore the expectation among many that out of this apparently
common historical experience must arise a new and united Africa. It
is true that Africa's identity today is an outcome of an apparently
common historical, political and economic legacy: centuries of underdevelopment by the northern hemisphere; the scourge of slavery
and racism both of which have constituted a serious drawback on
Africa's economic development and undermined the dignity of the
African person; and, consequently, the relationship between these
historical factors and the current economic and political malaise that
together account for the African condition today. But even within this
broad sweep, there are important differences and specificities between
one African sub-region and another, and between one African country
and another. African scholars are nearer now to the consensus that the
African condition is an outcome of both internal and external factors.

But we need to examine more closely the specificities of these factors with particular reference to the social formations in individual countries. The study of individual countries and situations will help to highlight these differences and specificities and thereby contribute to both an overall understanding of the African condition and a possible development of a strategy for recovery. Hence the need for a methodology on the basis of which we might begin to understand the key and theoretical conceptual issues about which such a study on governance and democracy should be concerned: the relationship between the (post-colonial) state and civil society; and the contextual nature of democracy.

Within the South African situation in particular, it becomes self-evident why the issue of governance and democracy cannot be understood outside the context of the post-white settler colonial state and the inherited economy. Here it is necessary to go beyond the mere characterisation of the post-colonial situation as one falling broadly under the concept of neo-colonialism. There is need to define its specificity in a given society in motion: both the nature of the state and the extent (and extant) of the civil society. Like other post-colonial states, the post-white settler colonial state is caught between the continuities demands of old, as reflected in the economic power of both the former white settlers and international capital (including the overall hegemony of the US and its major Western allies in Southern Africa). On the other hand, there are the inherent and growing economic and social demands of the mass of the people whose consciousness has already been aroused during the colonial period, particularly given the expectations associated with the nationalist struggle for independence. Within this broad contradiction should be considered the new and emergent social and class forces in civil society: the various elements of the petty bourgeoisie, the wage earners and other mass organisations; and the complexity of the relationship between internal and external forces within this historical process. Such a methodological framework provides an insight into, and indeed explains, the political and economic conditions that almost inexorably propel the post-colonial state towards a one-party-state (de facto or de jure). It also helps to explore the conditions and means whereby the civil society can create the space, to overcome those negative aspects and factors with a process of democratisation. The Zimbabwe debate on the one-party state and democracy should give us a deeper insight into the problematic of the state and democracy in the post-colonial situation.

The Historical and Ideological Bases of the One-party State in Africa

Colonialism and Liberal Democracy

The study of the post-colonial state in Africa has been a pre-occupation of scholars for as long as this phenomenon has been with the continent. The field has been dominated by two broad and sometimes conflicting perspectives. As I will attempt to illustrate, both methodologies might have had a profound influence on the nature and conduct of the post-colonial state, particularly the extent to which both have been used as the ideological or theoretical justification for the one-party state in Africa. First, the conventional model based on the modernisation theories found their origins in the Rostowian model of traditional Western political science. According to this school, the state and society in developing countries was inherently given to conflict and strife. Therefore, development, based as it is on Rostow's simplistic but ahistorical theory,[2] was conceived and perceived of a stage by stage process whereby the developing society gradually approximated the (development) model of such developed societies-e.g. USA and UK -as were characterised by stability, consensus, equilibrium and harmony. This is the school of thought that pervaded political science in the nineteen sixties and the development models of post-colonial Africa. Indeed, as contentious and controversial as such a submission is likely to be viewed by many in the northern hemisphere, it is this Western-type development model that has been the major source of the one-party state in Africa. It sought to provide both the historical and theoretical justification for a centralised and authoritarian system of governance on the grounds that there was a necessary link between the three phases of African history: the pre-colonial period when Africans were governed by centralised and authoritarian kingdoms and chiefdoms all of which invariably assigned a definable and even stable system; the colonial period during which Africans were introduced-however unfortunately and with whatever consequences-to modernisation and development by a centralised and authoritarian colonial system that nevertheless tended to bring together, all the various pre-colonial groupings within the new territorial boundaries in a kind of a stable and unified system, and the post-colonial period during which it was, therefore, imperative that this newly found unity be maintained under a strong state and strong leader, as a guarantee of stability and development. There was an implicit - not explicit, otherwise how could Africans lament colonialism and celebrate independence day - acceptance of continuity between the three periods. But as we will argue shortly, a major basis of the current African condition is also the extent to which these features and phases of Africa's recent history are so inextricably bound as to be reflected in the socio-economic and political structures of our contemporary societies.

There is an aspect of African political philosophy that tries to conceal this historical reality of continuity and yet is definitely an off-shoot of the Western philosophical thinking of which this development model (of *unity, stability and development*) is an outcome. This has been the philosophy that has underpinned the theory and practice of government in much of post-colonial Africa. It is inherent in that complexity we call the post-colonial state which has been Africa's legacy for the last thirty years. As is illustrated in the writings of Julius Nyerere in particular, this philosophy sought to conceal its link with Western political thought by the apparent rejection of any kind of continuity between the three periods of Africa's recent history: pre-colonial, colonial and post-colonial. Instead, there was the attempt to forge an umbilical link between the pre-colonial and post-colonial periods. According to the philosophy that inspired and guided this early post-independence period, the attainment of national independence was a return to the blissful past in which Africa was devoid of classes and characterised by *consensus, stability, and unity*. Hence Nyerere's celebrated book at the time, *Uhuru Na Umoja: Freedom and Unity*.[3] From it came not only the view that unity was the basis for attaining freedom but also that multi-partyism was inherently given to disunity and instability. And so it was that for most of the Africa of nineteen sixties and seventies, one-party-one-leader became the currency. (In fact, it would appear anomalous to speak of one party without one leader as its corollary.) At worst, the one-party-state (read one-leader-state) was viewed as the necessary price to pay for *stability and development*.

Now all should concede that the Nyererian thesis was as mythical as it was romantic. The impression, that appeared to wash for a while in Tanzania, must be attributed less to any claim of historical validity than to Nyerere's own style of leadership (not to mention his important contribution to the liberation struggle in Southern Africa). Also the fact that Tanzania was predominantly peasant in character made it extremely receptive to the *paternalism* of a father figure, the *mwalimu*! Yet it was also on the basis of one party one leader that Africa has produced those life-long personal fascist dictatorships that we need not mention here. But how does one distinguish between the paternalism that underpins or seeks to extol the one party state as the only basis for political life on the one hand and, on the other, that of the colonialist who believed that Africans were good for nothing unless nurtured like little children? Not surprisingly, it was not so much the Africans as the Europeans and North Americans who sang praises in the nineteen sixties and nineteen seventies (read the political science books of the day) about the one party state as the guarantor of development. Invariably, the pursuit of a one party state on the part of those concerned in Africa has been less a response to the mass demand for freedom and democracy than an attempt to silence and arrest a democratisation process that began in the struggle for national liberation and seeks a full resolution of the national question. So far, the overall negative aspects of the one party state in Africa is more than sufficient evidence that this is a political system which is out of step with the realities of our continent.

In short, Western *liberal-democratic philosophy* and its model of development provided the resource base upon which such non-leftist but Western-aligned post-colonial African states were born and nurtured. The oft-cited conclusion that one party states were born only out of the last leftist and Marxist-oriented leaders of Africa is not only a partial perspective but it, also reflects a certain level of dishonesty or the extent to which the analyst himself/herself was subject to, and therefore blinded by, the liberal ideology we have just outlined. For, the central feature of the *post-colonial state* is that it is *essentially a continuation of the colonial state*. This is particularly so with regard to the essential organisation of the state itself and its structures. As Ali Mazrui and Michael Tidy point out:

> Most new African states emerged into independence with relatively strong legislatures. The nature of the nationalist struggle during the colonial period had given the old Legislative Councils a central position system, and a mystique had grown round the idea of parliament. Much of the rhetoric of African nationalism was saturated with liberal democratic dicta..[4]

However, the same authors reveal their own bias when they equate the development of the *one party state* with the gradual evaporation of the "faith in parliamentary institutions".[5] As has already been pointed out in the foregoing, the vagaries of the post-colonial state invariably forced the latter into an inevitable modification of the Westminister model. The issue was not so much whether the state was *multi-party* or *one party,* but how continuity was to be maintained and sustained with regard to those essential elements of the state that defined the form and content of the emergent nation. It was the colonial state that in most cases carved and defined the form and content of a given emergent post-colonial state. This had to be sustained within a system which, while it rejected colonialism for what it was, nevertheless adopted the very elements that held the territory together. The achievement of unity and stability became the overriding objective of the new nation, regardless of how this might run counter to the democratic process that was inherent in the struggle for national independence.

The point here is that the rejection of the Westminster parliamentary model did not necessarily constitute an essential breach with the colonial era. Nor did this rejection cause undue concern to those former colonial masters who had bequeathed the parliamentary model to their African successors. For much of the 1960s and 1970s, it was really a question of whether the one party state ruled in the image and interests of the former colonial masters or sought, through a leftist Marxist one party system, to cut that umbilical cord in both the political and economic spheres. Thus, there would have been no essential difference in the nature of the Ghanaian and Kenyan states under Nkrumah and Kenyatta respectively. Each sought to use the one party state towards "leftist" and "non-leftist" goals respectively. However, whereas Nkrumah earned the wrath of the West, with Ali Mazrui himself dubbing the Ghanaian leader a "Leninist Czar"[6] not until the 1980s do we see the emergence in liberal democracy of a generalised critique Western-oriented one party states in Africa. This is, perhaps, an outcome of the end of the cold war, suggesting that the old dichotomy between "leftist" and "Western" in Africa was as shallow as the entire post-colonial record has illustrated. We will return to this theme after a critique of the other school of thought that gave rise to another version of the one party state.

The Liberation Struggle and Marxism-Leninism: The (Sole and Authentic) Vanguard Party and Socialism

Marxism-Leninism has provided the main philosophical basis for modern political economy, particularly to the extent that the latter has so far constituted, perhaps, the best methodological framework for the study of society. At the same time, Marxism-Leninism has been subjected to a variety of interpretations, the main one, for our purposes here, relates to those of its key elements that have influenced and pervaded the political process in many parts of post-colonial Africa. We refer to the inter-related concepts in Marxism-Leninism: the vanguard party, the dictatorship of the proletariat, and socialism. Of course, it is true that there is not a reference at all to one-party state system in Marxist-Leninist theory; and it is often forgotten that the Bolshevik Party of the October Revolution was only one among several other parties, receiving less than a third of the votes in the elections for the Constituent Assembly in 1918. But no doubt, both the import and theory of the vanguard party under the dictatorship of the proletariat did contribute to the process whereby the one party state acquired vigour and sought legitimacy in the leftist and Marxist-oriented regimes of both Europe and the third world. For, implicit in this theory of the vanguard party and the dictatorship of the proletariat was that of a sole and authentic party, infallible and therefore synonymous with the State and masses alike. Accordingly, it is not difficult to see how such a theory became distorted conveniently, in search for some kind of philosophical justification for one party states which were invariably outcomes of the social and political processes of the respective countries concerned. Likewise, within the intellectual and academic sphere it gave rise to that genre of scholars who were intolerant of the views of their counterparts, given to factionalism even within the left itself.

Yet it is also true that the Soviet Union in particular and the socialist bloc in general provided, through their support for Communist Parties and national liberation movements became a major resource base that tended to further reinforce the one party state regimes of the leftist type. In the early days, such parties and movements had to earn the recognition of the Soviet Union if they were to be regarded as "authentic"; but by the late 1960s, the Sino-Soviet split left most these parties and movements of the third world evenly divided between the Soviet Union and China their main supporters, particularly with regard to military training and supplying arms.

That was indeed the pattern in Southern Africa, with the Soviet Union baptising six of the national liberation movements as the "sole" and "authentic" movements among the various groups that were involved in the struggles for national liberation. The six were the ANC (including its concomitant organisation, the Communist Party) of South Africa, ZAPU of Zimbabwe, SWAPO of Namibia, the PAIGC of Guinea Bissau, MPLA of Angola and FRELIMO of Mozambique. Likewise, China baptised its own "authentic" organisations, usually those which had been labelled "rebel" movements by the Soviet Union and its allies:

ZANU, PAC and UNITA of Zimbabwe, South Africa and Angola respectively. Both the dynamics of the struggle itself as well as the decline of the Sino-Soviet conflict, would distort this bifurcation which was hitherto more reflective of this super-power rivalry than of any ideological differences between movements in the countries of Southern Africa. Besides, there is so far little evidence that the national liberation movements, some of whom are now in power, really imbibed and internalised the ideological persuasions of either the Soviet Union or China. At the end of the day, it was a question of which of the two would provide material support for a struggle that was essentially nationalist in character.

At any rate, to the extent that the main thrust and nature of the liberation struggle in Southern Africa purported to be based upon Marxism-Leninism and the idea of a "sole" and "authentic" vanguard party, so too, did this provide both the justification and the impetus for a one party state in the post-colonial period. The most logical application of this thesis was in the Mozambican case when Samora Machel declared that FRELIMO was a vanguard Marxist-Leninist party. With few exceptions, all national liberation movements which assumed power tried to impose the imprint of the "sole" and "authentic" one-party on society. More importantly, this emphasis on the principle of the sole and authentic liberation movement provided the rationale, and indeed the licence, whereby the party in the post-independence period could ride rough-shod - in the interests of the masses! - over the interests of the very people it purports to serve. In particular, it is the militarist element - regrettably the most dominant feature of most liberation movements - which fights against democracy, places limits on the civil society and, ultimately, provides a dubious justification for all that is done in the name of the "people", under the banner of the "noble tradition of the heroic national struggle"! It is a problem that is most pronounced in liberation movements. As has been the case with respect to those of Southern Africa, they have had to operate in exile, away from the home base (or the civil society) which might have provided the element of accountability the absence of which has led to "atrocities" and "detentions" at the hands of certain fascist elements within the liberation movement itself. As will be argued shortly, it is the civil society - of which the educated petit-bourgeoisie is an important element - that can help temper this political instinct on the part of the African petit bourgeoisie once it has attained political power in this era of the dominance of international capital. Conversely, it is this same political instinct, based as it is on the weakness and compradorian tendencies of this class, which propels the development towards a one party state in most of our societies.

There was, of course, the obvious relationship between the pursuit of a one-party/vanguard state and socialism. But as in the case of the theory of vanguard party, there was likewise no clear conception of the theory and practice of socialism. It is enough that Marxism-Leninism has generally been abused in practice in most of those countries that purport to be socialist. This has also been so with regard to the post-liberation struggle societies of Southern Africa. Here ideological commitment alone - no matter how emotional and romantic - became synonymous with socialism; there was no essential difference between that conception of socialism as a "state of mind"(viz. Nyerere[7] and "African Socialism"; and the social democratic conception of socialism) and the rhetoric that oozed out of countries such as Angola, Mozambique, Zimbabwe, South Africa, and Namibia. To begin with, the liberation movements of Southern Africa reveal no attempt to deal with the theoretical considerations of socialist construction, particularly with regard to those aspects that are essential to the process. Unresolved is the theoretical and practical question of whether it is possible to advance to socialism with an essentially peasant base. Joe Slovo asserted, some twenty years ago, that it was possible to advance to socialism through the non-capitalist road.[8] This implicitly meant that the peasantry and not necessarily a large proletariat as would be associated with a capitalist path to socialism, could constitute such a basis for socialist construction. Twenty years later, Slovo accused FRELIMO of "premature transformation of the movement into a communist vanguard"[9] (referring to Samora Machel's declaration of 1979). The point here is that there is as yet no clear guideline as to the means whereby the socialist transition is to be effected, particularly in the post-white settler colonial societies of Southern Africa, including South Africa itself. Clearly, the national liberation movements of Southern Africa have almost all lacked the wherewithal to deal with economic issues in preparation for independence. Despite their statements about liberation, they have been unable to produce even a vague blue-print - an economic plan of action - when it comes to the question of translating political independence into even some form of national control of the commanding heights of the economy. To that extent, the oft-cited claim that the armed struggle would foreclose neocolonialism now rings false and worthless against the reality we have experienced so far in Angola, Mozambique and Zimbabwe; and, as appears inevitable, also in Namibia and South Africa. Indeed, it can be argued that all these countries are not essentially different from what prevails in such countries as Zambia, Malawi, Swaziland or Botswana.

The historical reason for this indictment of the post-independent period is now well-known; and has been adequately illustrated with particular reference to the history of white settler colonialism in Southern Africa. In the light of the latter, it would have been sheer madness- if not tantamount to suicide - for the independence government of Zimbabwe or Namibia to confront the economic issues head-on. The nature of the settlement itself constituted a dilemma: how to pursue political independence to its logical conclusion without reaping economic instability and courting the disfavour of the international community. Yet even the legal and constitutional obligations to which independence was tied did not constitute a complete iron-wall against which a well-considered programme of even gradual change could not have been implemented. Analysts will have to consider carefully why most post-independence governments have been able to Africanise the public sector through a degree and level of affirmative action whereas they have allowed the private sector to continue as before.

But our initial observations about Zimbabwe in this regard point to factors which might also be applicable to Namibia and South Africa. First, there was the reality of the poor technocratic base with which the national liberation movement would have to tackle the issues of the economy. That is, the tendency to seek first the political kingdom in the hope that all else would follow. Second, there was ideological confusion over the relationship between the public and private sectors, between the state and the economy. This was tied to the question of how to begin the process of building a national economy out of an economy that was so essentially insecure given both its reliance on a transient and itinerant white community and its dependence on international capital. The confusion over these became evident in the debate over the "Leadership Code". The code premised on the naive assumption that if leaders were clean and exemplary, then in due course the entire society might learn to accept and practise the virtues of socialism. However, it was at best understood popularly as a law to which only those in power should adhere, while others, particularly whites were free to amass fortunes. It is interesting to note that the average member of the public will raise eyebrows at a Minister who amasses a fortune while expressing little or no concern for the wealthy members of the private sector. This is also because the post-colonial state is still viewed as a gateway to power and wealth for the blacks who hitherto had no other way of attaining bourgeois status. Therefore, members of the state are envied rather than critiqued by most of those not yet fortunate enough to gain access to the state. The state remains ambivalent about the reality of the Zimbabwean economy: sometimes accepting capitalism as something to be tolerated in the interim, and, at other times, insisting that socialism is on the agenda. Therefore, how can the state promote black control in the private sector without appearing to favour capitalist development even among its own people?

From this arises a third factor. This is the inherent fear of the post-colonial state concerning alternative centres of power in society. Invariably, therefore, the objective is to try to ensure that those who became rich, particularly outside the state, do not become prospective contenders for state power. And hence the attempt by the State to direct and regulate the level of capitalist accumulation and likewise also the pace of black advancement among its indigenous population. As a member of the governing class, it becomes part of your mission to ensure that only those of your kith and kin, or those likely to support your political enterprise, should wax rich and advance in the private sector.

At the end of the day, the issue of black advancement is caught in the myriad of post-colonial petty bourgeois political wrangling: the blacks, mainly the middle classes, are politically pre-occupied with how best to contain and constrain each other while the former white settlers continue to control and dominate the economic field. It is a sad indictment of the history of national liberation in Southern Africa that the post-independence struggle should be reduced to a call for black advancement and not black control. This is the legacy of white settler colonialism and the post-white settler colonial situation. At what stage and how will this whimper for advancement be transformed into the self-assertion of control?

Reference has already been made to the thin line of distinction between radical and right wing one-party state regimes in Africa. But it needs to be highlighted here that the exaggerated distinction that hitherto existed conceptually should be attributable to some elements of the leftist movement in the northern hemisphere and its "revolutionary mythology".[10] Together with some of the radical intellectuals of Africa, leftists in Europe and North America helped to project the liberation movements as revolutionary and Marxist-Leninist. Their aim was to present such governments-to-be as far better alternatives to the reactionary nationalism of other liberation movements who, in the view of these leftist elements were likely to be as "tribalist" and "corrupt" as their counterparts in those countries of Africa which had not undergone a violent armed struggle. Such a conception was meant to de-emphasise and conceal those aspects of the Marxist-Leninist tradition to which most people of the northern hemisphere were opposed. It also created a strong basis for consensus within the northern hemisphere, about how an inherently unstable, tribal and backward Africa might better be re-designed and re-shaped through strong centralised states, preferably those supporting the Western model of development.

In general, any movement that remained uncompromisingly black nationalistic in its outlook would find itself with fewer friends in the northern hemisphere than one which purported to be Marxist-Leninist while extolling the virtues of "non-racialism", "multi-racialism", etc. More than three hundred years of imperialist and racialist domination of Africa (and the third world) has meant that the average white person in the northern hemisphere feels uncomfortable about the subject of race and black nationalism. Accordingly, both the left and right in the northern hemisphere have sought to recreate Africa in their respective images. It is also a feature of the current conjuncture that African (or black) struggles have seldom been viewed as having their own individuality in a world dominated historically and culturally by an aggressive and dominant northern hemisphere. This has given rise to a kind of white paternalism (both of the left and right) which views as its major mission the need to patronise and even dominate the struggles of the oppressed and exploited peoples of the third world. Indeed the latter is in itself the" raison d'etre" of modern racial paternalism and liberalism. Likewise the objects and subjects of this paternalism have themselves invariably compromised the very issues upon which the struggle was based: black nationalism and the national question both to survive and be able to mobilise international support in a world of limited friends and resources. The resulting de-emphasis of these two key issues has and will deprive the national liberation movement, particularly that which declared itself to be "sole" and "authentic" Marxist-Leninist of the means whereby it might build a broader nationalist coalition, as the basis for an emergent new nation in the post-independence period. In pursuit of being seen as "reasonable" and "rational", African leaders and their movements have had to pretend and speak tongue-in-cheek about the issue of racism which is essentially a product of the history of the northern hemisphere and its relation with the third world. Whereas it should be those of the northern hemisphere that feel guilty about racism and therefore preach the gospel of non-racism among themselves, it is now Africans who feel even more guilty about any political expression which might be misconstrued as being anti-white, even though it is inconceivable that there can be such a thing as black racism. All the same, it became a major objective of governments borne out of the liberation struggle to seek to prove ad nauseam that they were "non-racist". In so far as this sometimes meant making concessions to the former white settlers (e.g. including a disproportionate number of these in the Cabinet), this became a bone of contention between the ruling party in government and other contending nationalist groups. In short, "non-racial" types of concessions often reflect a failure to deal with the national question on the part of post-liberation governments. This, in itself is an important cause for internal conflict and has led to the gradual erosion of the legitimacy and power of the post-colonial state. The last fifteen years of Angolan and Mozambican history is but a confirmation of the contradiction and/or antithesis between, on the one hand, ideological declarations designed to pander to international public opinion and, on the other, the commitment to a nationalist coalition which, by definition, is borne out of the acknowledgement of political diversity and is the basis of nation-building.

A brief historical analysis will reveal the extent to which the demise of UNITA in Angola was far more an outcome of Europe and North American propaganda that projected it as a reactionary and racist movement than the fact that it later aligned itself with the South African state and the imperialists. With little or no scrutiny, the dichotomy between MPLA and UNITA was accepted among African and non-African radicals alike. It required another fifteen or more years, of immense bloodshed and suffering before this dichotomy was to be exposed as largely superficial. The current turn-around towards multi-partyism in the post-liberation societies of Angola, Mozambique, Zimbabwe, Namibia and even South Africa is testament to the fact that there was something inherently wrong with the tendency towards one-partyism. As President Chissano stated recently when he announced that FRELIMO had decided against the Marxist-Leninist one party system:

> The fundamental point is that we believe that no-one has the right to deny its citizens who want to form political parties within the law.[12]

Likewise, dos Santos of Angola, speaking on the occasion that his government declared multi-partyism, emphasised the need

> to ensure that the different opinions, interests and aspirations which exist in civil society are expressed.[13]

More than that, this might also reflect favourably on a civil society whose very nature and composition is antithetical to the one party state. The decision by Chissano, dos Santos, Mugabe or Kaunda against a legislated one party state is not a matter dependent upon the whims and fancies of a given leadership. Wise leaders are those who demonstrate a capacity to respond to the yearnings and grumblings of a civil society. By responding in the manner that they have, these leaders have strengthened civil society in these countries. The Namibian experience so far proves that nation-building is very possible with eight parties in Parliament. And all the indications are that our South African comrades will learn from both their neighbours and the totality of the global experience in governance. Again, it is with respect to South Africa that there exists a tendency within some of the elements in the northern hemisphere, whether from the left or right, to anoint a particular party as the sole and authentic. It is true that the socialist bloc characteristically recognised no other group than the ANC and its concomitant organisation, the Communist Party. All other parties and groups particularly the PAC and those of the Black Consciousness persuasion were regarded as reactionary. Likewise in the rest of the northern hemisphere the prevailing tendency has been to focus on the ANC to the exclusion of all other parties. Thus it was not enough for some in the northern hemisphere to discredit black consciousness as either false consciousness or "conservative". It also became essential to try and demonstrate that it had no roots in the black society of South Africa and that the South African state would rather "live with black consciousness" than with the radical ANC. This is the import of those analyses characteristic of the kind of tendencies to which we have referred earlier. For, Julie Fredrickse's book *The Unbreakable Thread*: *Non-Racialism in South Africa*[14] amounts to no more than an attempt to reinterpret South African history, even in the face of the reality that is unfolding in that country. As Patrick Laurence asks of Julie Fredrickse:

> Why then did the Vorster regime ban and detain a succession of black consciousness leaders from 1972 onwards? Why did the state try key black consciousness leaders for terrorism in black consciousness trial of 1975-76? [15]

The historical record, concludes Laurence, demonstrates:

> the strength of black consciousness in 1977 rather than its weakness. One need only think of the student demonstration at the time. They

were conducted under the banner of black consciousness, not of the Freedom Charter or of the ANC. [16]

Of course, there has always been continuity in the history and development of black protest and struggle in both South Africa and the rest of the continent. It is only mechanistic historiography that will seek to fragment that process between one phase and another, between one party and another. No member of one movement including the Black Consciousness Movement could claim that their struggle was autonomous from that of the ANC or PAC. And yet it is a clear reflection of that negative tendency in political analyses to seek to balkanise the liberatory process by both over-zealous partisanship and the attempt to anoint certain organisations as the sole and authentic. Happily, the events of the last year alone, not to mention the totality of the South African experience, might put an end to the kind of subjective analyses that have so far characterized writings of the white left in both South Africa and elsewhere. The indications are that the African leaders of South Africa have acknowledged the political diversity that is in their country and are intent on creating a broad nationalist coalition. As Itumeleng Mosala (of AZAPO) stated recently:

Ideally, it would have been nice to have had one homogeneous united liberation movement. It would have been nice for obvious reasons. For example, there would have been little if no tensions at all among those opposed to the same enemy. Mobilisation of the masses of the people behind the gigantic task of overthrowing the system of apartheid capitalism would have been made easier. Fewer people would get killed in internecine political strife. The prospect of divisions among the oppressed as a result of the work of the oppressors in our midst would be greatly diminished. Above all, the Witdhoek incidents in 1985/86 would not have happened; the massacre of black people in the violence that has gripped Natal in the last few years would have been made difficult. Indeed, the carnage in Thokoza, Vosloorus, Kagiso and Soweto just recently, would probably never have happened.

Unfortunately, idealism, like logic is not truth. The fact of the matter is that there is not one homogeneous, united liberation movement in our country. And it is doubtful whether it is ever desirable that there should be one, homogeneous, united liberation movement.

Like other people in the world, blacks are thinking, creative and diverse people. They are not intellectually or conceptually homogeneous simply by virtue of being black. Like other people, they are products of history and society and many times, victims of history and society.

The plurality of liberation movements is therefore, a blessing and not a curse. It is a welcome development of the black struggle for liberation in occupied Azania. It was right that different traditions of struggle should have evolved in the course of our resistance. It is a good thing and not a bad thing, that different liberation movements should have come into being to reflect the nature of our wrestling with the problem of our liberation.

I would like to put it to you that each of the traditions of struggle, represented by the various liberation movements, is not only a product of particular historical circumstances, but in fact represents a development on the struggle of our people for national and social liberation.

This means that the plurality of liberation movements is not in itself to be regarded as unfortunate. After all, we are involved in a struggle for liberation. Struggle means that we are to struggle for freedom not only against the oppressors but even against those of our own whose souls and minds are in the pockets of our exploiters. This we must do for, as Steve Bantu Biko so aptly observed:

The most potent weapon in the hands of the oppressor is the mind of the oppressed. We must not allow the detractors of our struggle, especially the self-righteous white liberal types and their servile black lackeys, to induce a paralysing sense of guilt on us by deliberately, maliciously and in typically populist manner, confusing our plurality with our disunity. There is, of course, disunity in our struggle. There is debilitating disunity. But surely it is the height of racism to equate black political plurality with disunity while treating white ideological and political plurality as democratic diversity.[17]

The Problem of Democratising the Economy in the Post-Colonial Situation

The foregoing account has tried to demonstrate that narrow and romantic leftism has invariably been the cause of as much autocratic and authoritarian rule as rightism has produced in Africa. The interesting difference in the current phase, however, is that it is such "leftist" regimes and post-liberation struggle societies such as those of Angola, Mozambique, Zimbabwe, Namibia and South Africa, that have demonstrated a capacity to respond to the yearnings of the civil society. In this category should be included Zambia whose leadership has acceded to the call for multi-partyism and Tanzania where one partyism remains only nominal. By contrast, such countries as Malawi, Swaziland and even Lesotho, remain largely unresponsive to the pressures for democratic order. The contrast however superficial between, such countries as Tanzania and Zimbabwe on the one hand, and Malawi and Kenya on the other, is interesting in this respect. It is not that the civil society in the latter societies is non-existent or weak as compared to those of the former. It might be simply a question of the weight of the unresponsiveness and rigidity of the state and key elements that constitute it. But it does suggest that democracy is not given, not to mention the fact that there can be no "pure democracy" as long as different classes exist ("we can only speak of class democracy").[18] In the final analysis, it is not a question of one party or multi-party state. Herein, it has been important to demonstrate the political and economic conditions that almost inexorably propel the post-colonial state towards such undemocratic/ tendencies as are expressed in the one-party system. But these conditions are evidently present even in those societies like Botswana which declare themselves to be multi-party. This alone should dispel the oft-cited correlation between multi-partyism and democracy. The struggle for democracy in most of our countries in Africa involves the need to steer carefully, creating space, developing fora, informing and highlighting the main elements of the political and economic reality that all progressives are intent upon transforming. The problem of the state and democracy in Africa has to be considered in the context of the historical, socio-economic and political factors that constitute the totality of that social process. Any attempt to abstract and isolate issues relating to this process might assist only in highlighting particular problems without however explaining their bases. The historical and political bases of the post-colonial state can also be explained in the context of the contradiction between what might be considered to be a clearly defined mandate or policy framework on the part of African Nationalist Struggles for National Independence and the failure to fulfil and carry out that mandate as evidenced in the current political and economic crisis now gripping the continent. For, the post-independence track record and, therefore, progress in development has to be assessed in relation to the new state's capacity to resolve the national question, land question the issue of wages and an improved standard of living, democratisation of education and health systems, the restoration of the dignity of the African individual after centuries of white domination and, in general, liberation from those forms of oppression and exploitation which characterised the colonial period. These were the very issues about which the liberation struggle was waged. During the struggle there was general consensus between the leaders of the liberation movement and its mass base that these demands would be met. More than that, even the detractors of the liberation movement expected that this would be the agenda of the new government, and had done everything possible to forestall that development. To what extent, therefore, was this agenda a mere ploy, a smoke-screen behind which the leadership could secure this support of the masses towards the fulfilment of its own class interests, to the exclusion of the mass of the people?

Clearly, the question of the economy is central to that of democracy. But, as has already been pointed out as characteristic of most of post-independence Africa, it has been easier to implement reforms in the social sectors than it has been to attend to economic transformation issues. There is, perhaps, as yet no match in modern post-independent Africa to Zimbabwe's progress in social development: i.e. the democratisation of education and health systems. Indeed, the increase in the number of schools, roads, clinics and water utilities in the rural areas have all tended, for the time being, to submerge the state's failure to resolve the land question. These achievements continue to project a favourable contrast with the acute deprivation of the colonial era of just eleven years ago. The state's resolve to grapple with the land question will determine whether this pattern of progress in rural development will continue to be acknowledged by the rural masses.

Progress in social development in Zimbabwe reflects the need for the new state to respond to mass demands mainly because of the visible contrast with the privileged condition that the white settlers enjoyed. The prevailing ideology stressed that social development, particularly education, was a precondition for both economic achievement and equality. I has in fact taken more than ten years for the population to realize that economic power still remains largely in the hands of the former white settlers. Aid for social development programmes was in part an attempt by international development agencies to contain demands for radical economic change.

As a recent analysis of the Zimbabwe economy has concluded, only 4% of the population owns 90% of the wealth.[19] The State has become a mediator between capital and labour, between the aspirations of the people for the "fruits of independence" and the imperatives of capital and its quest for more profits. Accordingly, the transition itself has been confined to strict and narrow parameters of change and transformation, principally to benefit the nouveau riche who have been integrated into the hitherto white only society. There is a relationship between this constrained capacity to answer the demands of the urban wage earners and disgruntled members of the African middle class and the low turn out of voters in the 1990 General Election. The question of wages, unemployment, and black advancement, (note, not black control!) are the issues that cry out sharply in the urban areas of Zimbabwe. It is a sad indictment of Zimbabwe's first decade that there should still be a cry for black advancement and not black control. In the meantime both the urban wage earners and the petty bourgeoisie (particularly the professionals, University students and intellectuals) must acknowledge that their role is less fundamental in post-independence electoral politics than that of the rural masses. It is a factor which has provoked other post-colonial states into a conscious and deliberate alliance with the peasant masses, against both the urban wage earners and the petty bourgeoisie. Besides, a large section of the urban wage earners still has strong linkages with the rural areas, a factor which, as Lloyd Sachikonye[20] indicates, constitutes a significant drawback to the development of the labour movement in Zimbabwe. But the proletarianisation of the peasantry is developing at an even faster rate; and one might add that the advances made in the field of education in particular will also contribute to, rather than detract from, the political growth of consciousness of the masses in general.[21] The question is whether in the years to come Zimbabwe will reject the white settler colonial legacy, resolve the land question, deal effectively with the economic transformation and lay the foundations for a national economy. There has to be democratisation of the economy. This must go beyond the creation of a comprador bourgeoisie. The danger with the current structural adjustment and liberalisation programmes in Zimbabwe is that they will strengthen the link between international capital and the emergent comprador black bourgeoisie. Such a development might in fact be an improvement on the prevailing dominance of white settlers throughout the economy in cohorts with international capital but without a commitment to the national project in Zimbabwe. However, the central question is whether there exists a capacity within the state to develop a policy framework for a national economy, based on classes who have a national consciousness and are therefore anti-imperialist.

Conclusion: The State and Civil Society

These are but some of the issues to be considered in discussing the African condition. Essential to its understanding is a methodology highlighting the nature of the post-colonial state and the class structure which it inherits. Analyzing the social process in Africa requires taking into account the relationship between the state and the civil society, not necessarily as diametrically opposed forces, but as factors which impinge one upon the other. The process will depend on the extent to which the totality of the civil society (i.e. mass-based social and political organisations, various factions of the petty bourgeoisie, intellectuals and students continue to temper the post-colonial state. The struggle for democracy and development is a complex process the outcome of which cannot be predicted. We have raised some of the issues concerning the relationship between the post-colonial state and the struggle for democracy. These are that the post-colonial state is so weak and dependent that it develops anti-democratic tendencies, as it is confronted with its own inherent failure to deal with popular demands; that the post-colonial state remains the terrain of contest, particularly between the various factions and fractions of the petty bourgeoisie; and the peasantry and wage earning classes are so disorganised by the combined impact of the state and ignorance that they variously and unwittingly appear to provide support for dictatorship.

After thirty years, the post-colonial state is now undergoing a historical metamorphosis, the parameters of which are not yet clearly discernible. However, the question is whether there will emerge a new and dynamic organisational framework which will respond to the enormous economic problems confronting Africa, and will promote democracy. It is likely that neither the personalities nor the philosophies which have but tressed the post-colonial state to date are likely to survive the 1990s. We must prepare for the future. It is essential that intellectuals continue at least to keep the debate alive and thereby make a modest contribution to the democratic process.

Footnotes

1. International Herald Tribune, 24 April, 1990.
2. W.W. Rostow, The Stages of Economic Growth, New York, 1960.
3. J. Nyerere, Uhuru Na Moja: Freedom and Unity, Oxford University Press, 1967.

4. A. Mazrui and M. Tidy, Nationalism and New States in Africa, Heinemann, 1984, p.285
5. Ibid.
6. Ibid., p. 69. But this account on Nkrumah is a milder one than that which Ali Mazrui presented in an earlier publication in Towards a Pax Africana, London, 1967.
7. J. Nyerere, Ujamaa: Essays on Socialism, OUP, 1968.
8. J. Slovo, "On the Non-Capitalist Road to Socialism", Marxism Today, 1969.
9. J. Slovo, Has Socialism Failed?, Inkululeko Publications, London, 1990, p.8.
10. See Ibbo Mandaza, "Introduction: The Political Economy of Transition" in Ibbo Mandaza (ed.), Zimbabwe: The Political Economy of Transition, 1980-1986, CODESRIA, 1988.
12. Cited in Karl Maer, "Outmanoeuvring RENAMO: The Motives Behind Mozambique's New Constitution" the Southern Africa Political Monthly (SAPEM), Vol. 4, No. 5, February, 1990.
13. Speech by President Jose Eduardo dos Santos, 25 October, 1990, published in the Southern Africa Political and Economic Monthly (SAPEM), Vol.4, No.2, November, 1990.
14. Julie Friedrickse, The Unbreakable Thread: Non-Racialism in South Africa, Ravan Press, 1990. Reviewed by Patrick Laurence, "No, the Nats Did Not 'Live With' Black Consciousness", The Star, Johannesburg, 30 January, 1991.
15. Ibid.
16. Ibid.
17. "Unity in Action Among Liberation Movements", The Southern Africa Political and Economic Monthly (SAPEM), Vol.4, No.1, October, 1990.
18. V.I. Lenin, "Bourgeoisie and Proletarian Democracy" in On Soviet Socialist Democracy, Progress Publishers, 1980, p.61.
19. Arnold Sibanda, "The Economy Since Independence" The Southern Africa Political and Economic Monthly (SAPEM), Vol.3, No.7, April, 1990.
20. Lloyd M. Sachikonye, "Worker Mobilisation Since Independence", Southern Africa Political and Economic Monthly (SAPEM), Vol.3, No.7, April, 1990.
21. For a more extended analysis of these developments and how they related to the 1990 General Election, see Editorial entitled "Zimbabwe's First Decade: What of the Next?", Southern Africa Political and Economic Monthly (SAPEM), Vol.3, No.7, April, 1990; and Ibbo

Mandaza, "Election Results a Barometer to Assess First Decade of Independence and Consider Future Prospects," The Financial Gazette, 12 April, 1990.

Chapter 7

30 YEARS OF AFRICAN INDEPENDENCE: THE ECONOMIC EXPERIENCE

Thandika Mkandawire

On the eve of independence, the African countries ranked among the least developed, the least industrialized, the least secure places in which to be born. In short they were among the poorest countries of the world. This was the record of three hundred years of foreign domination and about one hundred of colonial rule. The nationalist movements were acutely and painfully aware of this terrible legacy - a fact emphasized by the slogans they chose - "Uhuru na Kazi". It is important to bring out the nationalist stance because a deliberate misreading now dominates the interpretation of the nationalist perspective, so blinded by euphoria as not to have grasped the enormity of the task before them. To the best of my knowledge, no nationalist promised that independence would bring an utopic existence of laxity. Instead, all exhorted their people to ready themselves for greater work and greater sacrifices.

It is true there were tales of natives being seen surveying the magnificent villas of the settlers which they believed they would occupy on the morrow of independence. But these were at best merely apocryphal tales which more often than not revealed racist fears of the story-teller that the native's envy for the good life would lead to attacks on his/hers property. It was an aspect of the gallow humour of beleaguered colonisers.

What the nationalist promised was not less work and exertion, but a diminution of the discrepancy between effort and reward. What dissipated people's enthusiasm and fervour was the wasteful deployment of their energy, the privatisation of what should have been social gains, and the marginalisation of the people from critical development decisions.

In retrospect, if Africans were naive about anything it was about the prospect for democracy and accountability by their new leadership and not about expectations of instant material prosperity. They were also naive about the benign nature of the international system to which they were joining. The first signs that all was not well with the system were already apparent with the murder of Lumumba. This marked the beginning of the loss of innocence for much of Africa.

Having said this, it still is necessary to recapitulate the African economic experience since independence. This is an important exercise. Brief though this period is, the interpretation of what transpired is fraught with controversy.

Low Levels of Industrialisation

One of the outcomes of colonial rule was a low level of industrialisation. Table 1 gives figures for a number of African countries. Economists have developed models for describing patterns of industrialisation across countries and time. They have established certain norms which indicate what would be the normal level of industrialisation for a country of a given population size and per capita income. Using these norms, it can easily be shown that colonial rule had severely "underindustrialised" Africa. As an example, Gulahati has shown that on the basis of regression analysis linking manufacturing's share of GDP with GNP per capita and population, Zambia's, Kenya's, and Tanzania's rate of industrialisation was below the "Chenery norms". On the basis of Chenery norms, the observed share of value-added in manufacturing to GDP in Kenya was 45 per cent less than expected Tanzania's shortfall was 80 per cent while Zambia's was 50 percent.[1]

Table 1 - Selected Economic Indicators of selected
African Countries at Independence

	Pop.	GDP $m	Per Capita	Manufac-turing Production	Share of manu-facturing in GDP %
Cameroon	4.7	511	109	30.6	6
Cote d'Ivoire	3.2	584	181	31	5.3
Ethiopia	20.7	1021	49	61.3	6
Gabon	0.4	131	294	8	6.1
Ghana	6.8	1503	222	94.7	6.3
Kenya	8.1	641	79	60.9	9.5
Nigeria	40.0	3500	88	157.5	4.5
Senegal	3.1	678	218	64.4	9.5
Sierra Leone	2.3	316	133	19.9	6.3
Sudan	11.8	909	77	43.6	4.8
Tanzania	9.6	671	67	20.1	3
Togo	1.6	150	92	6.2	4.1
Uganda	6.7	583	87	37.9	6.5
Zaire	14.1	910	58	127.4	14
Zambia	3.2	511	155	28.1	5.5
Zimbabwe	3.6	751	206	120.2	16

Note: Manufacturing excludes utilities and construction. All values
    expressed in U.S. Dollars.

Source: P. Kilby, "Manufacturing in Colonial Africa" in Duigan and
L.M. Gann *Colonialism in Africa* Vol. 4, The economics of Colonialism
(Cambridge, 1975). p. 472

All in all then the historian Boahen's summary of the colonial
experience with industrialisation is apt:

> All African states were... in accordance with the workings of the
> capitalist colonial economy, turned into markets for the consump-
> tion of manufactured goods from the metropolitan countries and
> producers of raw materials for export. It is this total neglect of
> industrialisation by the colonial powers which should be chalked up
> as one of the most unpardonable indictments against colonialism. It
> also provides the strongest justification for the view that the colonial

period was the era of colonial exploitation rather than the development of Africa [2].

A simple nationalist reflex response was to embark on some kind of industrialisation and not surprisingly, the right to industrialisation entered the nationalist agenda. Even the most "neocolonial" of African countries embarked on industrialisation.

The Industrialisation Strategy

The basic industrialisation strategy pursued by most countries was that of "import substitution" which involved providing special incentives to industry. These incentives included protected markets, cheap credit, favourable exchange rates, and subsidies. The expectation was that in the early years, these "infant" industries would not generate much surplus. Instead surpluses were to be obtained from other domestic sectors or from external aid, foreign investment or borrowing. More often than not, the domestic sector that was to generate the surpluses was agriculture. However, in some countries such as Zambia and Zaire, the mining sector was expected to foot the bill. In the not too distant future, the infant industries were to grow up, generate their own surpluses, be self-sustaining, and competitive on the world market. They were to contribute to the eventual diversification of exports moving the economies away from the colonial monocultural pattern of enforced bilateralism. In the event, in many countries these infant industries never grew up and when they did they were disappointingly retarded.

Origins of Strategies Pursued

There have been many explanations of strategies pursued by African countries since independence. In the seventies the dominant explanation attributed the strategy to the "capital" logic of the world system or the designs of transnational corporations which managed to squeeze out concessions and protection from dependent states. Even today, most explanations stressing internal factors still lay much of the blame on this strategy. Others trying to explain why African states pursued a strategy which ineluctably led to economic disaster use the following range of explanations: personalism, urban bias, and the venality and petty bourgeois character of Africans .

Rather than rehash these explanations, I will directly go to my interpretation of what happened. Suffice it to note that each of the above explanations contain part of the truth but only part and do not always highlight the most salient factors.

Political origins

The experience of import substitution in Latin America, India, South Africa and Rhodesia during the Great depression and World War II had demonstrated that import substitution could lead to industrialisation. To be sure, this experience did not constitute a strategy, if this meant a deliberate and calculated deployment of economic resources for the attainment of a particular objective. In most cases the import substitution was in response to the "delinking" that the collapse of international trade had imposed on these countries.

As we have argued elsewhere, colonial Africa did not have the means to respond to such delinking by industrialising [3]. By the time African countries became independent what had started out as an unplanned response to crisis, had been elaborated into a full strategy of development by Raul Prebisch and the Economic Commission for Latin America.

"Economic development" was an important item in nationalist programmes. Both history and contemporary theorising clearly suggested that economic development involved industrialisation and as we noted, partly because in no other sector was colonial blockage to accumulation so transparent, the struggle for independence closely linked nationalism with the "right to industrialise". [4] And so, in no other policy pronouncement does nationalism assert itself as conspicuously as in the demand for industrialization.

It was only with the attainment of independence that Africa could initiate industrialization through import substitution by first removing some of the cruder colonial barriers to industrialisation. This, however, did not specifically entail the pursuance of import substitution. Hypothetically, the perception of backwardness could just as well have called for a transformation of the structure of exports and the adoption of an export-oriented industrialisation programme. At least this is what the neoclassical economists claim would have been the right path and that

that is how they have incorrectly interpreted the experience of the "Four Tigers" of the East.

And so why did the strategy assume a "statist" character in virtually all countries regardless of the ideological proclivities of the leadership?

First, there was an intellectual endorsement of an activist state policy. The dominant intellectual tradition at the time Africa achieved independence favoured an activist role for the state in the process of industrialisation. By the time Africa became independent the Latin American experience had been condensed into a "strategy" of import substitution industrialisation. Also, the developed countries themselves were under the spell of keynesian economics, which advocated state intervention to correct various "market failures", such as those which led to the great depression of the 1930s. The nationalist and the populist bent of nationalist movements tended to ineluctably push them in that direction.

The quest for industrial development, national control, and the absence of a national bourgeoisie further reinforced the case for a statist option.

Historians lent further intellectual weight to the statist option by pointing out that the "late industrialisers" of Europe had relied heavily on the state (Gershenkron Thesis). *A fortiori*, the "late, late industrialisers" would rely even more on the state.

The state was to nurture infant industries with a whole battery of policy measures: tariffs, cheap capital, quantitative restrictions on competitive imports, subsidies in terms of cheap infrastructure, services, and manpower training.

In addition there was the Soviet experience of rapid industrialisation through central planning and state control of the economy. Even for capitalist economies, the War demonstrated that market economies could be redirected towards a set of goals determined by the state.

The point of departure for African countries was not that of "laissez faire" management of the economy, but a statist tradition inherited from colonial rule. Furthermore, the post-War period witnessed furtive attempts at colonial planning, if only to appease the nationalist pressures for a better deal.

This statist view of the management of the economy through import substitution was reinforced by the experience of African countries in trying to stimulate private investment. The nationalist expectation that their good behaviour would attract foreign private capital proved to be grossly unfounded. Virtually every nationalist movement embarked on a strategy of what has been termed "industrialisation by invitation".

The new nationalist governments removed most barriers to investments from non-Metropolitan countries. However, all efforts to attract
foreign investments led to naught. In most cases, the new channels for
the free flow of capital became veritable conveyer belts for shipping out
our surpluses from the ex-colonies. The cases of Tanzania and Zambia
are illustrative of this process.

Despite government willingness to offer protection, and a xa which
gave guarantees of compensation if assets were nationalised, the inflow
of capital was less than the profits being exported. Some have argued
it was this experience rather than Nyerere's socialist inclinations that
persuaded the state to move towards its version of "socialism". Kaunda's
humanism was also provoked by similar behaviour on the part of
foreign capital. In the case of Zambia, Turok argued that the state
became predominant "not because of ideological predilection on the
part of the rulers but seemingly as a pragmatic response to the behaviour
of private capital". It was this that pushed UNIP towards a statist
political stance.[5]

**Table 2 - Gross Profit Outflows and
Inflows of Private Capital (1961-8) in Mill. shs.**

Year	Profits Capital	
	Inflows	Outflows
1961	-71.2	50
1962	-73.0	58
1963	-123.0	155
1964	-93	79
1965	-110	-6
1966	-114	+138
1967	-159	-66
1968	-114	+76

Source: Andre, Cuulson, : "The State and Industrialisation in Tanzania"
in Fransman, (Ed.) *Industrialisation and Capital Accumulation in Africa*,
Heinneman.

This unexpected reticence of foreign capital and the outflow of capital
from Africa forced states to seek indigenous solutions.

In the case of Africa, these could hardly be based on private capital as colonialism had seen to it that no indigenous African capitalist class emerged. This was in sharp contrast to the case of India where a national role in the industrialisation policy invariably led to a greater role for the state. In the more "leftist" countries, the active participation of the state was attributed to socialist goals while in the "rightist" ones this was simply viewed as nationalism or indigenisation.

Performance

The first years of independence witnessed rather impressive rates of industrialisation even when one takes into account the low levels of industrialisation characterising the initial point of departure.

Between 1960 and 1975 Africa industry grew at the rate of 7.5% annually. This compared favourably with the 7.2% for Latin America and 7.5% for South East Asia. However three things should be borne in mind. First is that Africa's starting point in terms of manufacture value added (MVA) was extremely low. Secondly, within Africa itself there were and are great disparities in the levels and rates of industrialisation. Nigeria, Egypt, Algeria, Libya and Morocco together account for about 53% of Africa's industrial production while 27 others have a share in regional MVA of less than 1%. Obviously performance by the above four countries tends to exaggerate Africa's overall performance. Thirdly, growth rates over the fifteen year period mentioned above were far from steady. Much of the growth actually took place in the first decade of independence as the most rudimentary type of industrial establishments began to produce such things as beverages, matches, and textiles. The second decade saw Africa lagging behind the rest of the third world as most countries registered much lower rates of industrialisation than those achieved in the first decade of independence. Between 1970 and 1976, out of forty three countries for which information was available, ten had negative growth rates in the manufacturing value added, another fourteen had less than 5% and of the ten with more than 10%, seven based their high performance on petroleum (Nigeria, Gabon, Congo, Libya, Algeria), new mineral finds, or investment (Botswana and Mauritania). Table 1 tells the story of uneven development quite clearly.

Although one can look at the first post-independence period as a veritable "golden era" Africa still is the least industrialised continent in the world. Table 3 shows the gap between Africa and other developing countries.

Table 3 - Share of Industry and Manufacturing in GDP

	Manufacturing		Industry	
	1965	1986	1965	1986
Ethiopia	14	15	7	10
Burkina Faso	20	22	—	—
Malawi	13	18	—	12
Zaire	26	36	16	—
Mali	—	13	—	7
Mozambique	—	12	—	—
Madagascar	16	16	11	—
Uganda	13	6	8	5
Burundi	—	17	—	10
Tanzania	14	10	8	6
Togo	21	20	10	7
Niger	3	16	2	4
Benin	8	13	—	4
Somalia	6	9	3	6
Central African Rep.	16	12	4	4
Rwanda	7	23	2	16
Kenya	18	20	11	12
Zambia	54	48	6	20
Sierra Leone	28	22	6	4
Sudan	9	15	4	7
Lesotho	5	27	1	13
Ghana	19	17	10	12
Mauritania	36	24	4	—
Senegal	18	27	14	17
Chad	15	—	12	—
Guinea	—	22	—	2
Liberia	40	28	3	5
Morocco	28	30	16	17
Zimbabwe	35	46	20	30
Nigeria	19	29	7	8
Cote d'Ivoire	19	24	11	16
Egypt, Arab Rep.	27	29	—	—
Botswana	19	58	12	6
Cameroon	17	35	10	—
Congo, People's Rep.	19	54	—	6
Tunisia	24	33	9	15
Mauritius	23	32	14	23
South Africa	42	46	23	22
Algeria	34	44	11	13
Gabon	34	35		
Low-income economies	28	35	21	24
China and India	31	39	24	27
Other low-income	18	20	10	11
Oil exporters	31	33	14	15
Sub-Saharan Africa	19	25	9	10

Agriculture

Agriculture became the Achilles heel of Africa's industrialisation strategy. Much has been written on how the "urban bias" of the strategy was to thwart the efforts at agrarian transformation and how this was tantamount to killing the proverbial goose that led the golden eggs - in this case foreign exchange. There is therefore no point in rehearsing the arguments here. One should however confront the argument that African states inherited successful agriculture which they somehow foolishly destroyed.

Colonial agriculture was a failure in many ways. First, it transformed nothing technologically leading Walter Rodney to remark that if the African entered colonial rule with a hoe, he/she emerged at independence with a hoe. Much of the colonial success involved expansion by mere extension of the territory cultivated. Little investment was made in agriculture, leading the colonialists themselves to pat themselves on their backs for having provided the African with a "vent for surplus" a surplus generation that was not preceded by any prior investment by colonial powers. For it did seem to the colonialists that they were getting something for nothing. Countries were exporting surpluses without ever having received any capital from the colonial powers. The true story was of course different. The "surplus" that so thrilled the colonialists and their apologists was produced by dramatic changes in the division of labour and in the allocation of resources. This lead to the steady contraction or food crops in favour of export crops.[6] By the time Africa became independent, the seeds of later famines had already been planted. Africa, which had been a net exporter of cereals for much of colonial period, was barely self-sufficient at independence.

It was also in the nature of the political economy of colonialism that the emergence of an indigenous agrarian capitalist class was blocked. There was a preference for capitalists being either white settler farmers or peasant farming tied to various private and state mercantile siphons of surplus.[7]

We have noted that the strategy adopted was that of import substitution and that it was premised on the extraction of capital necessary for industrialisation either from agriculture, mineral rents, or foreign aid. The effects of this strategy has been widely discussed.

Another problem with post-independence agriculture was the ambivalence of the state as to what mode of production was to be encouraged in African agriculture. Everything was tried: state farms, cooperatives, kibutzis, private plantations, peasants smallholders schemes, kulak farmings etc. Some of these thrived side by side, however, in other cases the simultaneous attempt to promote all these led to disasters. It was also one of the paradoxes of the post-independence era that the radical regimes, in their fight against the emergene of an indigenous agrarian capitalist class, tended to pursue the policies of their erstwhile colonial masters.

The net effect of the policies pursued in agriculture was that in many countries agriculture stagnated Africa's share in a number of key crops. And even more politically salient was the fact that in many cases, food self-sufficiency fell at the same time when the foreign exchange earnings of most countries were feeble. The ultimate result was hunger, undernourishment, and famine.

Table 4 - Food Self-sufficiency Ratios

	1974	1984
North Africa	66.1	49.1
Sub-Saharan Africa	83.6	68.0
Central America	71.3	66.5
South America	84.9	94.2
West Asia	63.6	33.9
South and East Asia	88.1	94.2

Source: FAO, Agricultural Issues in Structural Adjustment Programmes, Paper 68, 1987.

Social sectors

African states did fairly well in tackling colonial neglect in health and education. Increases in school enrollment were nothing short of revolutionary in most of Africa, excepting Malawi where enrollments fell in the first two decades after independence.

Expenditure on social services by African states has been much maligned. It has been attributed to the wasteful distributive propensities of patrimonial states where clientalism was the guiding principle of resource allocation. I believe that in many cases expenditure on social services was motivated by genuinely nationalist aspirations of nation-building. The focus on education reflected the conventional understanding that human resources were vital for development. It also demonstrated a faith in the egalitarian function of education. Most nationalist leaders were men of humble origins whose own social mobility had been facilitated by education. There was thus a belief that education would serve the same purpose for others. In the event, the "Matthew Effect" (to those that have more shall be given) was to undercut the egalitarian thrust of education.

Thus, reversals in the provision of education and other social services is particularly painful and politically difficult to swallow given that these were the only "fruits" of independence the majority of the post-independent population ever tasted. It is also here that the callousness and the political insensitivity of those who now hold Africa at ransom has been most conspicuous leading others to scream for "adjustment with human face".

Regional Integration

In additional to combatting the "unholy trinity" of poverty, ignorance, and disease, the nationalist movement also promised African unity. Pre-independence structures and movements such as the RDA for Francophone Africa, PAFMECA for East Africa and the Pan-African Congress in Accra in 1958 were seen as not only constituting the pan-African rampants against colonial rule, but also viewed as harbingers of a united Africa. Here more than perhaps anywhere else, African nationalism failed to deliver. Thirty years after independence, Africa is even more fragmented than it was in the colonial days. The colonial monetary and travel arrangements that allowed for greater mobility have been replaced by rigid currencies and narrow-minded travel restrictions that make travel between countries a luxury only available to those who have access to passports, visas, and foreign exchange. Micronationalism has frozen what were to be temporary arrangements into permanent fortresses behind which little empires have been constructed.

With the help of hindsight, one can see that the expectations of an immediate movement towards African leaders would have sought African unity. For some the achievement of national independence was a life-long quest for which they had made enormous personal sacrifices. They were not ready to embark on other new adventures. For others, having tasted the perquisites of power which came from being head of state, the prospect of being a regional governor of some backwater state was not particularly attractive. Nkrumah and his talk of a unity government did not make African unity any more palatable.

Secondly, there was no strong economic interest in regional cooperation. There was no national bourgeoisie desperately in need of
national, let alone regional markets. The few indigenous capitalists
who existed were either more than satisfied with their lilliputian
markets or were more interested in comprador links with global markets than with regional markets. For bureaucrats who ran the new
parastatals, the choice was for the quiet life of protected markets and
excess capacity in preference to greater competition.

Politically, African unity had been removed from whatever little
national politics remained. Under the new authoritarian arrangements
that emerged everywhere, African unity was the preserve of the head
of state and a few ministers. Treaties signed with other states were
subject to no discussion, were never ratified by parliaments, and no
referendum took place concerning new regional arrangements. And
also new arrangements were entered into or abandoned entirely according to the whims of heads of states.

The few schemes which made any headway were run by international
bureaucracies (ECA) and donors. By definition, these could not involve
matters of distribution which would require critical political decisions.
Not surprisingly, it was the costless, and often the most trivial aspects
of "integration" which worked.

The Crisis and Adjustment Years

Because of their extreme "openness" and the great vulnerability to
global changes, African countries were badly hit by the economic crisis
of 1973. The combined increase in prices of oil, inflation in the developed countries, and later the high interests rates were to rudely push
African states off the course of industrialisation.

One often forgotten story is that quite a number of countries have
been "adjusting" for close to a decade now. The adjustment has taken
place under the tutelage of the International Financial Institution (IFI).
Even in those cases where strategies have been "home grown", the IFI
has kept a close eye on countries to see whether or not they approve of
what is happening. The standard package has included reduction in
public and private consumption, wage freezes, hikes in interest rates,
devaluation, privatisation and opening up the economy to international
trade.

In the early years, it was simply assumed that getting prices right would do the trick". The orthodoxy underpining these policies was contemptuous of the kinds of concerns that had preoccupied development economics.

I believe when the history of Africa's economic development of the eighties is written the eighties will go down not only as the "lost decade" but also as a decade in which the influence of the international organisation were to cost too much to too many for no reason other than dogma and arrogance. For as was predicted by critics of these orthodox policies, the programmes were recessionary.

The Bretton Woods institution has been at great pains to point to the light at the end of the tunnel. And in one case they have been caught by ECA fiddling with figures to suggest that "strong adjusters" were enjoying higher rates of growth than "weak adjusters". As it turned the contrary seems to have been the case. The good performance of "strong adjusters" could just as well have been attributed to greater financial flows as to favourable climatic or trade conditions.

Things have not been easier by the outcries from some of the IFI's students. When last year one of the favourite students of IFI policies, Jerry Rawlings, indicated that he had enough of them and that he was quite unimpressed by the results, the aid establishment was shaken. Ghana was an ideal choice in many ways. The country had sunk as low as one could when IFI came in to rescue it. It had the manpower and was not in a difficult position to improve agricultural output. In addition, the regime had the "political will" to push through its policies unencumbered by the political clamour of different social groups. Donors poured in vast amounts of money into this "experiment and they had used the country as a prime example of the virtues of "strong adjustment". And so in the eye of the donors, Ghana had to succeed. Rawlings backpedalling was therefore viewed as unconscionable. However, in some ways Rawlings had donors tied down. More money had to be poured in and programmes supposedly receptive to the outcries against the social implications of SAP were quickly slapped together, albeit poorly funded.

What went wrong?

The first explanation for what went wrong was the continued dependence of African economies. The full force of the dependence was felt following the "crises" of the 1970s in the developed countries. What had started as economic dependence began to be more translated into forms of political dependence. International financial institutions virtually took over the fiscal and monetary roles of the state in Africa. Political conditionality was added to economic conditionality.

Second, were the problems internal to the state itself.

Industrialisation in Africa was not a class project but rather that of nationalist politicians and bureaucrats. These two elements were engaged in a process of accumulation which was contradictory. On the one hand the broad nature of the coalition constituting the nationalist movement meant that state policies tended to be chaotic and highly improvised to accommodate the various interests constituting coalition. The "nation-building" that was the objective of this coalition could assign the same priority to a bewildering array of objectives, if only to be seen to be moving on all fronts and to keep the coalition together.

The bureaucratic wing of the coalition in its turn tended to favour nonmarket solutions. Such a preference was sanctioned by "Development Planning" à la mode, and demanded by donors usually as a precondition for aid.

The combination of inchoate objectives, lack of democratic accountability, and the understandable preference by the bureaucracy for these objectives by bureaucratic means set the stage first for short-lived post-independence booms and the later for the inflexibility of African economies in face of the devastating crises of the mid-1970s and 1980s.

Undisciplined neither by the market nor by political forces, the bureaucracy and its cohorts the "political class" essentially ran amok. They set up projects that had no economic rationale whatsoever. They entered into all kinds of shady deals to set up industries most of which never even took off. They realised their mad dreams of grandeur but only through monumental waste. Choices of technology, location of industries, and products were either completely arbitrary or reflected a highly idiosyncratic understanding on how industrialisation takes place. Rarely did they reflect anything hinting of the national interest.

Another interesting aspect of the African tale is the role played by foreign advisers. Partly because of the dearth of skilled manpower at independence, but more because of Africa's reliance on foreign aid, the continent became a veritable hunting ground for "developers". It is now fashionable among donors to disclaim for what really happened. But the fact is that in all too many countries key economic advisory posts were occupied by foreign experts. Most of them knew nothing about the political economy of the countries they were advising, partly because they did not stay long enough to learn. However, given the nature of the donor-recipient relationship, it would have taken extreme humility for these experts to admit ignorance. And so the blind continued to lead the blind and apparently they still do.

Lessons for Namibia

I understand that one of the reasons for choosing this country as the venue for the conference was the belief by the organisers that Namibia as a new member of the independent African states might draw on some lessons learned from the African experience to date. I would therefore be remiss in my duty if did not extract some lessons from the drama of Africa in the last thirty years.

The first lesson is that there is no one recipe for successful development. It all depends on the historical conditions under which one embarks on industrialisation, on the structural features of the economy- both economic and social, on the political arrangements that are possible at a given conjuncture, and on a dose of good luck.

The second lesson, which follows from the above, is that most of the peripatetic advisers who will come to Namibia with impressive testimonies of their experience in Africa have learnt little and in many cases are partly accountable for the ruins that litter the African economic landscape. So, watch out for them.

The third lesson is that it is extremely unlikely that you will develop on your own. And given the hostility of the international system you will do well to strengthen ties with your African neighbours. Namibia as a new member may be able to put new life in to some of the fledgling schemes of regional or pan-African integration.

The fourth and perhaps most important lesson, is to tie your development efforts to democracy and pay attention to the voices of your own people.

Footnotes

1   Gulhati R. and Sekkar, "Industrial Strategy for Late Starters: The Experience of Kenya, Tanzania and Zambia,"Washington D.C.: World bank staff working paper No. 457, 1981.
2   A. Adu Boahen "Colonialism in Africa: Its Impact and Significance," in A. Adu Boahen, *Africa Under Colonial Domination: General History of Africa.*Vol VII Heieneman and Unesco, 1985

3   See Thandika Mkandawire, "De-industrialisation in Africa, Africa
    development
4   Ibid., See also Samir Amin, *Class and Nation*, New York: Monthly
    Review Press, New York.
5   Ben Turok "Zambia's System of State Capitalism" Africa
    Development.
6   R.H. Davis "Agriculture, Food and the Colonial Period" Art Hansen
    and Della McMillan(ed.)
7   We have argued this point at length in Thandika Mkandawire,
    "Political Independence and Agrarian Transformation in Africa",
    CODESRIA (Mimeo, 1989).

──────────────────────Chapter 8

ECONOMIC ASPECTS OF THE CRISIS IN AFRICA

Jumanne H. Wagao

"The economic channels of the young state sink back inevitably into neo-colonialist lines. The national economy, formerly protected, is literally controlled. The budget is balanced through loans and gifts, while every three or four months the chief ministers themselves or else their governmental delegates come to the erstwhile mother countries or elsewhere, fishing for capital" [Fanon, 1965: 135]

1.0   Introduction

Sub-Saharan Africa (SSA) has so far failed to formulate and consistently follow a proper policy of development. The limited growth of per capita GDP that has been achieved during the last thirty years is largely the result of a favourable set of circumstances rather than the result of a policy of development.

From 1960 to 1980 the continent's economic policy has been formulated by groups disinterested in defending the interests of the toiling African masses. The 1990s provide an opportunity to ask: What exactly is meant by a policy of development? More specifically what particular conditions are necessary for development to prevail in SSA?

The next section of the essay discusses the background to this question. This is followed by brief notes on the SSA economic situation. We then review existing responses to the region's crisis. The fourth section outlines the conceptual framework to identify the key obstacles to SSA's development momentum. In the final section, means of improving SSA's economic performance are examined.

2.0   Background

Stereotyped theories of development must be discarded. The crises experienced in Africa over the past decade provides enough documentation to support a fundamental theoretical shift in development thinking as indicated by Rudolph Bicanic's use of the phrase "turning point"

By "turning point" one is referring to observable and measurable qualitative and quantitative changes in essential developmental variables that reverse their original direction. The importance of such points is that they require adequate changes in economic policy primarily because measures which may in the past have produced positive effects become ineffective and may even cause damage to development.

The complexity of this process arises from a growing awareness that because the evolution of development is intricate, it happens that important changes escape the attention of policy makers. This is to be expected in a distorted environment where political decisions lag behind economic changes. Consequently, many errors are made before this lag is noted and eliminated. What is especially damaging in this sphere is the premature anticipation of economic changes by political decision makers, who often take measures which are not appropriate to the real economic situation.[1]

Therefore, the need for long-term social and economic planning is widely recognized today. The future of developing countries in Africa cannot be left to a spontaneous process of development.

Celso Furtado (1965) is deeply conscious of this awareness, noting: "When conceived as a strategy for modifying an economic and social structure, the policy of development can only be pursued with a society fully cognisant of the problems that face it; one which has worked out a project for its own future, and which has created an institutional system capable of effectively furthering the aforesaid project".

Unfortunately, post-colonial SSA is far from enjoying the conditions necessary to establish a policy of development as conceived in these terms.

3.0   Poor Economic Record

SSA's socio-economic and political crisis is a well-documented record. Sharp falls in per capita income since 1980 have followed a decade in which growth per head was either negligible or, in the case of the poorest countries, negative.

SSA's low level of productivity stems in part from the low yields of its agricultural sector, owing to its heavy dependence upon highly vulnerable weather conditions. For many countries in the region, chronic food shortages are the most serious aspects of the crisis and are the outcome of a failure of production to keep pace with population growth in the 1970s. But this too is also the result of a significant, largely drought-induced, fall in agricultural output since 1981.

3.1 Macro-economic Performance

Economically, SSA has a poor performance. Without underestimating the negative effects of the global crisis on Africa's economy. It should be noted that the continent's economic troubles predated this crisis of the 1970s and 1980s.

The economic conditions in many African countries started to deteriorate in the 1970s and subsequent trends have shown even greater rates of decline. In the 1960s, SSA's growth of output and of exports were greater than its population growth. Deficiencies in human conditions were severe, but still improving. This was closely correlated with and resulted from growth as well as broadened state intervention.

Between 1970 and 1975, SSA as a region had growth rates below the average of other least developed countries. The decade of the 1970s can be divided into three periods, 1970-1973 was poor for almost all African economics, especially in terms of growth. For most countries, the period 1974 -1975 was one of short-term crises dominated by drought, rising import prices, fiscal imbalance, and threats to public service maintenance.

The rest of the decade, 1976 - 1979, was characterised by a rapid recovery from the drought of 1974 and from the economic decline arising from the earlier hike in oil prices. GDP growth rates averaged 5 per cent per annum. The weakening of the public service was arrested in most countries while policy formulation was dominated by setting ambitious new targets. There was also a greater concern with employment and basic needs.

A turning point appeared in 1980. The period from 1980 to 1984 was almost uniformly disastrous. The second increase in oil prices, a sharp rise in interest rates, drought and war were among the main causes considered.

Consequently, the average GDP growth rate ranged between 1.5 and 2 per cent between 1980 and 1984 rising to an almost 3 percent between 1985 and 1989. However, by 1990, GDP per capita had fallen to almost 25 per cent below its 1980 level.

3.2   External Environment

SSA's external sector's performance during the 1970s had disturbing dimensions. The period was characterized by growing balance of payment deficit. While the deficits were largely due to external factors such as the declining terms of trade, protectionism in industrialized countries, and heavy debt they also affected by domestic factors. These included declining or stagnating demands for primary products which also explains the loss of SSA's shares in total world trade.

For example, the export sector in Africa grew at an annual rate of only 0.6 per cent between 1970-1980 compared with 6 per cent over the period 1965-70. Africa's share of non-fuel exports is estimated to have declined from more than 18 per cent in 1970 to about 9 per cent in 1978.

The deterioration in the world economy since 1979 has also had an adverse effect on the economies of African countries. Even though one cannot conclude that Africa's poor performance is due solely to external factors, the coincidence of a poor African economic record with the general recession in the industrialized countries inclines one to think that external factors explain a good deal of the declining economic performance of these countries. As the external context worsens, African countries face more radical cuts in imports, public investment, and in the provision of public services.

Broadly speaking, therefore, the current situation is the cumulative result of a downward spiral which resulted from the interaction of poor domestic policies and adverse external events.

3.3   Diminished Import Capacity

A severe 10.6 per cent cut in real imports in 1982 followed a decade of low import growth for SSA import volumes stagnated in 1980 and declined in both 1981 and 1982.

The contraction of imports has reduced output, caused excess capacity, and led to rising unemployment in industry, agriculture and the tertiary sector.

Problems of low import capacity would have been more acute had inflows of foreign funding not risen over fourfold in nominal terms since 1970. This included a significant increase in export credit and an appeal for SSA countries to reduce their foreign reserves.

3.4 External Debt

In low-income Africa, growth was estimated at 3.1 per cent in 1988. However, per capita GDP growth in SSA was zero in 1988, following an absolute decline since the early 1970s. Consequently, per capita income is now only three-quarters of its level in the 1970s while per capita investment has fallen by around 50 per cent since then.

Difficult historical and natural circumstances and years of unimpressive policies have been compounded by external shocks in the late 1970s and early 1980s. This combination of factors has left a legacy of debt.

Foreign aid also appears to have stagnated while foreign private investment cut in half. In the meantime, large debt service payments are falling due with import arrears having risen to unmanageable levels. The escalating magnitude of SSA's debt and debt-serving obligations raise major challenges.

Africa's external medium and long-term borrowings increased from US$ 12.7 billion in 1972 to US$ 99.7 billion in 1983. Nominal interest payments by African countries increased from US$ 0.2 billion in 1972 to US$ 4.9 billion in 1983. External debt rose from US$ 55.7 billion to US$ 102 billion between 1980 and 1986. As a proportion of all developing countries debt, SSA's debt rose from 9.6 per cent in 1980 to 10 per cent in 1986.

During 1987, SSA's external debt was US$ 129 billion, out of which 57 per cent was owed to official creditors. Debt on concessional terms, as a proportion total debt, fell from over 38.7 per cent in 1985 to 37 per cent in 1987. External debt was 47 per cent of GDP while scheduled debt service on liabilities other than short-term debt and use of IMF credit, was US$ 10.5 billion in 1987. This amounted to more than 30 per cent of exports of goods and services. That amount compared with actual payments of US$ 7 billion in 1986 or 21 per cent of exports of goods and services.

Many of the new loans have merely gone into servicing debts and not into new investments or rehabilitating African economies. External debt now stands at nearly US$ 175 billion. Debt service actually paid rose to US$ 17.8 billion by 1989 or 23 per cent of US$ 76 billion exports.

If existing debt were fully serviced, it would eat up over US$ 30 billion out of the total continental exports of over US$ 80 billion.

Total debt figures in SSA might seem modest, relative to other debtor countries like Brazil, Mexico, South Korea and Argentina. these are countries whose debts are owed mainly to private sector. Yet SSA's debt is more burdensome than that of major debtor nations. The impact on the region's economies, is just as devastating as those of the large debtors which attracts more global attention. In addition, the burden of servicing debt is more acute in Africa because per capita incomes in the region on average are lowest.

Debt service ratios have soared so fast that SSA, as a whole, had more than thirty-two reschedulings in less than three years before the mid-1980s. Growing arrears have become so manageable that as of 1985 twenty SSA countries reported payment arrears. Underlying the debt-problem has been a widening gap between debt-servicing capacity and debt-serving obligations. This is approaching the 50 per cent mark in many countries.

To date the international economic environment is characterized by deteriorating terms of trade for exporters of primary commodities, rising costs of imported goods, declining capital flows, high interest rates and growing protectionism in developed countries. It is an environment which has sharply declined Africa's capacity to service its external debts.

Small wonder that rising indebtness in SSA has coincided with an erosion of countries ability to maintain debt service as their export revenues declined. Estimates show that debt service obligations actually falling due in 1988 amounted to 47 per cent of the region's total export revenue. But the actual debt service ratio was 20.5 per cent in the same year. The wide discrepancy between scheduled and actual debt service has occurred in spite of import levels that have remained below what prevailed in 1981.

Those involved in policy formulation recognize that Africa's debt constrains its ability to surmount the current crisis. Most official creditors and donors have therefore began to provide special assistance to SSA countries through increasing concessional aid and through devising innovative options for concessional rescheduling. Alternative solutions require major policy shifts in debtor countries and large increases in concessional aid. However both options are difficult to implement.

4.0   Responses to Africa's Predicament

Africa became independent with high expectations. Governments believed that rapid progress would be made in raising incomes and improving welfare. In the early years many African countries successfully expanded their basic infrastructure and social services. Much effort was also spent on consolidating the fragile new nation states.

After an initial period of growth, however, most African countries faltered, with minor exceptions, then went into decline. SSA has now experienced almost a decade of falling per capita incomes, increasing hunger, and accelerating ecological degradation. All have disrupted the growth-oriented initiatives of most African countries.

The 1980s in particular has been a period marked by continued decline for economies already in decline. This includes failure for those attempting to surmount stagnation through debt financed investment and a disappointing record for economies seeking for externally-funded bridging programmes. In almost all countries, the earlier progress made in social development is now being eroded.

4.1   *Adjustment and Stabilization Measures*

In an attempt to reverse declining economic trends, many governments have begun stabilization and adjustment programmes. By the end of 1983, about 25 countries had adopted some form of adjustment measures.

In the past, the disruptive effects on Africa were somewhat contained by frequent resort to external financial assistance. This was coupled with efforts to increase the production of exports to compensate for the decline in world prices for primary commodities. However, by the late 1970s multilateral financial institutions and bilateral donors became much more pessimistic about the ability of African countries to service their debts.

To date, the measures adopted to counteract the effects of the crisis have worsened the living conditions of large parts of the population. Most of the programmes have overlooked the qualitative dimension of the adjustment process in fields such as employment generation, income distribution and the provision of basic needs. It is now widely recognized that the situation of the poor in Africa is not likely to improve for some time to come.

The stabilization process advocated by the IMF in Africa has entailed 'shock cures'. The policy environment has been dominated by reduction of external, fiscal, banking, exchange rate and price imbalances. Real wages have fallen with widespread cuts in real public spending, excepting that needed to service external debts. Most countries now face lower real credit for enterprise working capital, sharp currency devaluations, and high interest rates. These are the typical instruments in practice.

The World Bank's adjustment process has had an adverse effect on countries institutional set up, social fabric, and market. Instant trade liberalization as opposed to phased liberalization has been a prominent feature. It has also been difficult to secure large enough soft external funding for a sufficiently long period to allow a less compressed time scale for the adjustment process to take place. In addition, most adjustment programmes continue to be underfunded.

4.1.1. *Appalling Human and Social Conditions*

SSA had made some impressive improvements in the period immediately following independence. Notable areas included education, sanitation, public health, transport, and communication. But to date the performance on the whole leaves a lot to be desired. It is the unquantifiable human dimension of the adjustment process which tells an even sadder story.

Living standards in African countries have declined steadily for more than a decade and are now far lower than at the end of the 1970s. The 1980s was a period characterized not simply by erratic GDP growth but also by increases in the proportion of Africans living in absolute poverty. The 20-30 per cent decrease in average real GDP in SSA has been a cause of continental poverty.

Conservative estimates reveal that 30 per cent share of the population is absolutely poor, with women disproportionately represented in this category. Nationally, absolute poverty ranges from as high as 60 per cent in Mozambique and Ethiopia to under 20 per cent in Mauritius and Botswana.

Rising food insecurity at both household and national levels is a growing threat with female-headed households predominating. Moderate and severe child malnutrition in SSA ranges from 25 per cent to nearly 70 per cent. Food imports have risen dramatically to about 6 per cent of all calories.

The problem of food insecurity is even more daunting. In the 1970s, the proportion of Africans with deficient diets increased slightly. In the 1980s barely a quarter of SSA inhabitants lived in countries in which food consumption per capita was increasing. In the 1970s, the corresponding proportion was about two-thirds.

There is also evidence of serious deterioration in the social sector. Primary school enrolment rates have declined since 1980. Despite a slow down in economic growth, government spending per person in the social sector continued to rise in real terms until the early 1980s. From 1981 onwards, however, these expenditures began to fall, reflecting the acute financial difficulties faced by an increasing number of governments.

There is growing open unemployment in almost every African country. This is partly a consequence of urbanization which is transforming rural underemployment into open urban unemployment. In addition, the number of educated unemployed is also increasing reflecting the fact that the educational system is not responding to real local needs.

4.2   World Bank and Critics

As SSA's crisis deepened, the world became aware of the difficulties faced by countries in the region. The nature of the economic malaise confronting SSA has been described in numerous documents. Two reviews of Africa's problems were published by the World Bank one in 1981 and the other in 1984. Other institutions responded promptly to the region's dim economic prospects. They included the O.A.U., the U.N., the E.C.A., and the O.E.C.D.

Recommendations for reforms by African governments in economic management were provided by the World Bank. However, its experience in assisting the expansion of export crops in East Africa from 1972 to 1982 was not particularly impressive. This was a period when the Bank's total investment in agricultural projects accounted for 30 per cent of its total lending.

It is of interest to note that there were successive shifts in emphasis of the Bank-assisted agricultural development projects World Bank sought to identify a complementary programme of action for the decade of the 1980s to achieve the objectives set by the O.A.U. in its Lagos Plan of Action. The programme envisaged a major increase in economic assistance in real terms in the course of the 1980s as well as sweeping reforms in economic policy and management.

The Bank's review of past trends and its projections for the 1980s were based primarily on the annual World Development Reports (WDRs), particularly that of 1981. The Bank had presented four scenarios for the 1980s based on 'with or without policy reforms' and coupled with 'small or substantial increase in aid.' (See Table 1)

Table 1: Projected Performance of Oil-Importing African Countries, 1980-90

Performance Indicator	Average annual growth 1980-90 (%)			
	Without policy reform		With policy reform	
	small aid increase	substantial aid increase	small aid increase	substantial aid increase
GDP	2.4	3.1	4.2	5.0
GDP per capita	-0.5	0.2	1.3	2.1
Agriculture	2.3	2.8	3.5	3.8
Exports	2.6	3.3	4.1	5.2
Imports	0.7	2.3	2.3	3.9

Source: Projections based on World Bank data

It was suggested that the rates of growth of GNP per capita would improve progressively from -0.5 per cent per annum in the worst case projection which assumed no policy reforms and small aid increase to 2.1 per cent per annum in the alternative scenario with both reforms plus substantial increases in aid. Thus the adoption of the World Bank's 'agenda for action' was to transform SSA's economic prospects from stagnation or decline in the 1970s to vigorous economic growth. As the Bank put it:

> "With continuation of most present policies and only a small in-
> crease in aid...per capita GDP is projected to fall throughout the
> 1980s.... Without policy improvement there is insufficient structural
> adjustment to get the economy back on to a faster growth track.
> ....All that higher aid can do is help to sustain the level of imports and
> also that of investment. ...With appropriate policy reforms the

prospects brighten ...(but) policy reform without substantially increased aid does not provide a satisfactory solution.... Policy reform
can boost growth but without greatly increased aid there will be
insufficient foreign exchange and investment funds available to
allow full structural adjustment".[2]

The disappointing economic performance of the African economies in
the 1980s has generated a search for fresh policy approaches to the
future of SSA. Concern has been voiced that the adjustment record has
involved unwarranted welfare losses, at least in the short-run.

For example, the World Bank/UNDP's report, "Africa's Adjustment and Growth in the 1980s" painted a relatively favourable picture
of the development of SSA, excluding that of oil exporting countries.
Between 1985 and 1987, the region recorded an average economic
growth rate of 2 per cent per annum. But this rate of growth was, as
claimed by most commentators, hardly enough to offset the increase in
population. Infact, the GNP of SSA rose by barely 0.5 per cent in 1989.

A more pessimistic vision of Africa's adjustment-with-growth scenario is confirmed by the "World Development Report of 1989" which
forecasts an average economic growth rate of 3.1 per cent p.a. from 1988
to 1995. This projection is based on the assumption that African
countries will not take adequate adjustment measures (variant I). But
even if appropriate measures were implemented (variantII), the rate of
growth in GDP would rise only marginally to 3.2 per cent p.a.

Most of the adjustment programmes have not had a significant
impact on the general growth trends in Africa. Instead, they have
tended to prolong and intensify the hardships in most countries. As the
World Bank's Chief Economist for Africa, has noted, "we did not think
that the human costs of these programmes would be so great, and
economic gains so slow in coming"[3]. Africa should, therefore, expect
limited gains from rigourous adjustment in accordance with recommendations of the World Bank and IMF.

The reactions to the Bank's and IMF's recommendations have stressed
the fact that the policy and management reforms dictated to Africa
constitute bitter medicine. Indeed, adoption of some of the recommendations has involved serious political risks in a period in which political
instability has been endemic in SSA.

It has been insisted that the policy measures have so far proved to be
unpopular and have endangered declared national objectives of equity
and welfare for the poor. More specifically, measures such as the
devaluation of African currencies and ending or greatly reducing

subsidies on food and essential services have also adversely affected the urban poor.

The political objections to the Bank's recommendations also stem from the feeling of most African leaders that in the prevailing hostile international economic environment, the reforms are insufficient to the economic prospects of African countries.

5.0 Scope for More Clarity and Care

In different ways most recent efforts to understand the problem of SSA countries have tended to concentrate almost exclusively on short-term concerns and on 'nonsensical' decisions by African political and economic leaders. That it is desirable to reverse domestic policy inadequacies which are considered to have impeded economic growth flows logically from this perspective. But from the standpoint of an interpretation which seeks an explanation about the historical development of contemporary SSA, excessively concentrating on domestic policy inadequacies is not very fruitful.

Until recently, this narrow focus has distorted analysis to such an extent that problems of SSA have been defined superficially. Attempts to apply mainstream orthodox monetary devices in the African context have so far proved ineffective, if not disastrous. The adoption of Bank-Fund sponsored structural adjustment programmes has obscured the real issues confronting SSA. They shed no light on concerns related to development problems, strategies, and policies.

A more serious consideration of the development problems of SSA requires a detailed examination of fundamental questions of the historical roots of the region's underdevelopment. The first and most daunting challenge is to develop a proper analytical framework which addresses African questions. Such a framework should provide an adequate basis for the elaboration of policies aimed at facilitating the achievement of an internally-generated process of development, with foreign trade ceasing to be the dominant variable. Instead the development needs of the people and the continent as a whole became the vital issues. The satisfaction of these needs is a major concern among policy makers and executors.

5.1 *Salient Features*

We have reached a moment in African history which is characterized by a severe crisis. This has been characterized by several notable features.

(a) *Structural Obstacles*

There has been no major shifts to horticulture as a way to diversify agriculture in SSA. Most output growth over the past twenty-five has come from cultivating and/or grazing more hectarage. In most countries this cannot be counted on.

In the immediate short-run major productivity breakthroughs are unlikely because of a lack of viable technologies. SSA has very limited access to short-run measures such as better access to markets, transport, seeds, hand and animal drawn tools and fertilizers, all essential to raise output.

In industry unit costs, output trends, and the structure of manufacturing plants in almost every African country are unsound. Deferred maintenance has amounted to low capacity utilisation, due partly to the collapse of the import capacity and the excessive dependence on borrowed capital. All this was done in the context of high interest rates and high real devaluation costs in the case of external borrowing.

Often times, industrial plants are too large for national markets and are characterized by high unit costs. Real wages and salaries are also below the minimumly necessary wage. The outcome of the above are absenteeism, low morale, disincentive to improve skills, and corrupt practices. All these make lower wage per worker raise labour costs per unit of output.

(b) *Drought*

The drought of the last few years has worsened the above situation. Originally confined to the Sahelin areas, drought has now spread to many areas in Eastern, Western, Central and Southern Africa.

It is now estimated that 36 countries are affected by drought. The human dimensions of this are incalculable. In Ethiopia, about a million people are reported to have died, and many more are reported to have perished in Burkina Faso, the Sudan, Niger, Mali, Senegal, and Mozambique. The drought has aggravated an already bad food and agricultural situation.

(c) *Sectoral Bottlenecks*

The poor performance of African economies has been amply demonstrated in four most crucial sectors.

In *agriculture*, the crisis manifests itself in declining output per capita, declining land yields, growing food imports, stagnant commodity exports, declining food availability per capita, and spreading malnutrition. Agricultural production across SSA has been growing slowly since the 1960s. It is estimated that the African region now produces only 20 per cent of its cereal requirements.

Per capita grain production in the 24 countries affected by drought has been falling on average by 20 per cent per year since 1970. The sector's inability to keep pace with the rapidly growing population has led to a persistent and worsening food crisis. Because of the slow growth of output and the acceleration in the rate of population growth - from 2.4 per cent per annum in the 1960s to 2.95 per cent in the 1970s and over 3 per cent in the 1980s - there has been a continuous fall in the level of per capita food production across the region dating back to the 1960s. For instance, food production rose by only 1.5 per cent during the 1970s whereas population was increasing annually by 2.7 per cent.

For sustained recovery and less inadequate nutritional levels combined with reduced dependence on food aid, SSA needs a 4 per cent agricultural growth rate annually from 1990 to 2010. For export production, 5 per cent annual rate keep imports from declining.

It is not only agriculture that has done poorly. *Industry* has also been an abysmal failure. Much industrial capacity now lies idle with industrial initiatives foundering. SSA remains one of the least industrialized regions in the world. Relative to world manufacturing output, Africa has had a share of manufacturing value added of less than 1 per cent. In addition, it does not look as if the figure is going to increase in the near future.

African industry did fairly well from 1965 to 9185, with an annual growth rate of 8.8 per cent. However, from 1980 to 1987, the growth rate for manufacturing in SSA fell to 0.6 per cent. This industrial slowdown was largely confined to low-income economies where substantial under-utilization of capacity had emerged. Foreign exchange for imported inputs and equipment was more severely rationed and domestic demand fell. The squeeze on modern industry led to considerable unemployment, with some of the unemployed seeking refuge in formal sector and/or underground activities.

The *energy* sector poses two quite distinct problems. There is, first, an excessive dependence on petroleum. Limited attempts have been made to increase the use of alternative energy sources such as hydro-electric power, coal, and natural gas. The other problem relates to wood fuel. Deforestation is making wood/charcoal costlier in urban locations and has contributed to growing soil erosion and desertification.

Transport and Communication is a sector which has gone backwards since the late 1970s. Deferred maintenance and frequent civil disorders have wrecked many once adequate routes and lines of communication most rural areas never had adequate access to transport, or to markets. Poor transport and communication internally has impeded the spread effects of developmnet initiatives. Furthermore SSA is unlikely to regain the 1970s basic transport and communication standards in the coming future.

(d) *Declining Governance*

Good governance has direct positive economic benefits. In most SSA countries, there has been a breakdown of the administrative machinery in part because state financial and personnel resources have been inadequate or are poorly developed.

Lack of people's participation in governance has increased the inefficiency in the use of resources and has generated low morale. It has also led to low productivity and an unwillingness by communities to augment public resources for basic services and small scale infrastructure.

There is a sense of growing insecurity. Law and order, in the sense of being able to go about one's daily livelihood and life without threat, is weak, even in non-war SSA countries. The economic costs of a break down of order and of civil disorder are high. Properly executed, law and order which is increasingly absent in many African countries, is necessary, but not a sufficient condition for development.

5.2 *New Outlook*

There is one central question for the 1990s: What do analysts have to say about African countries attempting structural transformation from their own resources?

Such an enquiry would require the past economic performance of

SSA to be subjected to critical historical reappraisal. Such a reappraisal would require an awareness that policy discussions about the crisis in SSA must take into account the political and institutional factors to define and deliver policies.

In the 1960s, it was noted that "there are a number of underdeveloped countries where the concentration of economic power and political power is in the hands of a small class, whose main interest in the preservation of existing wealth and leisure rather than mobile productive investment, rules out the prospect of much economic development."[4] In the absence of addressing this issue, the analysis of SSA non-development record would involve no more than the usual reproduction of some familiar analyses of the African continent.

A preliminary study to develop a conceptual framework which would capture the essential features of the existing African reality could well begin with a three-way sectorisation of a "typical" African economy. The three sectors can be identified as: privileged activities (P), under-privileged activities (U) and the state apparatus (S). All these three sectors are directly or indirectly related to an external sector (E). This classification could highlight interdependence between the obscure sectors in the production and circulation processes; the latter being a process which inhibits both the generation and realisation of surplus.

Activities (P) and (U) are distinguished in an economy having access to scare resources. Unlike P-type activities which are best placed to generate a larger total surplus, operators engaged in the U-category of activities have limited access to the most strategic resources which include foreign exchange, domestic savings and the requisite tertiary services.

In between (P) and (U) lies the 'state aparati' (S) equipped with all sorts of tools to mould or protect the various operation carried out in (P) and (U). Contrary to a popular belief upheld in dual models, the type of activities we have in mind here do not necessarily exist or occur as separate entities. Instead, they should be treated as complementary operations with dynamic tendencies to reinforce each other subject to the active hand of (S). In this task, the state machinery is bound to take account of the varying socio-economic interests of existing classes.

Another key issue is to identify the principal social groups according to whether they are linked directly or otherwise to activities (P) or (U) or (S). This distinction must indicate both beneficiaries and non-beneficiaries. The importance of this exercise lies in tracing the way different socio-economic groups have access to income generated, and in particular the proportion of the residual income left behind in an economy which is appropriated by the different social groups. In this regard, transfer mechanisms through the operations of the state become critical.

Here, it is particularly important to emphasize the role of the state after colonial rule. The expansion of the state bureaucracy has been enormous in some countries and Rene Dumont was correct in labelling the state machinery as 'principal industry' in the post-colonial contexts.

Yet typically African bureaucrats do not confine themselves to salaried jobs. Some top bureaucrats often find ways and means of penetrating sector (P) through the norm of 'one-man-jobs'. Following Cowen (1977), such individuals occupy the more lucrative position "which straddles the boundaries of administration with the state and accumulation within private enterprise".

When one deals with questions of income generation and its distribution within an African economy, extent of foreign collaboration is inevitably a problem area deserving attention. Experience shows that any positive steps which lead to various forms of guided external dependence work to increase the portion of surplus which is left for redistribution domestically.

However, experience also demonstrates that like in most other peripheral societies, the post-colonial state in SSA has remained more or less as "the adequate expression of the given social set-up upon which it reacts and thereby causes change. Conditions which are not already present in society cannot be created by the (new) state". Moreover, under Latin American conditions there is evidence that the "state and the bureaucracy are not seen as necessary instruments to improve the national position in the world competitive market; on the contrary, it is the world market; by means of the dominant powers, which imposes the conditions of existence on a given country. No internal class is able, therefore, to see...economic development as a reason of the state". Reversing existing forms of foreign collaboration in SSA, therefore, wont be an easy course.

Secondly, in the course of commodity circulation the relationships between activities in (P) and (U) often turn out to be asymmetric. This follows the one-sidedness nature of the transfer of income from sector (U). It is for this reason that considering the state's transfer mechanism becomes extremely essential. Depending on the nature and character of the state, either of the two activities may or may not benefit from the state's transfer mechanisms of the 'new middle class'.

6.0   Issue Areas

A consensus on the most desirable development strategy to overcome the crisis confronting SSA countries would be difficult to achieve. Thus, the framework we have proposed in Section 5.0 above does not presume to offer blanket solutions to the present impasse facing the continent. The limited underlying aim behind this formulation is to provide a layout on orders of magnitude and some of the more important relationship.

Our approach raises a whole series of interesting questions with respect to a large agenda of Africa's economic environment. This is in line with A.D.B's President Ndiaye's observation that "the Bank, recognizing that the development process extends beyond project lending, has long ago embraced the idea that a vitally important parallel feature of the development process is the fostering of an intellectual climate conducive to the re-examination of old paradigms and to the search for new solutions to the problems which confront this region". (1989)

I believe that five main issues of concern for SSA deserve comments in this concluding section. These are: resource constrains, market forces vs interventionist failure, ownership and control, external debt and aid modalities.

6.1   *Resources Constraints*

Paul Baran's classic work, published 33 years ago, is still relevant. Baran's exposition emphasizes how 'potential economic surplus' is utilized in low income countries. The surplus, according to him, is not utilized productively but for luxury consumption and unproductive investment. It is sometimes simply siphoned off abroad as tribute, dividends, or remittances.

Baran stressed the fact that the entire social fabric in such countries supports such a mode of surplus extraction. Subsequently, the same point was stated more explicitly by Stephen H. Hymer (1970) in these remarks: "The major problem of capital accumulation in underdeveloped economies is not so much a shortage of savings but a lack of institutions to channel the existing or latent surplus into productive investment". Part of the answer to the failure of development may thus be provided by the mode of utilisation of the economic surplus.

In the African context, for example, the ability of agriculture to generate surplus is crucial to the sustainance and acceleration of the growth process. As Samir Amin (1987) has it: "Africa as a whole has not even began the essential agricultural revolution, which is the prerequisite to any other development, of whatever form: and that, concomitantly, it has not yet entered the industrial era".

Explicit reference to alternative development initiatives in SSA serves to emphasize a threefold approach: generation of surplus, its realisation and its disposition. It hardly needs to be emphasized that in a situation obtaining in SSA where there is a persistent problem of surplus scarcity, the pattern of its allocation becomes all the more crucial. The challenge would then lie primarily in the ability to transform the production structure to meet the neglected needs of the mass of people in the continent.

6.2   Market Forces vs Planning

Before the 1980s, the desirability of adopting conscious planning in SSA was not questioned. There was general agreement that approaches to SSA's problems should not be based wholly on market considerations.

By the mid-1980s, the private sector came to be seen as the prime mover of development in SSA. For people in some quarters, progress in debureaucratisation in all its forms needs to be much faster. It is further recognized that while overseas private investment is important in some countries and sectors with government -to- government external assistance are still useful, activities of the indigenous private sector will largely determine how SSA develops. Today, there is frequent mention of small farmers, artisans, informal traders and small-scale enterprises. These activities, it is claimed, are more important in generating employment and form the most dynamic component of economies in SSA countries.

African governments are under pressure to ensure that an appropriate enabling environment is created in which the private sector can flourish. In a recent stimulating discussion on markets and the state in SSA James Pickett offers the following judgement : "The main thrust of the Berg report was that macroeconomic policy should encourage and facilitate microeconomic freedom and that the state should retrench on many of its economic operations. ... It is therefore not surprising that economic liberalization has been at the heart of IMF and World Bank supported stabilization and adjustment programmes, so that in this and other ways African countries are being encouraged to let the market rather than administrative decision allocate resources".

There is a belief that aid should be directed to sector activities closely aligned to those in the private sector. An extreme view holds that a bigger portion of external assistance to SSA should assist the private sector more directly. Such a view strongly emphasizes the role of non-governmental organisations (NGOs).

Two questions must be posed. These are: Would free markets be equally suitable in all economies, regardless of ideology or level of development? Is the market a particularly suitable instrument for the development of SSA?

Recent calls which entail rolling back the frontiers of the state may not be the answer to all problems faced by Africans countries and governments. It is true that oversimplified solutions were advocated in the past for Africa and it may now be very important to review them. For example, economic planning as opposed to the free market and the state as opposed to private enterprises have been viewed as alternatives to each other.

Yet in practice the state and private enterprises or planning and the market needed to be combined. And each of them has had important roles to play. Indeed, the central question at hand becomes one of finding the most suitable way of blending them. In dealing with present and future challenges, planning clearly has a very important role to play. In the process of introducing structural changes in domestic economies and in negotiating for reform in the structure of international economic relations, both the state and planning could play a vital role.

There is a clear need for change and there is need to learn from Africa's past experience. It is equally important to realize that short-term problems cannot be dealt with in isolation from long-term concerns. In other words, the vulnerability resulting from the current crisis should not divert attention from the future. What may be at stake is to improve the planning process in SSA in order to achieve a realistic harmony between the approach to solving immediate and more pressing problems and other concerns aimed at medium and long-term challenges. Clearly planning has a role to play in each of these tasks.

Planning is not incompatible with the fact that private enterprises and the free market can also perform their functions without unnecessary bureaucratic impediments. The question then becomes one of identifying, those activities that are best left to the market and those that are best undertaken by the state.

6.3 Ownership and Control

In the view of G. K. Helleiner (1989), "The weakness of the indigenous business class is probably even greater in Sub-Saharan Africa than it was in Latin America. Africa will therefore certainly continue to rely on foreign firms for many of its development needs. Pragmatism and moderation are the obvious prescription for Sub-Saharan African policy approaches to direct foreign investment"

One might agree with Helleiner concerning the poor performance of the public sector. Nevertheless, it should be noted that recent concerns with different policy perspectives and analytical frameworks for SSA are not similar to those advanced by Helleiner concerning the role of foreign direct investment.The picture portrayed is one in which a new strategy for SSA would evolve similarities with standard socialist thinking. And here, nationalization of some of the key means of production will be undertaken in order to assure that the first priority in production, and in the utilization of surplus, is given to the satisfaction of basic material needs for those most in need.

The structure of ownership and control of the means of production also has direct bearing on income distribution. There would certainly be differences among countries depending on whether ownership and /or control favours external or internal private interest groups. But it would still be in the interest of real economic development if SSA countries aimed to both own and control the leading means of production.

However, any such transfer of ownership and control from external owners should not necessarily favour the internal minority beneficiaries. In one sense, "a transfer of ownership of foreign firms to local private hands may actually hinder the 'transition to socialism' by creating a stronger political base for the private sector which is likely to oppose state ownership. It is often politically easier to expropriate foreigners than local enterprises". (see Penrose, 1976: 148)

Yet even state ownership through partial nationalization needs to be pursed more consciously. There is ample evidence to suggest that nationalization per se has of late been accommodated by major actors in the global investment scene. Zambia's copper case was most illustrative when concern was voiced on the need to "take a closer look at what is really happening beneath the familiar rhetoric of nationalization".

6.4   External Debt

We all know that the external debt crisis is a real one. And for countries of SSA the choice is between rescheduling and defaulting. The fist option, however, amounts to temporary relief without curing the disease. Many SSA countries have had their debts rescheduled on more than one occasion, but the problem continues to grow.

There are clear indications that creditor countries are gradually endorsing the idea of writing off Africa's large debts. It is usually the case, however, that any moves to implement an expanded programme of concessional debt relief for low-income SSA countries should complement domestic policy reform supported by additional aid.

There is a general endorsement of the principle of concessional relief for the poorest countries in Africa. Partial debt forgiveness, reduced interest rates, and longer maturities are some of the proposed options available in rescheduling arrangements for low-income African countries. However, much more needs to be done.

Our proposal would be the following: for SSA, a country -by - country approach to the debt problem would be desirable. In countries where external loans have benefitted the majority of the population, the solutions lies in retroactive terms adjustment (RTA) along the following terms: for the poorest ones, you simply convert past official loans to grants. An alternative could take the form of providing additional grants and soft loans commensurate with the debt service due. For countries considered to be relatively 'rich' the option might be to bring terms into line with those of current concessional lending. This would imply an easing in the terms of repayments.

There could be difficulties in other countries where foreign funding has benefitted regimes instead of the population at large. The choice wont be easy because pressing for prompt servicing of external debt would be undesirable if this means a further squeeze on essential imports. It is for creditor nations to make firm decisions, knowing that they cannot "expect large and growing repayments on their claims and at the same time impose barriers to the importation of goods and services from the developing countries. The developed nations must either continually refinance interest payments and maturing debt or permit better access to their markets. Both activities will be necessary to assure the future progress of many developing countries."

6.4.1   Foreign Exchange Myth

There is a need for foreign exchange throughout SSA. People sometimes think that there is a one-to-one correspondence between scarcity in foreign exchange and growing mass poverty.

That is not to deny that a country's ability to consume what it does not produce domestically increases with the availability of foreign exchange. This is stated succinctly l y Paul Streeten: "But we ought to think very carefully before we universally preach 'grow more food for your consumption' rather than, say, go in for more manufactured industrial exports and import the food from countries like United States and Europe, which have enormous food surpluses and where, apparently, high productivity in food is very easy to achieve,...Many countries, as we know, have done terribly well by industrializing, by growing relatively little food and by exporting their manufactured products".

But does reality match the typology described above. The question - Is foreign exchange the answer? - has taken on a new twist with the emergence of the oil-rich states and their emerging development problems.

The development record of OPEC countries reflects what Galal Amin has dubbed 'The Modernization of Poverty'. These countries reveal the inherent danger of the propensity to over-rate foreign exchange scarcity as the leading development bottleneck.   Indeed, availability of foreign exchange as such is not an end in itself; so that - as Darwin Wassink puts it -"the problems of economic development in (OPEC) countries include inflation, port and transportation bottlenecks and manpower shortages. ...While most development planning continues to be based on capital constrained growth models, the experience of these countries draws attention to the absorptive capacity constraints in development".

Almost all OPEC countries have experienced very rapid economic growth by historical standards. But much of this growth has occurred in the oil sector. Other sectors have encountered numerous obstacles. Hence the relevancy of Henry Bruton's remarks that " What foreign-exchange-rich countries are now learning is that foreign exchange really is not the heart of the development matter. The heart must be the indigenous resources and their commitment to the nation's development".

The experience of revenue-rich countries deserves the attention of development theorists and practitioners. In the end, we should realize that the disappointing development experience of SSA results from overstressing the 'forex' constraint. This is best explained in Streeten's words: " I think one of the best and most useful things is to increase the indigenous capacity of the African to discover and research into what it is that they really need and how to achieve it". This line of thinking considers "development as the growing capability of people themselves to determine their future society"[31].

With the present development malaise choices must be guided by the principle of relying on one's resources.

The harsh truth is that African planners are operating under very unusual conditions. SSA faces a crisis of economic management. This state is gradually breeding an unusual sense of hopelessness throughout Africa. However, we must guard against growing impatience and despair.

6.5 Aid Modalities

It is appropriate to conclude this paper by considering whether current aid strategies for SSA are really new.

Most of the policies under discussion must be considered in light of the complementing policy reforms being pursued by African governments. The nature of these programmes is well known so that only a brief mention needs to be made here.

Assistance for emergencies consists of providing humanitarian assistance. Examples here include emergence assistance programmes to Ethiopia and Sudan. External responses to emergencies have often been widespread and positive. One question remains: Should long-term development assistance be sacrificed for short-term relief? In this way both African Governments and donors end up dealing with appearances at risk of overlooking the root causes of the emergencies. Programme support for specified problems is another form of support. Instances here include WHO's Global Programmes on AIDS, Tropical Forestry Action Plans, and Population Programmes. Such initiatives are definitely valuable, but only if they do not direct policy attention and local resources from the broader issues which govern the need for medium - and long-term transformation.

Initially, both bilateral and multilateral aid donors emphasized project aid. There has been less emphasis on project aid since the late 1970s, with most assistance being converted to fast-disbursing support earmarked for reform programmes. This is considered essential to redress past mistakes of external support to SSA.

The essence of reforms with help from the IMF, the World Bank, and bilateral donors entails minimum controls, reduced inflation and a decline in the growth of balance-of-payments deficits. In practice, these reforms have amounted to cuts in state subsidies, raised agricultural producer prices, a streamlined public sector, currency devaluation, and liberalization of foreign exchange and trade regimes.

However, reforms of this nature rarely work in practice. Tanzania's *Daily News* of March 16, 1989 reported a similar worry by drawing evidence compiled in two reports:

(1) report by the House of Representatives sub-Committee on Africa based on research conducted by the staff of the House of Representative Committee on Foreign Affairs; and
(2) the report by the UN Commission on Social Development presented in Vienna. A similar scepticism is evident in the 'World Development Report' of 1988.

The need for substantial assistance from the international community is desirable. The argument is clear enough: it is in the interest of donor countries to meet the financial needs of Africa.

In the case of Britain, for example, Africa's share of the country's exports dropped from 8 per cent in 1980 to only 3.5 per cent in 1987. But Africa's import bill from Britain was more or less constant for the same period, notwithstanding high price of imports. Furthermore, in 1987 alone Britain received procurements valued at 1.7 per cent for each one per cent Britain subscribed to various multilateral agencies.

In other words, Britain's financial support to bodies such as the World Bank present a window of opportunity for British firms to consolidate and develop their trade relations with Africa. As everyone knows, "bourgeois economists argue over aid's effectiveness in promoting development, while in business and political circles its defenders make the only really telling arguments: that markets and resources are secured, and a climate conductive to world wide private investment is created and strengthened.

More complex is the lesson drawn by Helleiner, leading him to conclude that " the prospect for direct foreign investment in Africa today is quite bleak, regardless of governmental approaches. With the exception of some petroleum and mineral developments, some tourist development potential, and some reinvestment on the part of long-established foreign firms in trade and manufacturing, foreign investors are at present very chary of investment in a crisis-ridden continent with massive debt and payments arrears".

Foreign assistance could play a greater role in ending this state of affairs by filling the gap. However, the prospects are not promising. Recently, programme aid has recorded a relative increase to the extent that it has exceeded spending on project aid. Although useful for the kind of short-term relief it provides, programme aid has the drawback associated with aid that is provided to what are requested as "key" areas. What is considered as "key" may vary both between countries and over time. Moreover, what appears to be a "key" sector by donors need not be what African governments themselves view as leading sectors.

7.0   Summing Up

When, at the beginning of this essay, I cited Frantz Fanon, I was aware of the challenge set in his conclusion: "Let us decide not to imitate Europe; let us combine our muscles and our brains in a new direction". It is my hope that the above analysis lives up to the same concern.

There is widespread conviction that Fanon was as much of an economist as a social theorist. He, therefore, holds a paramount role in the development of social thought in the context of underdevelopment.

While this is acknowledged, Fanon is more often quoted than actually read.

Fanon's work is, however, relevant to SSA today. Should not one be mindful of the following: "The peasant who goes on scratching out a living from the soil, and the unemployed man who never finds employment do not manage, in spite of public holidays and flags, new and brightly-coloured though they may be, to convince themselves that anything has really changed in their lives". This was the precise description of Africa's position immediately after the 1950s. Thirty years after, one could still raise the concern that, is it not the same position today? This is a matter of judgement. Nevertheless, some of the indications provided in this essay give hints towards arriving at a more accurate judgement.

Footnotes

1   In the concluding lines of *The General Theory*, it is interestingly stated that "Practical men, who believe themselves to be quite exempt from any intellectual influence, are usually the slaves of some defunct economist. ...; for in the field of economics and political philosophy there are not many who are influenced by new theories after they are twenty-five or thirty years of age, so that the ideas which civil servants and politicians and even agitators apply to current events are not likely to be the newest". Keynes, 1965: 383. Some of these ideas are of more relevance today than perhaps Keynes and his successors envisaged, and it is my belief that such ideas should be picked up given more thoughts. Cf. A. M. Babu's contribution in Rodney, 1976.

2   World Bank, 1981: 122 - 23

3   *Africa Recovery* June 1988: 23

4   Shah, 1964: 81 (emphasis original).   Also, as J. Meynaund - *L'Elaboration de la Politique Economique* puts it: "Most (economic policy) programmes amount to mere declarations of intent. Political parties are largely responsible for this confusion, since their desire to attract the maximum number of voters leads them to seek fairly vague formulas to avoid displeasing anyone"; cited in Lessa, 1979: 68/69. Without going any further into the matter, the reader should keep in mind that these remarks are extraordinarily rel-

evant to SSA's Social-economic and political facts. See, e.g. Brandt et.al., 1985 and contributions on the theme States and African Agriculture in: *IDS (Sussex) Bulletin* 17(1), 1986

5   Pinches, 1978: 139. Thus Perroux's remarks that "Neither capitalism nor socialism, however modified and corrected, can bring progress to the developing countries; the only hope of doing so lies in the efforts made by enlightened pragmatists to provide indigenous peoples with institutions of their own. It certainly seems that the need to set new standards and find fresh means of updating the old values without distorting them is the crucial problem of development". Perroux, 1983: 41. Also, cf.Furtado, 1978.

------Chapter 9

TOWARDS A DEMOCRATIC COALITION
AGAINST SAP

Ben Turok

Introduction

A curious paradox is haunting Africa's policy makers. Surrounded by
catastrophic economic crisis, there is nevertheless an appreciation that
the solution lies not so much in the economic as in the political domain.
Matters seem to have gone too far and the crisis is too deep for proposals
for economic adjustments to carry conviction by themselves. A new
focus is emerging on the need for democratic transformation. Whether
this momentum will gather strength and become effective is the major
issue of our day.

African governments are under two types of pressures to democra-
tise. First, opposition forces are harnessing their energies in a variety
of actions which are becoming ever more forceful. Second, foreign
governments and agencies are becoming increasingly insistent that
Africa needs better "governance" and more respect for human rights.
The genuineness of these pressures may be questioned, but they cannot
be ignored.

However, it is the internal pressures which preoccupy African
regimes, challenging their legitimacy and sometimes their very survival.
The demand for democracy has now struck a chord deep in society.
Two decades of political silence is being broken by a period of activism

which is spreading across the continent as the power and exuberance of politics is now being discovered by new generations. This politics is not traditional whereby conventional parties compete with each other over programmes and leaders. Rather, it is spontaneous in its diverse manifestations and loosely knit in its social composition. It is as though a new dimension unknown for decades is being given to the public domain.

Is there a country in Africa which is not experiencing rioting, protests, university closures, campaigns for multiparty democracy or public opposition to the work of the IMF and World Bank? A profound sense of dissatisfaction pervades Africa and almost all governments are at bay.

Zambia is a classic example of popular alienation and economic stagnation. It is being punctuated by social unrest, highlighted by "IMF riots", which are clearly the product of economic retreat. Since the story of Zambia's misfortunes is typical for the continent some details are worth recording here. In 1985, after a decade of close relations with the IMF, Zambia found itself with a massive external debt. The IMF imposed a programme of stringent financial measures which led to the lifting of price controls on mealie meal, the basic food for the majority of the people. Rioting against the state broke out on the copperbelt with the loss of 15 lives. President Kaunda ordered a break with the IMF programme on 1st May 1986. But only four years later, the programmes were back in place, price controls were lifted, and this time, the rioting led to hundreds of casualties in several cities, including Lusaka. A serious attempted coup followed as the country seethed with dissatisfaction. This soon found expression in a mass movement for multiparty democracy which saw mass meetings of over 100,000 people in Lusaka and other locations. These sights had never been seen before in Zambia and probably no place else in black Africa since independence.

Ivory Coast is another such example. The darling of the West, the Ivory Coast has been held up as a model of capitalist success under France's close friend President Felix Houphouet-Boigny. Dependent on commodity exports, the country remains extremely vulnerable to international prices. When cocoa and coffee prices collapsed, the country fell under the sway of the IMF and World Bank. When these institutions imposed a plan in January 1990 which included a 40 % cut in the salaries of public employees, a wave of protest erupted, led by teachers. Soon airport and other workers threatened to strike. Students and workers clashed with the security forces and 137 people were arrested. Opposition forces are becoming bolder and bolder, challenging the legitimacy of the regime which now seems to be highly vulnerable.

Around this time a wave of popular revolts also swept through Senegal, Gabon, Niger and Benin, all linked to the harsh economic measures of repressive regimes.

Togo saw the biggest anti-government demonstrations since independence in October 1990. Demonstrators had running battles with police and soldiers, vehicles were set on fire, several police stations were gutted, with four people killed and 34 injured. The Bar Association launched a 72 hour strike, and the country was overwhelmed with calls for political change.

Elsewhere in Africa, the same phenomenon troubled other governments. In Nigeria, almost all universities were closed in response to protests against the Government's acceptance of IMF programmes. The Nigerian Labour Congress was actually closed down for the same reason.

Unrest in Tanzania was small scale and largely confined to the university, but it is nevertheless indicative of serious problems as the country grapples with the harsh measures imposed by the IMF. Staff and students complain of the absence of democracy and accountability, a decline in the proportion of funding allocated to education, and corruption in the bloated bureaucracy, all of which has affected working and living conditions.

In Zaire, economic collapse coincides with the disappearance of administration. Government offices are virtually abandoned as civil servants no longer bother to go to work trying other income generating activities instead. The state is crumbling and Mobutu's power has eroded to such an extent that he relies on South African mercenaries. Even his erstwhile supporters, the World Bank and IMF are now denying him further loans. The time for the emergence of a new opposition seems to be at hand.

Government instability is therefore the rule across the whole of Africa. The harsh demands of the IMF and World Bank generally have been the immediate trigger for protest. But the origins of the process lies much further back in the character of the international economic order and which is now increasingly unjust, unequal, and undemocratic.

Political Conditionality

It is ironic that western institutions are raising the question of democracy in Africa, even making aid conditional on improvements in this respect.

The theory has it that "the connection between democratic practice and economic efficiency has become more and more apparent... Market systems need accountability, rule by law and transparency in decision-making" (OECD Development Assistance Committee, 1990 Report). The IMF, the World Bank and all the other major western institutions also reiterate homilies about democracy in tandem with their rush for free market economics and efficiency. These sentiments might be taken with a pinch of salt given that these institutions have themselves relied on the support of African dictators and their totalitarianism to implement their adjustment programmes. However, some governments such as Sweden are genuine in their demands for conditionality on those seeking foreign aid.

The Non-Government Organisations (NGO's) of the North are also being drawn into similar positions. The argument is that their projects in Africa are suffering from maladministration in recipient countries and that grassroots people are not benefiting because of state corruption.

Such emphasis has been placed on democratisation that African governments are now being forced to make at least same formal acknowledgement that democracy is on the agenda.

Salim Salim, the OAU Secretary General believes that Africa's record on democracy is poor and that much needs to be done. But his acceptance is nevertheless conditional; as he notes,

"We are told that our crisis is a result of years of poor administration, unwise spending, and simple disregard for tomorrow. We are councelled to open up government systems and make them accountable to the governed. We are also told to weed out corruption and inefficiency. I agree with all this. But if Africa did all this would development be certain?" (speech at House of Commons Conference, 6 June 1990)

He goes on to argue that the new conditionality is diversionary and at some level irrelevant to the development solutions of the continent. "For no matter how many political parties an African state may have, it will not change the price of coffee, cocoa, cotton, sisal or copper. "Nor will it reduce external dependency, or more consultation over the price of commodities or interest rates. It will also not stop the injustice of the poor of the South subsidising the rich of the North.

Would it not be more helpful, he asked, if the argument for democratisation of African societies were linked to the democratisation of the international system.

There is a great deal of evidence that the situation in Africa is deteriorating primarily because of the unfavourable terms of trade and the reduction in aid. This is in part due to the new preoccupation with Eastern Europe. The prospect is that a new united Europe will strengthen its own industries, and marginalise Africa further in the field of trade.

The Legacy of External Control

Western pressures for democratisation are also deeply resented because the present systems in Africa arose within the structure of economic relations rooted in the colonial period.

Nzongola Ntalaja has argued that the African crisis is basically a crisis of accumulation rooted in the export oriented process of surplus extraction established under colonial rule and maintained by the ruling class. After independence this production system continued with a deeper insertion of neocolonial rulers into the international structures of wealth and privilege in which they sought to find their place. (Presidential Address, African Studies Association, USA, October 1988)

In my view, it is not certain that African rulers were quite so willingly, integrated into the international system. One can also argue that they were coerced. There is evidence that "independent" governments were subjected to gross political manipulation and conditionalities to ensure that economic control remained with multinational corporations and former colonial powers. Do what they might, foreign interests remained dominant in Africa economies despite efforts to enhance domestic power. Nationalised enterprises were circumscribed by limitations relating to, capital, and market restriction leading to control from abroad. Conditions were unfavourable for the emergence of competent governments and good management.

Thus, the history of state intervention in Africa is one of relatively inexperienced and weak governments struggling to increase their powers vis-a-vis foreign owned economies. Their problems were compounded by activities of experts imposed by foreign interests or brought in by governments ill-prepared for the complexities they faced. Post-independence Africa was invaded by hordes of economic advisers lacking local know-how. They espoused the post-war-wisdom about growth and modernisation and encouraged Africa to build industries which would enhance the image of government and increase GDP statistics. But the import substitution model they advocated was not based on domestic inputs nor primarily directed to the internal market. The fallacy of this model became apparent when the terms of trade moved steadily against exporters so that less and less could be bought with the same amount of exports.

The urban based elite slotted naturally into this milieu. Increasingly they saw themselves as part of a modern society with little connection to or interest in the masses in the rural areas or in the urban slums. Many sought upward mobility through trade rather than through production. Even this did not suffice and politics became a vehicle for personal gain since official openings provided access to import licences and government favours.

Since growth and development was not rooted in an effort to harness national wealth, but in marginal activities, the economy faltered and scarcity set in. This was the breeding ground for corruption.

Also, Africa was faced with an acute management crisis soon after independence. Since top positions were held by colonial expatriates, strong pressures grew for Africanization. However, as many of these positions were considered "hardship posts" foreign managers were usually paid well above rates in developed countries, setting a naturally high standard for local personnel. In some cases, counterparts were appointed to work side by side with expatriates at the same salary scale to avoid the charge of discrimination. This led to increases in the number of superscale posts.

Yet the required management culture was not addressed. Dependency on expatriate managers continued as the quality of management deteriorated. Africanization of posts also applied lower down the scale. In colonial Zambia, the gap in skill and pay levels between white expatriates and African was huge. Union pressures and public opinion forced some changes which took the form of increased wages from below, thereby massively raising the total wage bill.

For the above reasons plus the fact that a self-serving elite steadily entrenched itself in power, independent Africa failed to deliver on the promises made during the freedom struggle. This was not the environment in which democracy could flourish. One party systems, at first dedicated to social mobilization faltered and soon turned into one-person dictatorships multiparty systems were replaced by military despots.

Primacy of the External Factor Now

The fact that the above is now the dominant pattern for all countries irrespective of ideological orientation shows that undemocratic practices have their roots in the economic crisis rather than in political ideology or the characteristics of individual leaders. All the more reason, therefore, to be critical of those International Monetary Fund whose Structural Adjustment Programmes (SAP) create scarcity of jobs, income, and goods. A decade of lending to Africa at rising interest rates and in circumstances of falling export revenues has meant that all Africa is now in debt and actually a net exporter of funds to these organisations. The poor are subsidizing the rich at the very time when world opinion recognizes the terrible deterioration of the conditions of the former.

The scale of transfers from the third world to the North is staggering. From 1982 to 1990 there was a net transfer of $ 300 billion from South to North. For Sub-Saharan Africa the figure is $156 billion for 1984-90. Most disturbing of all is the net transfer from Sub Saharan Africa to the IMF and the World Bank which was $4.7 billion for 1986-90. This has occurred despite these organisations' claims of being concerned with the development of the continent. It is clear that they operate as commercial banks and that they have no scruples about gaining from Africa's crisis. Indeed some African experts believe that this is the main objective of their SAP policies.

The three main external factors now constraining Africa's development are debt, unequal trade, and SAP. The debt burden takes the form of being required to pay rising service charges which now stand at $25.3 bn for SSA and which average at 40 per cent of total export revenues. In some countries it is much higher so that almost all income from exports is immediately paid to service foreign debts.

Repayment of external debt and debt servicing have become the single greatest burden on governments which have taken drastic measures to cut government expenditures and squeeze the economy. Debt servicing has therefore been a major factor in undermining democratic government and has helped to lay the ground for authoritarianism.

The debt issue is now often seen as the most cruel manifestation of an unjust and inequitable international economic order, generating undemocratic consequences in the countries of the victims.

According to the Frazer Report, Africa's non-oil commodity exports earned $18 billion in 1988, that is 35 % less than in 1970. Yet $17.2 billion was needed in 1987 for debt servicing and $13 billion for food imports.

The irony is that having saddled Africa with huge debts, which have devastated its economic performance, the North is now writing the continent off as an area with which it can have fruitful economic relations. At a conference held in London on 8 October 1990, the Deputy

Director General of DG VIII of the European Commission in Brussels explained that there was a degree of "aid fatigue", as the belief grew that funding only enriching Southern government officials and was therefore a waste of taxpayers money. Also, lending to Africa has declined dramatically because the returns are so poor and countries of the South are no longer deemed creditworthy.

Yet Africa is being driven into bankruptcy due to declining export revenues and falling world market prices. The price of cocoa alone fell 50 per cent in 1989. For Africa as a whole the terms of trade fell by 31 per cent between 1980-1987.

This is the price Africa is paying for failing to diversify its exports over the years, policies which have been encouraged by donors under the rubric of export led growth. Even now the World Bank and IMF persist in promoting exports as the means of "balancing the books" on external accounts. This places African governments on a treadmill from which there is no escape.

As Bade Onimode, Africa's leading expert on structural adjustment programmes, notes: these impositions of the Bank and the Fund are undemocratic in their mode of imposition, and in their effect. They are conceived within those institutions by groups of experts focusing on the short term adjustments they think are needed to sustain sound international financial relations. They are imposed on African governments under the threat of depriving them not only of loans and grants by these institutions themselves, but also of a "certificate of creditworthiness" which would lead to a financial blockade by other agencies and banks. Many governments which set out to resist the IMF package have been embargoed in this way until they have retreated. This amounts to a direct assault on sovereignty and a ganging up on the part of northern governments and institutions.

The damage done from SAP has been immense. It has worsened conditions for the poor by reducing employment and cutting wages. It has also increased the price of basic commodities, especially food, and had led to a reduction in government expenditure in basic services such as health, education, and sanitation in Africa between 1979 and 1983, expenditure per capita on health and other social services fell by 50% and continued to fall thereafter. Unemployment rates have also increased to 60 per cent among school leavers and 30 per cent among graduates.

This has led to such a chorus of criticism that representatives of the Bank have been forced to make damaging admissions about their own fallibility. The World Bank Vice President for Africa, E. Jaycox, admitted in an official publication that "neither the World Bank nor anyone else really had all the answers on what an effective adjustment programme should look like". Even more damaging is the admission that "it is very hard to predict the social impact of a given programme...it is incredible how little is known about where and how to manage the social side." (Africa Update, External Affairs Unit, Africa Region, World Bank, 1988/9)

In the previously quoted speech, the Deputy Director General of DG8 admitted that "although the World Bank has admitted failure with structural adjustment, the idea has not been abandoned." He added that the Bank works on the basis of trial and error with unfortunately too many errors. On the other hand, he argued that structural adjustment "necessarily involves a period of suffering and should therefore be related to aid policy so that social support can be given where needed". This is a similar argument to that of UNICEF which amounts to providing of ambulances to carry the victims of SAPs. The fallacy however is that not only are there too many victims for such palliatives, but that SAP, actually undermine the whole structure of a society including its politics. SAP can only be implemented by draconian means and that requires authoritarian, usually military governments. It is no coincidence that Africa is overwhelmed by military rule at this time of economic crisis.

Given this background, we are amazed by the new pronouncements of the Bank: about their concern for democracy, people centred development, empowerment of women and the like.[1] While a common defence of Bank documents is that there are different opinions within the Bank which find expressions in differing perspectives, this report is signed by President Barber Conable, and therefore carries the full weight of his endorsement. It is now impossible to give such documents much credibility.

Africa's Response

The failure of IMF and World Bank policies have fortunately found a countervailing voice in the United Nations Economic Commission for Africa. Professor Adebayo Adedeji has provided dynamic leadership in developing alternative policies throughout the continent and among Northern NGO's.

Implicit in these critiques is the demand for a new international system which might be called a New International Democratic Economic Order (NIDEO).

Following on the Lagos Plan for Action of 1980, and the APPER document of 1986, there is now in place the ECA's African Alternative Framework to Structural Adjustment Programmes of 1989. Also significant is the African Charter for Popular Participation in Development adopted at a meeting of African NGO's in Arusha in February 1990 which was sponsored by the ECA.

All these documents are using a new terminology of change and renewal. Suddenly there is even a recognition that the non-governmental organisations have a role to play in giving a lead to public opinion in a new attempt to generate an alternative development strategy. Their documents refer to "peoples participation", "empowerment", "democratic process", and "peoples charter", terms formerly confined to the radical movements of Africa, while the condemnation of undemocratic practices such as the "abysmal failure of past elitist and bureaucratic approach to development policy and planning", of "political repression, oppressive austerity" and "authoritarianism" was formerly the terminology of government critics and opposition. The central idea in all these arguments is "state power must open up to accommodate people's power". (See also the OAU Declaration of July 1990)

How seriously can these statements be taken? It is inconceivable that leaders and regimes which have been repressive and abitrary for decades will readily change their practices at home, no matter their protestations abroad. Nevertheless, new scope is now available for public pressure for democratic alternatives, for human rights, multiparty democracy and political pluralism.

An important milestone in this regard has come from Zambia where the one party state has come under serious pressure. The Report of the Special Parliamentary Select Committee of 9 July 1990 examining multipartyism noted that "a country which glorified its existence on falsehood in all normal circumstances was bound to collapse". This dishonesty arose because some leaders wanted to secure their continued existence. The party leadership as the only political party took it for granted that nothing could go wrong with their system and their authority would not be challenged. There was attempt to enforce accountability in the party. There was inertia. The majority of top officials were appointees and the majority of the membership of the party congress were either appointees or employees of the party and government. Similarly the National Council's agenda was solely based on the Opening Speech by the Party President, thereby foreclosing open debate.

Julius Nyerere has articulated the anxiety of many about the one party system. These ideas are being taken up even in countries like Kenya where the single party has been the vehicle for undemocratic rule since independence.

It is once again a paradox that the most vocal forces in the multiparty movement are those of businessmen, petty bourgeois elements, and non-political public figures such as churchmen. The African left has not figured strongly so far. Yet, socialists have always understood that if the struggle for socialism parts company from the struggle for democracy serious distortions will arise. The fact that this truth was forgotten in Eastern Europe does not diminish the fundamental principle involved. Socialists will have to accept the fact that under present conditions in Africa they do not have a monopoly on the struggle for democracy, especially as almost all sectors of society have suffered from its denial.

Nevertheless, attention and resources are being diverted to Eastern Europe, while protectionism and inter-North trade is increasing. Africa's needs are hardly receiving attention now, forcing its leaders to realize that they must allow the participation of the masses rather than trying to suppress their participation.

A proverbial wind of change is sweeping across the continent removing dictators from office and providing scope for popular opinion to surface for the first time in decades. There are signs that Africa's leaders cannot face an increasingly hostile world economic order without the support participation in development, in decision making, and the new emphasis on self-reliance.

These sentiments echo those of Salim Salim, OAU Secretary General, who said that "a society's ability to mobilise its creative abilities and to apply its abilities and resource positively to development is determined largely by its degree of democratisation." "Democracy is the involvement of people in the process of governance" "I am absolutely convinced of the imperative need of democratising our societies, that human life is scrosanct. We must build societies, where human rights is an automatic right, a right which governments do not dispense or withdraw at will but which they are obliged to protect and defend. We must instil the notion of the rule of law into our political life, and a political culture in which dissent is not taken to be treason but a right of citizens and essential to constitutional rule."

What Democratic Future?

In short, there is a new spirit aboard, fuelled by public demonstrations which is also being encouraged by the activities of social movements and NGO's and is even being supported by official pronouncements. Essentially it is anti-authoritarian in sentiment, reflecting Africa's malaise, deep concern about the failure of Eastern European socialist regimes, and finding inspiration in the mass rejection of apartheid in South Africa.

But the concept of democracy is easily manipulated and carries many meanings. What future does democracy have in Africa? What might be its shape? And what alternatives does it offer?

1. Intrinsic to the current demand for democracy is that government and the state must reflect the will of the people and not be a substitute for it.
2. Although the state in Africa has almost universally developed into a coercive instrument, it is generally accepted that the state will remain an important institution. The state must retain an important defensive role against external economic penetration, but it must also facilitate and intervene in the economy. It must also lead in the provision of public services and social welfare.
3. However, the overblown post colonial state has become a serious obstacle to development since one of its main functions is to satisfy the interests of a self-serving parasitic bureaucracy. Hierarchy and complex procedures of delegating responsibility has made the system prone to corruption.

   In multi-ethnic countries, the state has become a site for serious ethnic conflict as different groups try to bolster their own privileges and positions.

   As resources dwindle, the state apparatus becomes less efficient and civil servants lose their commitment to public duty. However, there is hope of transforming the situation without seriously assaulting the power of the bureaucracy.
4. It is now well understood that development cannot come from above, but must find its momentum from below. While there are many examples of economic growth being achieved as a result of state coercion or from a strong capitalist class, this does not benefit the people as a whole, nor are its achievements sustainable in the long run. Indeed one central lesson of the Marxist legacy is that while state centred growth may build the productive forces in the

short run, it cannot create an economic system which will expand
steadily and evenly serving the people as a whole.

Development is about extending the capacity of the people and
developing a country's resources in an integrated manner. It is a
total process.

5. While the debate about the contradictions between the state and civil
society are most important, we should not think in terms of polarities.
The state must be curbed, but civil society cannot be seen as its
antithesis. Both must be combined in a harmonious totality in the
best interests of society as an organism.

6. At the same time, we should be cautious about the reification of the
grassroots concept. Clearly we want to empower ordinary people
and build strong democratic structures from below. But many
conceive of this in a utopian way, as though fragments of social
structure can become thriving communities in isolation. We know
from concrete experience in Africa that isolation does not bring
strength, that communities have to trade with each, join in the
exchange of goods and services, and benefit from economies of
scale. African people desperately need social services including
health and education, which can only be established nationally as a
public service.

7. In the same way, while we must encourage the rapid growth of
NGO's, the voluntary sector, and the informal sector, we also know
that local, small scale development efforts are severly limited in
scope and are easily derailed by micro-economic constraints.

8. Finally, while many have derived enormous inspiration form the
ideals of socialism, it is apparent that Africa is not ripe for socialism
now, nor could it be given the underdevelopment of its productive
resources. Indeed the polemic between capitalist and socialist
options has not on the whole been helpful. For many, the socialist
perspective remains valid despite the trauma of Eastern Europe.
But, Africa cannot develop its material base by neglecting the profit
motive or self-interest, provided they do not take command of the
economy and society. The democratic path is the path to development and provided democracy means the interests of the people as
a whole, it is a sufficient guide to economic and social policy.

In Conclusion

The serious constraints imposed on Africa by the unjust international
economic order has created a basis for broad coalitions within Africa in

defence of its resources and peoples. The imposition of structural adjustment programmes by the IMF and World Bank, the further penetration of Africa planned in the Uruguay Round of GATT, and the harsh policies adopted by the G7, all continue to generate a sense of desperation on the continent.

Footnote

1 World Bank Report: Sub Saharan Africa- From Crisis to Sustainable Growth, 1989.

Chapter 10

AFRICA'S DEVELOPMENT EXPERIENCE UNDER THE LOME CONVENTIONS

Results and Prospects

Dani W. Nabudere

Introduction

Africa's developmental experience over the last thirty years has clearly produced no positive results. Indeed, its rate of growth in the late seventies was negative. It grew so much worse in the nineteen eighties that this is now being called "the lost decade". This negative experience cannot be attributed entirely to the mismanagement, corruption, and mis-allocation of resources by African leaders and their governments. These domestic problems have intensified rather than caused the negative developmental experience. Indeed, one can say that the corruption and the mismanagement are themselves the result of this negative experience. In fact, Africa's present day problems can be traced to five hundred years of slave trade and colonisation. One nevertheless has to concretely examine, the mechanisms and relationships which have characterised this experience over the last thirty years.

Apart from the Bretton Woods system which supervised the world economy in general, Africa has had a peculiar relationship with the former European colonising powers under a series of economic arrangements which have included the Lomé Conventions. The relationships between the Africa (and the Caribbean and Pacific-ACP-countries in general) and the European Economic Community-(EEC) have, if anything, intensified the old colonial division of labour in the post-colonial period of independent Africa instead of rectifying the situation. It is the purpose of this paper to examine these relationships to reveal some of the fundamental structures which have impended Africa's development over the last thirty years.

The structures which were intended to entice Africa back into the womb of colonial subservience were part of the Rome Treaty itself. This created the basis for a united Europe to the extent that the link was seen as an inevitable component of the European unity. According to the verbiage of the period, this relationship was seen as creating a continuing linkage between Europe and Africa in a kind of "Euro-Africa". Under Part IV of the Treaty, provisions were made for the Community through which a regime of "liberalised" trade could be developed with the former colonies. In addition, an "Implementing Convention" was annexed to the Treaty giving procedures for continuing these old relations in a new way and providing for the notion of "aid" within it.

In 1958, the first European Development Fund was set up under the European Development Bank, with an initial fund of 581 million "units of account" (the forerunner of the ECU). All of this was to be spent in form of "grants" for economic and social infrastructure projects in the colonies, particular the French ones. In 1960, a number of these colonies were "granted" independence after Ghana had opened the way in 1957. In these early days, Senegal's groundnut economy began to experience low prices in the French markets. Because of this, France pressured other members of the EEC to use this fund to assist Senegal. This was the beginning of new relationships between Europe and formally independent African states.

These early activities were soon consolidated in formal arrangements which came to be referred to as the Yaounde Conventions, named after the capital of Cameroun where they were formalised and signed. The Implementing Convention provided for a form of "unilateral association" between the EEC and what were then called "Overseas Countries and Territories"-(OCT). After independence, these states also created their own structures to enable them to maintain and extend their relationships with the EEC in line with their new status. The 18-former French colonies (excepting of Somalia and Madagascar) formed the Association of African States and Madagascar -(AASM) for this purpose. In July 1963, they concluded a Convention with the Six EEC states which at this time were France, West Germany, Italy, the Netherlands, Belgium, and Luxembourg. This Convention referred to as the first Yaounde Convention, was cushioned by the increased second

European Development Fund of 800 units of account which included grants and loans.

Not wanting to be left out, Nigeria signed, but did not ratify, its own agreement with the EEC in 1966. This was due to the debate that erupted about the neo-colonial implications of the idea of "Euro-Africa" which was then current. In 1969, the three East African states of Kenya, Uganda and Tanganyika, signed their own agreement with the Community called the Arusha Agreement, at a time when they themselves were still part of the East African Community. There were strong hopes this would lead to the establishment of an East African Federation, but as we know these hopes were soon dashed. So as not to be accused of being drawn into neo-colonial relationships, the Arusha Agreement concentrated on trade relationships, particularly on preferential trade arrangements which came into effect in 1971.[1]

These arrangements must be viewed against the backdrop of the booming enthusiasm of the 1960s. For Europe, this period was referred to as "the Golden Sixties" and the period 1963-1973 as "the Golden Decade", because of Europe's unprecedented economic growth deriving from the Marshall Plan and its post-war recovery. African countries, having contributed to the financial soundness of the metropoles during the war years, because of the high commodity prices of this period, also were convinced that they too could "take-off" in line with W.W. Rostow's visions of the time.[2]

Indeed such visions did not appear to be unfounded, as the growth rates which were achieved at this time by most African countries appeared to confirm this enthusiasm. Between 1960 and 1967, ten African countries, representing 25 per cent of the continental population, had per capita GDP growth rates of 2.5 per cent per annum. Another thirteen countries with 38 per cent of the population also registered had a per capita growth rate ranging between 1 to 3 per cent. While for seven countries with 14 per cent of the population the GDP per capita was only 1 per cent or less, with the remainder having negative growth rates. The overall picture looked promising.

Hence it was not surprising that the African states, influenced by the mood of the period, saw all these new arrangements as opening up new possibilities, despite the fact that they seemed in fact to consolidate old relations. Europe, also experiencing boom conditions, saw the possibility of a new world economic order. Britain which had not taken part in the Treaty of Rome, began also to be interested in joining the EEC. Their initial efforts were blocked by President De Gaulle of France, but by 1973 (together with Ireland and Denmark) they had managed to join, bringing the total of EEC members up to nine, from the original six. When joining, Britain wanted her former colonies to associate themselves with the EEC on "favourable terms" comparable to those of the ex-French colonies. This was taken care of in Protocol 22 of Britain's Act of Accession to the Community. After considerable bargaining, twenty Commonwealth countries–African ones included–were included in the Protocol. Even then, the EEC saw no reason why it should not offer similar conditions to any African country which was neither part of the AASM nor within the Commonwealth.

1. Lomé I and II Conventions

It was at this stage that 43 African, Caribbean and Pacific countries,(ACP) as a group, began to negotiate for a more comprehensive arrangement. The second Yaounde Convention which had been renewed in 1970 was due to expire on 31 January, 1975. The African countries, in preparation for the negotiations, had in May 1973 announced their negotiating principles at the OAU Summit held at Addis Ababa. These were as follows:

1) the EEC should not expect reciprocal tariff concessions from Africa for whatever concessions they made;
2) any rights of establishment granted to Europe should be available to other countries as well (due to pressure from the USA and Japan);
3) rules of origin in the Yaounde Conventions should be reviewed;
4) rules in the Yaounde Conventions relating to capital movements should also be reviewed;
5) Africa should have free access to EEC financial and technical assistance;
6) there should be free access of African goods to the EEC market whether or not they were covered by the Common Agricultural Policy-CAP;
7) stable, equitable, and remunerative prices for Africa's products should be guaranteed;
8) any agreement with the EEC should affect intra-African cooperation.

These principles became the basis of the negotiations which followed. The negotiations ended with the signing of a new umbrella convention called the Lomé Convention, named after the Togolese capital where it was signed on 28th February, 1975.

It should be noted that 1973 was a significant year. It had signalled the exercise of economic power by the Arab petroleum producing countries after the Arab-Israels war of that year by blocking the supply of oil to some western countries. Although the consequent rise in oil price rises had negatively affected African countries, there were hopes that this collective power could be exercised over other raw materials. In official circles, therefore, Lomé I was seen by all sides as constituting a new "beginning" of economic relations between industrial and non-industrial countries based on partnership and equality.[3] This "equality recognized the sovereignty of each side which was reflected in the contractual character of the relationship.

In fact, both conceptions were false. Neither took into account the basic inequality stemming from their previous historical relationship. In historical and political terms, the new relationship was clearly significant, at least in the formal recognition of the independence of the ACP states by Europe. Nevertheless, the relationship was still situated within the context of the continuing contradiction between the ACP states and the EEC. The contradiction of the economic subordination could not be resolved simply by a judicial act such as the signing of the Lomé Convention. All this was clear from the beginning.[4]

The above historical contradictions were reinforced by a series of provisions in the Convention. These provisions in turn became the real pillars on which these one-sided exploitative relationships were built. The provisions were: first, those relating to trade which although superficially conceding the principle insisted on by the African states of non-reciprocal advantages, nevertheless obscured the fact that this "non-reciprocity" was itself the reality of Africa's dependence on Europe. The U.S. and Japan then demanded non-reciprocity, because the two viewed the EEC-ACP Lomé Convention as establishing a closed door relationship which would jeopardize the principle of non-discrimination in international economic relations. However, the EEC's acceptance of non-reciprocity was seen by the ACP states as a major "victory" for them as compared to the situation under the earlier Yaounde conventions and the other arrangements referred to above.

The second provision was the linking of trade to economic aid which was supposed to supplement development finance from export earnings. This was accomplished by continuing the European Development Fund (EDF). Already funding from this fund had been channelled to support the groundnuts crisis in Senegal and later it was structured as an element in the Yaounde Conventions with the AASM. This provision was used to sustain the old division of labour in Africa which Europe had imposed on the African people.

The third provision was the creation of an export-earnings stabilisation scheme (STABEX) which was supposed to strengthen the foreign earnings of cash crop production in the ACP states. This was used to strengthen the second provision by reinforcing "aid" under the EDF with a separate scheme to the cushions export earnings of certain crops. This, as noted below, was an impossible objective to achieve. Fourthly and finally, there was the provision of industrial and technical co-operation under which it was agreed that Europe would support the industrialisation of the ACP states. This could not materialize as it would have weakened at Europe's competitive advantage in its African former colonies. As it turned out, none of the measures undertaken to assist industrialisation in the African countries under the Conventions bore fruit. Thus, the idea that the above four provisions were capable of interacting and creating a basis for a sustained economic development could not be realised. In the analysis below we examine why this was so and why the relationship instead resulted in the consolidation of neo-colonialism, leading to the crisis that characterised the negotiations for Lomé III and IV Conventions.

A. Trade and Development

One of the earliest hopes of the new states was that development could be achieved on the basis of equitable trade relationships. This was consistent with the theory of comparative advantage and the new post-war economic system. Hence, in the negotiations for the first Lomé Convention ACP states demanded that their products would have access to European markets. However, the EEC was more concerned about the need to protect their farmers, a policy guaranteed under their Common Agricultural Policy (CAP) of the Treaty of Rome.

The central provision which emerged was the 'granting' of duty-free access of ACP exports to EEC markets. This "non-reciprocal concession" was, qualified, however, in that all the African agricultural products competing with the EEC's farmers' products were not given "duty free" status. They were instead subject to import quota restrictions and import levies. This, in turn had the effect of raising the prices of these products in the EEC and creating an export subsidies fund for the European products to the ACP states. The ACP states had, therefore, 'preference' over non-EEC countries in the export of products not met by European producers. There were two other provisions that curtailed the 'free-duty access' principles of the Conventions. The first was the limitation imposed by the 'Rules of Origin' provision. The second was the 'safeguard clause' which allowed the EEC to withdraw the special privileges which had been granted to the ACP states if these were judged by the EEC to be causing a "serious disturbance" in that sector of the production or in any member states' economies.

The "Rules of Origin" were more extensively defined in a special protocol under which the concept of 'originating products' was applied to those products which were 'wholly' obtained in one or more ACP states. This meant that products which had undergone a certain level of processing of working and which contained not less than 50 per cent value-added within the ACP states would be excluded. The effect of this provision was to restrict ACP states from exporting products to the EEC which were not produced within their own countries. The provision also restricted the ACP states from purchasing parts of products from third countries other than EEC countries. The significance of these provisions was to further restrict the export of ACP states' products to the EEC. They also inhibited the processing of these products, thereby undermining manufacturing and the development of and forward and backward linkages in the African states.

The experience of fifteen years under three Lomé Conventions makes it clear that African states have not benefited from this arrangement. Between 1975 and 1982, the current value of ACP exports grew by an annual average of nearly 11 per cent. However, this achievement was, undermined by the inflation of EEC exports to the African countries. In the ACP states themselves, inflation also increased. The result was that the real growth in ACP exports was never more than 1 per cent, and in some cases was negative.[5] Indeed, when compared to the EEC exports to the ACP countries, the ACP countries' trade balance shifted from a surplus to a deficit between 1975 (600 million ecu) and 1980 (1 700 million Ecu). The share of ACP trade with the EEC in fact fell from 6,7% in 1975 to only 5,5% in 1981[6]

Whilst factors within the ACP states themselves may have accounted for this negative picture, the overall picture is nevertheless significant. Another factor which exacerbated the situation was the use of transfer pricing by EEC transnational corporations. This made it more difficult for African states to raise capital for further development. Table 1 below provides a picture of this generally deteriorating trade situation.

Table 1 - Share of ACP Countries in EEC Imports: 1975-1982

	1975	1976	1977	1978	1979	1980	1981	1982
As % of all extra-EEC imports	7,0	6,6	7,3	6,7	6,8	7,0	5,4	5,5
As % of imports from LDCs	17,0	15,7	14,8	16,5	16,6	16,3	12,7	13,8

Source: EUROSTAT

The total picture becomes even more revealing if one looks at the commodity breakdown of ACP products exported to the EEC. Its shows that the bulk of ACP exports to the EEC were primary products, many of which fell under the STABEX scheme. The single major export product was oil which accounted for 40 per cent of total ACP exports to the EEC. Other products (mainly traditional crops) such as groundnuts, cocoa, palm, cotton, sugar, etc. accounted for the rest. In all, primary products accounted for over 95 per cent of all ACP exports while manufactured goods accounted for a bare 3-4 per cent. Most of these primary commodities were also restricted to one of two products from particular countries. In 1977 for instance, a single cash crop constituted 50 per cent or more of its exports to the EEC for 33 of the 53 ACP states.[7] This of course reflected the monoculture of African agricultural production which the EEC wanted to continue under these economic arrangements.

Table 2 - Share of ACP Countries in EEC Exports: 1975-1982

	1975	1976	1977	1978	1979	1980	1981	1982
As % of all extra EEC import	7.0	7.2	7.8	7.5	6.2	7.2	6.9	6.4
As % of imports from LDCs	18.5	19.3	20.1	19.0	16.8	18.6	16.6	15.6
As % of imports from ACP	93.0	94.0	100.0	106.0	80.0	83.0	113.0	103.0

Source: EUROSTAT

Table 2 shows that EEC's exports to the ACP states slightly fell in those years. However, the fall was in manufactured goods. This is why the EEC transnational enterprises were able to overcharge ACP countries, with the result that the pattern of production and trade between EEC and ACP states remained the same as the pattern existing during the colonial days. What is most revealing, is that the 'surplus' of the EEC exports to the ACP states did not arise from an increase in the volume of goods and services, but rather from the over-pricing of its exports and the under-valuation of ACP imports including increases in shipping costs. Furthermore, the trade pattern was dominated by a small number of ACP countries. In 1982, ten of the 53 ACP states accounted for 70 per cent of all ACP exports to the EEC and 66 per cent of EEC exports to the ACP. These were countries which were exporting products financed under the STABEX system. What is the reason for this dismal picture? The main reason stems from the restrictions imposed under the Convention itself. The "Rules of Origin", safeguard clauses, the inherent bias within the production process the international division of labour against manufacturing, and the process of industrialisation in African states clearly account for this situation. Most of the restrictions against the export of ACP primary products affected products like sugar, beef, cereals, rice, fruit, many of which were produced by African countries. These restrictions were intended to protect .European farmers, however, they effectively ensured that African countries would thereby be limited in their ability to develop these products. Paradoxically, it also ensured that Europe would attack the very areas where Africa had a "comparative advantage". This not only undermined the pretension to "free trade", but also the very basis of their economic existence.

B. Stabex and Price Support

The Stabex schemes and other price stabilisation schemes attached to the Convention under various protocols, were seen as the means by which ACP countries could cushion themselves against endemic price fluctuation of primary products countries in the world markets for it was intended to stabilise the income of the direct producers, increase their productivity, and help diversify the agricultural production. Originally Stabex covered twenty nine commodities which fell into twelve categories of products: groundnuts, cocoa, coffee, cotton, coconut, palm, palm-nut and kernel products, raw hides, skins and leather products, wood products, bananas, tea, sisal, and iron ore. These were listed in Article 17 (i) of Lomé 1. Iron ore was the sole mineral included although there were demands to include copper as well. The EEC rejected this on the ground that it did not favour the inclusion of minerals in the scheme. It accepted iron ore "only for the sake of reaching a general agreement".

Later, other commodities were added under Lomé II bringing the total to forty four products. The mechanism for operating the schemes however became the real bed-rock on which the system foundered this; "corrective mechanism" went against the very grain of monopoly pricing of industrial goods from the EEC. As we have already noted above, monopoly pricing of manufactured products from EEC transnational corporations continued. This in effect undermined the purchasing power of the African countries. For this reason, the Convention tried to make the system as cumbersome as could possibly be to frustrate meaningful implementation. To begin with, to "trigger" the provisions of the scheme in their favour, these countries had to show that their export earnings from the listed products were 7,5% of their total earnings from commodity exports during the twelve months prior to the year of application (5% for sisal and 2,5% for land-locked countries and island).

The above was called the dependence threshold and was supplemented by an additional stipulation to the effect that for African states to qualify for actual entitlements, their real earnings from each individual product must at least be 7,5% (2,5% for land-locked and Island countries) below the reference level. This was called the trigger threshold. These percentages were later reduced to 6,5% (2% for LLICs) under Lomé II. A reference level was calculated for each ACP state and product to correspond to the component of export earnings during the four years preceding each year of application in a kind of moving reference points. This was called the reference period. The difference between the reference level and the actual earnings constituted the basis of the financial transfer which, at least, was assumed to be automatic once all the above elements were present with a number of minor restrictions.

'Minor' as these may appear, the restrictions in fact went a long way to weaken the ability of the scheme to meet its objectives. In addition to the cumbersome prerequisites outlined above, further restrictions in the application of the scheme were laid down:

First, only commodities destined for EEC "home use" or which were "under (an) inward processing arrangement" would be eligible for

Stabex treatment. Although this restriction was lifted for some countries at the discretion of the EEC Commission, the restriction excluded shortfalls in export earnings to other countries. Lomé II tried to improve the situation, but it limited it to exports from ACP states to other ACP states which in most cases were minimal.

Secondly, a further restriction fortified the "Rules of Origin" requirements. ACP states had to certify that the Stabex products had "originated" from their countries inhibiting African countries from developing trade with other nations.

Thirdly, a limitation was imposed concerning the volume of the resources available for the scheme. Here, it was stipulated that requests for the transfer of resources under the scheme would be examined "in the light of the volume of resources available". As will be seen later, this gave considerable discretionary power to the EEC Commission despite the contractual character of the Convention.

Fourthly, there was a restriction that Stabex resources could not be used to meet shortfalls (a) if these shortfalls were "the result of trade policy measures of the ACP states which adversely affected exports to the Community", or (b) where "the total exports of the requesting ACP state showed a significant change". This was later defined by the Commission to mean a ten per cent change or divergence in export earnings.[8]

The funding for Stabex under both Lomé I and II was to be through the EDF and this amounted to Eua 375m for Lomé I and Eua 550m for Lomé II, representing a 12 per cent of all the 'aid' given through the EDF. The scheme seemed to have operated 'satisfactorily' in the eyes of the EEC and some observers.[9] However, the financing problems which began to emerge in the early 1980s, were in fact connected with the way the whole Convention was structured to reinforce the very economic structures which were later blamed for the 'failure' of the system. In this respect, it is important to note that the commodities which received the most funding in terms of percentages were those which reinforced the old colonial division of labour. These were groundnuts (54%), iron ore (16%), cotton (11%), and rough timber (10%). Five states that produced these commodities and others such as Senegal, Sudan, Mauritania and Niger received 43% of total disbursements. Senegal and Côte d'Ivoire between them received over one-third of the funds from the first two Conventions, although the money had in theory been set aside for the forty eight ACP states!

By the time of Lomé II, the scheme was running into trouble. In 1981, the EDF could only pay 53% of the legitimate claims submitted by the

ACP states (Eua 138md instead of Eua 261m), while in 1982, only 40% of all claims could be funded (Eua 183m instead of Eua 453m). Again, in 1987, funding provided under the Lomé II Convention was also inadequate. Out of a total of 70 which were submitted, the Commission decided that only 43 were eligible and of these only 29 were funded, notwithstanding additional resources from the interest earned in earlier reserves and the reserve funds for national programmes. These developments clearly exposed earlier illusions; the EEC could not in fact have 'guaranteed' the export earnings of African producers. To have done so would have undermined the very basis of EEC monopoly in African countries.

The EEC Commission in its later evaluation and assessment of the period tried to establish the reasons for these difficulties. It pointed out that there were a number of 'underlying factors' among which was the 'globalisation' factor which had seen to the 'sharp fall' in the prices of the commodities covered by the Stabex scheme. This, according to the Commission, had brought the 'price factor' sharply in the forefront of the crisis with cocoa and coffee accounting for the largest share of this sharp fall. The Commission noted, however, that this downturn stemmed from the 'aftermath of events' that had occurred during the life time of Lomé I. This had led to a 'sharp rise' in the prices of the Stabex products between mid-1975 and mid-1976, followed by an equally 'sharp fall' between early 1977 and later 1978 for coffee and a substantial rise but steady fall for cocoa. This characterised the period 1975 to mid-1977 followed by a corresponding slide in prices afterwards. According to the Commission it was this that the system had found difficult to cope with. The Commission did not appear to understand that the 'recoil' itself the result of the earlier 'recoils' and the 'favourable' performance between 1975-76 was a reflection of a previous decline in prices.

The Commission came nearer to the real issues when it suggested that the problems were connected with the "loss of competitiveness," of the commodities covered by Stabex. It noted that African countries had become "more dependent" on the EEC "over the decade" under the Convention, than before and that this was a matter of "serious consideration for the future"![10] Clearly, any future consideration of the issue could not resolve such a fundamental contradiction. Indeed it could be concluded from these events that the Convention had achieved its basic aim: to perpetuate Africa's dependence on Europe. Thus, although by 1982, the scheme had been extended to 46 of the 63 ACP states, its "guarantee" to primary producers had become non-existent.

Significantly, although the funds disbursed under the two Conventions were supposed to be 'reconstituted', i.e. refunded as of 1980, only Eua 5,9m had been. Hence, the EEC decided to turn the amounts into outright grants for certain countries. This demonstrated that these countries were falling into a state of dependence arrangement. This was inevitable because the Convention tied Stabex funds to a narrow range of primary products which the EEC did not produce, but their ex-colonies did. The funds concentrated on a very limited number of countries which produced these commodities. Diversification had not been achieved nor had rural productivity been increased. This demonstrated the neo-colonial nature of the scheme.

Furthermore, even with this level of price support, there was no evidence that these funds had been of any help to direct producers themselves. On the contrary, existing data suggested that funds went into balance of payments support. This stemmed in part from the need to pay for the increased bills for imports from the EEC as well as for military expenses and bureaucratic privileges in the African countries themselves. The Commission's report had suggested that in its survey of 10 states which had received 42 transfers, only one had passed on the funds to the producers, whilst the vast majority had used them for other purposes.[11]

As the crisis of the African states widened, even those countries which had considered themselves "safe" also came under pressure. These were countries which had mineral wealth. As noted earlier, the EEC had resisted any attempt to include minerals in the scheme, except for iron ore which was accepted at the last moment as a "compromise". By the time of the negotiations for the Lomé II Convention, the mineral producing countries were also suffering from effects resulting from a loss of productive investment in their mines. Europeans pointed out the dangers of increased investment in African mines due to the limitations of European ownership and control over mining industries. Although 'nationalisation' had not in fact interfered with their exploitation of the minerals for European markets, the EEC nevertheless used political risk as a major argument against the stabilisation of mineral products under the Convention.

Finally, under Lomé II, a new system called SYSMIN (System Minerais) was agreed upon and some 280m Ecus was set aside not for stabilising mineral prices, but for maintaining the productive capacity of the ACP states that depended on an agreed list of minerals. These included copper, cobalt, phosphate, manganese, bauxite and alumina, tin roasted iron, pyrites, and iron ore. The system became more stringent. It was biased towards 'traditional exporters' such as Zambia, Zaire, and Gabon, while energy minerals were excluded. No new investment in minerals was allowed except on condition that 'risk capital' was applied which allowed investors to hold equity shares in the mines. The scheme was, therefore, used to re-privatise the mines under EEC control.

The implications of the sugar protocol on ACP production also should be mentioned given that EEC countries are also producers of beet sugar. Protocol 3 guaranteed the price of sugar for a number of former British sugar producing countries and India (not a member of ACP). In many of these countries, sugar was the sole export crop. Under the agreed arrangements, ACP states were to receive guaranteed prices for 1.3 million tonnes of which Africa would supply 51%, the Caribbean 35% and Pacific 13% with India taking up the balance. The price was to be negotiated annually, taking into account the range of sugar prices and 'all relevant economic factors'. Although ACP states were paid world market prices, the EEC has nevertheless increased its subsidy for sugar beet production within the EEC. Furthermore, the EEC has insisted that the ACP states should pay for the transport costs made under the protocol. Production and freight costs have thus increased by over 150% for ACP states.

At the same time, the EEC has continued to dump its excess beet sugar on the world market. This has further depressed the price of sugar in non-EEC markets where many ACP states sell the remainder of their sugar. Such disruptive competition, which goes against the idea of "free trade" and the theory of comparative advantage cannot be said to be encouraging development in Africa. This demonstrates the impossibility of the EEC stabilising the prices of primary commodities. In fact, EEC's dumping only increases the very problem STABEX was supposed to cure!

C. Industrialisation and Technical Assistance

Under Lomé I and II, the EEC committed itself to assisting industrialisation in Africa. A whole title in the two Conventions was devoted to this issue. However, the Conventions failed to put forward a concrete programme to assist the process. For example, Lomé II contained 16 articles (Articles 65-80) devoted to industrialisation. However, all were statements of general intention and nothing more: the EEC did no more than give aid to hold trade fairs and exhibitions of ACP products.

One institution established under the Conventions for industrial co-operation was the Centre for Industrial Development (CID). Its aim was to promote industrial co-operation and a transfer of technology for ACP states. A council of 16 members was manned on the EEC side by industrial executives of EEC enterprises, directors from financial institutions as well as people from industrial promotion groups. However, its main activity has been to try to find partnership or outlets for EEC business interests wishing to invest in ACP states. Instead of encouraging industrialisation, the CID has, as its declared policy, encouraged the processing activities of food products and other raw materials intended for exports.

A policy statement issued by the CID's chairman, Micheal Delefortie, states: "The top priority for CID action has been the processing of the raw materials of ACP countries and the maximum use of local resources. But those resources must first be available. It is, therefore, necessary that agricultural development... should be the main objective of every country...It is indispensable that agricultural development be co-ordinated with agro-food industries above all to satisfy domestic needs, but also to provide exports to neighbouring and overseas markets."[12] It is clear that the real content of the Lomé arrangement was to consolidate the role of African states as raw material and food producers. What the CID has been doing has been to go even further to subjugate this 'specialisation' to agribusiness interests centred in the EEC. This took the form of an ideological offensive because of the food crisis in the African states. Indeed speaking for the EEC Commission, its Director-General for development in charge of DG VIII department, openly declared that "since the African ACP states in particular are among the world's least developed countries, industrialisation represents more of a long-term target programme, than a present possibility".[13] This reveals the real official position of the EEC.

As we have already noted earlier, the application of the 'Rules of Origin' has kept Africa in the position of exporters of raw materials. Exports of manufactured goods such as textiles, clothing, shoes, etc. were restricted under safeguard clauses under which African states were asked to exercise "voluntary restraints" in these areas. The implication was clear that if they did not do so, "safeguard measures" would be taken against them to prevent them from exporting such products. The rules have gone beyond their 'legitimate use of avoiding 'trade deflection' to offering actual protection to EEC exporters. This was achieved with a procedural requirement which stipulated that apart from ACP manufacturing products being required to undergo processes which show that there has been a substantial transformation of the product under the Customs Cooperation Council Nomenclature (CCCN), the ACP product must additionally undergo a change in the tariff heading.

'List A" which was annexed to the Lomé II Convention is 35 pages long which is ten times the size of the Convention itself. The list excluded most products which were called 'minimal processes', 'simple mixing of products' and the 'simple assembly of parts of products' from permissible products. These terms were not defined and were left to the discretion of the customs officials of each of the EEC member states. This discretion in fact has been used to keep out ACP manufactured products from entering EEC markets. As if this was not enough, 'List A' went on to stipulate further processes and percentage criteria intended to make the meaning of value-added criteria of the Convention itself even more stringent. Under the additional process requirements, for instance, an outer garment which would have qualified for duty-free entry into EEC markets was excluded under the new rule if it included yarn as the starting material which was imported from a third country.[14]

A further analysis of the 'List A' items reveals that the list is concentrated in 'sensitive' and 'semi-sensitive' areas of products such as textiles, footwear, leather products, wood, electrical and electronic goods, toys, musical instruments and 'miscellaneous manufactured goods' under which almost any product considered undesirable by the EEC Customs authorities would fall. These products involve processes where significant labour intensive techniques are used. Furthermore, 'List A' includes products which are multistage operations in which the implicit value added, using the cost structure of most ACP states and the techniques used, would require a very high valued added, estimated at between 76-86 per cent, to qualify. The value added criterion of 40-50 per cent included in the Convention would thus in effect require a 150 per cent value added to the value of the imported materials. This procedure becomes even more impossible when applied to the category of 'electrical machinery and equipment."

Such stringent rules of origin have produced a result which assumed that ACP Countries were fully developed: "for if they could add 150 per cent value of wide range of imported materials, then they could hardly be described as (being) among less industrialised/non-industrial developing countries".[15] The rules were therefore intended to undermine the industrial development of ACP states, particularly the weaker African ones. If anything the 'footloose' industries that could be established under these circumstances would have been those transnational types of enterprises owned by EEC member states. To quote McQueen: "The combination of unrealistic rules of origin with the ability to count imports from the Community as originating products essentially creates a situation of 'tied trade' analogous to 'tied aid' with all the potential for monopoly pricing and inappropriate products and technology which have been identified with the latter".[16] Under these circumstances, it is indeed not surprising that Africa has made no progress in the field of industrialization, a field which continues to be dominated by EEC monopolies operating within African states.

D. Agriculture and Development

The evidence produced above indicates that the relationship under the two Lomé Conventions not only reinforced the old colonial division of labour, but in fact kept African countries from producing certain agricultural crops which competed with those of European farmers. It also shows that the EEC also prevented any meaningful processing or semi-processing of products thereby restricting manufacturing in the new states. This has been done to make sure that Africa remains a market for the EEC's industrial goods which are then exported at monopoly prices. Monopoly pricing has in turn reduced the purchasing power for Africa's primary products. Attempts to "cushion" the fall in the prices under STABEX and Sysmin have also proved to be impossible precisely because of these monopolistic practices. Thus, caught in a vicious circle of stagnation and retrogression, most African countries found they could not even grow enough food for their own populations. The reduction in the prices of their export cash crops under cash crop production compelled them to put more land to make up for the decline in prices. This, in its own way has also tended to undermine the prices even further.

In this "Catch 22 situation, the EEC began to blame African countries for "mismanagement" and exchange rate biases against agricultural producers. However, the "bias" was built into the monopolistic structure which Europe and other capitalist powers exercised over Africa. True, corruption and mismanagement was rampant, however, the EEC's pressure on African countries also encouraged these very corrupt leaders to carry out policies against the interests of their own people. With a new cynicism the EEC already began to push for the policy of 'ruralisation' as a 'new human 'approach to development. This new orientation in the EEC policy became more spelt out in a new 'special chapter' which was inserted in Lomé II Convention calling for 'agricultural co-operation', with a view to 'promoting rural activities.' These activities were now seen as being of 'prime importance'.[17]

Besides defining the objectives of the ACP-EEC cooperation in this sphere and listing the schemes that were to be implemented to achieve them, this chapter stressed the importance of stepping up technical assistance to African states to enable them to work out rural development policies and projects that were best suited to their needs.[18] With the passage of time it was clear that the EEC in fact wished to be involved directly in formulating rural policy for African states.

In the meantime, the policies that had been pursued hitherto were continued. Up to this point a third of all 'aid' had gone to agricultural projects. Now this effort was to be intensified "as a matter of survival".[19] The reason, according to Klaus Meyer, the EEC Development Director-General, was that the bulk of the gap in the supply of African food came mainly from the United States and to a lesser extent from Europe. Cities had expanded without development so that, according to World Bank reports, four out of five Latin Americans and one out of three Africans would live in cities by the year 2000. This, he added, made the development of agriculture in the Third World "a matter of life and death".[20] The plight of African people was now used as an important leverage: "Forget all about economic development, abandon all your grandeur schemes of 'national development', concentrate on rural activities of survival with our non-governmental organizations, all this for the sake of humanity in general ", seemed to be the new logic.

The EEC Commission perfected the new policy by insisting on the creation of 'micro-projects', a 'formula that had proven particularly well suited to schemes in rural areas.[21] These were to be expanded under a formula under which an overall appropriation of funds would be allocated to a set of schemes proposed by African states. The requirement was that these mini-projects were to be put forward by the 'communities themselves' who were required to provide some local financing as "counterpart funds"! In this way, the EEC bureaucrats in the Commission in Brussels began to mobilise rural resources for programmes approved in Brussels. By 1980 some 35 programmes involving 1,400 mini-projects were being processed in Brussels to be implemented by the African states. This was no doubt a process of 'recolonisation' as time was to make clear.

With this new approach in mind, the new Commissioner for Development, Edgar Pisani, began to formulate his 'Action Programme to

Combat World Hunger' in 1981. Under the 'plan', special food operations were to be undertaken for countries where there was a shortfall in food. Financial assistance was to be given to improve 'food security'. A 'novel' idea of using food 'aid' for food production was put forward and an agreement was entered into with four countries in Africa to carry out 'pilot schemes' to this end. These were Mali, Kenya, Zambia and Rwanda. Tied to these 'pilot schemes 'were policy directives aimed at 'liberalising the market'. Guide-lines which were issued included the redefining of the role of parastatal bodies, eliminating import quotas, creating extension services to the peasants producers including credit, improvement of storage, and processing facilities and promoting small holders access to inputs and research to enable them to produce 'marketable surplus'.

As time went on it was clear that the formulation of food strategies required 'policy dialogue' which was to become an important concern in the next phase. During these dialogues substantial matters such as the price of food products, credit and marketing policies of recipient governments, and the type of support to be offered by donor agencies were to be discussed". It also became clear that the new orientation in EEC policy was connected with the IMF 'stabilisation' conditionality as well as with World Bank 'structural adjustment' policies which were being pursued in the same period under multilateral institutions. In a later evaluation of the mini-project approach,[22] it was argued by the Commission that on its "surplus side" the approach had involved hundreds of village communities. In the Commission's view, these projects represented the "first direct benefit from official development aid" to the people. On the "minus side" the Commission noted cases where governments had imposed projects which fitted their own policy guide-lines "as distinct from the actual needs of the beneficiary community!". It added that there had been "inadequate consultation and participation.. on the part of the community" and this "tended to greatly diminish its impact."[23] This spoke for itself.

E. Aid and Financial Co-operation

The centre-piece of EEC intentions in the Lomé Conventions was the tying of African 'aid' to EEC approved economic projects. As we have already noted, the EDF was provided for in the Treaty of Rome itself and was first used to salvage the groundnuts crop during a crisis period.[24] Under the Lomé Conventions, 'aid' and financial cooperation were important aspects of assistance to ACP states. As we have seen, these objectives could not be achieved. The result is not surprising if one analyzes how the EEC handled the financial aspects of the Conventions. A central thrust of this aid was to finance only those projects which did not threaten the European economies. Another technique was to use outright grants to frustrate African development. Outright grants in the two Lomé Conventions constituted over fifty per cent of the total package. This in itself reflected a very high level of paternalistic dependency. Apart from Stabex and sysmin funding, which constituted part of the package, special loans for specific needs as well as risk capital appeared to represent a small part of the package. The rationale of the entire aid deal was to cheapen raw material production for EEC private capital.

Despite an apparent increase in the volume of the package between Lomé I and II public (aid) investment per capita declined if one considers inflation pricing, and other factors. It has also been suggested that Lomé I aid package was 20-25% below the level achieved under Yaounde II.[25] It is indicative of the heightened exploitation of African states exemplified by the low wages for African labour, monopoly pricing, and currency devaluations.

The above approach clearly exposes the parasitic and moribund character of EEC finance capital in African countries.

2. Lomé III and IV Conventions

As the above situation and international economic relations worsened, the EEC began to acknowledge that while Lomé II had contained a number of useful "innovations", the actual results had been "disappointing". The Commission observed that " by the time of Lomé III, it was obvious that Africa's decline was not merely a temporary phenomenon," but a permanent one. The question which was posed for Lomé II negotiations was to define the priorities to respond to the crisis and how to put them into effect in this declining atmosphere. According to the EEC, "a broad consensus emerged that self-sufficiency self-reliant development could only be achieved on the basis of food security and and that this could best be achieved by sectorial concentration".[26] Translated into practice this verbiage meant consolidated the continuing elements of the policy devised under Lomé II.

These continuing elements were built in the policies which were advanced by Edgar Pisani. The position was now advanced in the

"Pisani Memorandum" which advocated a 'grassroot convention' which was to be more 'human than the existing 'economic and commercial' one. The Pisani Memorandum was prepared and presented to the EEC Commission for approval in October 1981. This 'Memorandum on the Community Development Policy' true to its aim put forward a 'development' policy which the EEC wished to see the ACP states implement. It tried to substitute the new policy for the earlier Cheysson 'development policy' which was the work of the previous commissioner. This new policy was based on expanding EEC 'food aid' to the ACP states because the elements of the later crisis were already manifesting themselves as early as 1975.

The second facet of this aid was 'emergency aid' under which the EEC provided US$500 million to the countries affected by the 'crisis'. Cheysson had this to say at the time: "We have also initiated the elements of a world policy, what we might call a kind of fresco."[27]

By using the new crisis of ACP states and of African states in particular, the Pisani Memorandum attempted to steal the show from these leaders by appearing to champion the 'cause' of the 'people'. With this new paternalism of arrogance, the EEC argued that what was needed in Africa was a 'return to the land' with aid being extended to 'grass-root' communities. In the 'new development" guidelines, the basic aim was to support 'autonomous, self-maintained and lasting development'. The policy aimed at 'self-reliance'! The African states attempt to define "self-reliance" in the Lagos Plan of Action was snatched from them and Europe now began to articulate what this would be. Under the policy, special attention would be given to the least developed countries and the sections of the population most in need. The aim was to increase food production and the development of 'human resources. Emphasis was also to be placed on long-term programmes 'aimed at preservation and more rational utilisation of resources'![28a]

Advantage was also taken to define in much neater terms the manner in which "aid" would be extended under the new "perpetual" Convention. According to the Community's Director-General for Development, Dieter Frisch, in the past aid had been linked and limited to the 'simple transfer of technology' in ventures such as railways, ports, roads, hospitals and schools. Aid given in this manner had led to investments which these countries "did not always know how to use adequately". Dieter Frisch now admitted that the EEC had sought to implant European techniques and values "too deeply" in non-European areas. Forgetting for a moment that in putting forward this 'new' development philosophy for the ACP states they were in fact putting forward their own conception of development, Frisch continued: "We know better today than we did in the past and other financing agencies confirm our view that development is not only a problem of transfer of technologies which have proved their worth with us; not only even a problem of transfer of adapted technologies. It is much more a sociological and political phenomenon. Development is the mobilisation of a people within its own geographical framework, on the basis of its own social structure and cultural traditions, a mobilisation which is needed in order to take up the challenge of survival."[28b]

Thus having achieved their earlier objective of further marginalising Africa and exploiting it to the maximum, the EEC now took on a human face to advise how to bring about real "human development." "Big projects" large scale investments, and technological transfers were denounced as "inappropriate" after the EEC had already made billions. Because of such investments, African countries were caught in a debt-trap and new ventures could no longer be financed. The new wisdom was "small is beautiful": new forms of investment based on 'small' projects could be made profitable and these could, in the short-term, maintain the population and in the medium- and long-term, establish a new basis for repaying the old debts.

Emboldened by the weakness of African leaders, EEC bureaucrats began to talk boldly of an "everlasting Convention" based upon a 'common-heritage'. This ideology was part of a new humanitarian grass-root imperialism which was being pushed by European NGOs which had been operating in Africa for the last ten years: "Based on this approach we propose to direct ourselves progressively towards a new kind of relationship between the EEC and developing countries, and first and foremost ACP countries. What we desire is a qualitative change, a new way of approaching development activities. It will no longer be a question, as in the past, of a simple negotiation with the recipient country aimed at defining projects and their financial package: rather, the Community desires to engage in dialogue over the policies we will be supporting the policy dialogue."[29]

Further clarifying what this approach would mean concretely Edgar Pisani outlined four scenarios which were the essence of this new policy dialogue:

- The donor gives money without caring about how it is used. This is something the Community has never envisaged.
- The donor gives money and asks to be told how it will be used.

This is what happens at the moment.
- The donor lays the money on the table and asks to discuss how it is used. *This is the policy dialogue.*
- Lastly, Let us discuss and if we agree then you can have the money' (these are) the sort of conditions the Community does not want."[30]

Indeed as an experiment, the EEC decided to start on the four 'pilot' schemes referred to earlier in Mali, Kenya, Zambia and Rwanda. In these schemes, the EEC dictated the policy instruments to be applied by the four countries in agricultural development. The new approach envisaged long-term programme activities rather than the project approach of the previous period. Hence the idea of a Convention of unlimited duration as we have noted. It was these policy parameters which determined the kind of 'negotiations' that were to bring about the new Convention.

The Lomé III Convention merely reflected EEC policies Article 5 discussed the concept of self-reliant economic development: special efforts be made "to promote rural development, food security for the people and the revival and strengthening of agricultural production potential". 'Policy dialogue' is not referred to directly as the method to be used in implementing this approach, but it is self-evident in the above phraseology. Article 8 obliquely refers, to this approach: "With this in mind, they agree to pursue the dialogue, notably in the joint institutions, to seek ways of rendering the instruments ever more effective". Later in Part three dealing with the instruments of co-operation, the actual mechanics of implementation were laid down and these gave concrete meaning to the new procedures. In Chapter 4, Section One, dealing with programming appraisal, implementation, and evaluation it was stipulated that the financial operations of the community were to be integrated into the economic and social development plans of the states concerned. Consequently, ACP states were required to submit their draft 'indicative programme' to the Community. They were expected to indicate which sectors could be most amendable to financial support.

The concept of 'dialogue' is spelled out in greater detail in Article 215(5). The article stipulates that the draft indicative plan should be the subject of exchanges of views' between the representative of the ACP state concerned and those of the Community so as 'to ensure the maximum effectiveness' of co-operation schemes. The aim of the above dialogue was to enable the Community to learn about the development objectives and priorities of the ACP states. On the basis of the state's proposals both parties were to identify the sector or sectors which would receive support. The ACP states had to ensure that the operations thus agreed on were inserted harmoniously and effectively in their development strategies. If anything, this was a strategy the EEC to intervene in the economic management of the African countries.

The thrust of the EEC's development strategy was particularly evident in Part Two of the Convention. Attention was paid to attaining food security as well as to "guaranteeing" the rural population's participation in 'their own development by organising small farmers into associations and integrating them more effectively into national and international economic activity. The 'policy dialogue' tools for this sector were spelled out in Articles 29-32. They included the following: storage facilities for farmers of marketing arrangements 'underpined' by suitable producers' organisations, flexible market channels, adequate supplies of inputs, and credit facilities for small farmers. It was also laid down that 'food and operations' should be decided on the basis of the rules and criteria adopted by the Community 'for all recipients of this type of aid'. Thus, as can be seen, African states had been weakened to the extent that were there no guaranteed prices for ACP primary commodities. The EEC also used these weaknesses to insinuate the organisation into both rural development and food security.

Although attempts were made to improve the STABEX system, streamlining made it more stringent. The coverage was extended to include three new products: dried bananas, mangoes and shea nuts oil. The dependency and fluctuating thresholds were reduced to 6% and 1,5% for the least developed and island countries. Part of the method for calculating the transfers were revised to correct the effects of applying the method where excessive exchange-rate fluctuations occurred which worked two ways in the case of African currency: overvaluation or devaluation vis-a-vis the Ecu. If funds were not adequate to cover all the claims, the transfers were to be reduced. A provision was also made for annual instalments of the funds to be deposited by the EEC in the money market before it was claimed and for the interest earned on the deposits to augment the fund. Strict accountability for the use of the funds in the areas attracting Stabex transfers were reenforced. Satisfactory reports had to be submitted accounting for the use of the funds. Sysmin was redefined to include the restoration of mining capacity in additions to maintenance.

Other areas were also streamlined and played down even more. Aid was extended to activities such as tourism, fishing, cultural co-operation, human resources and communications. Aid to industry was directed at small and medium sized enterprises which could produce for domestic and regional markets. In the words of an observer, attention to industry was 'considerably downgraded'.[31] The ACP states promised to accord 'fair and equitable treatment' to the EEC investors, and to 'encourage and promote clear and stable conditions conducive to the participation of such investors. The ACP further promised to 'maintain a predictable and secure investment climate'.

However, the African economic situation in the 1980s offered little hope. From 1980-87, Africa's per capita GDP fell by an average of 2.6 per cent per annum resulting in an overall decline of 40 per cent. Capital investment also fell and there was a clear decline in the profitability of enterprises. From an earlier 30.7 per cent return on capital invested between 1960 and 1973, the rates fell to just over 2.5 per cent for the period between 1980-87.[32] According to the EEC's Commission: "The high hopes of a North-South partnership of equals were being eroded as, more and more, the international financial institutions took a leading role in managing the financial and developmental affairs of sub-Saharan Africa in particular".[33] The EEC of course included itself in this "take-over."

Having started with the idea of policy dialogue, EEC-ACP relations were "over-taken" by "drastic events" which increasingly necessitated introducing the World Bank and IMF's policy of structural adjustment. In addition, events in Eastern Europe in 1989 gave the impression that Africa might be "marginalised" or even ignored. As we have already noted however, the marginalisation of Africa had already been going on for generations. However, the threat of "marginalisation" by Eastern Europe and the advance of the Pacific Rim led a new panic which created favourable conditions for Europe to introduce Lomé IV on its own terms.

Discussions for the new Lomé IV Convention began in earnest. Whilst the ACP states criticised the record achieved under STABEX, they had nothing to hold on to except to demand "improvements". The EEC Commission was now even bolder in stating what should have been stated at the beginning of the Yaounde Conventions. In another evaluation of the scheme they were able to admit: "As an insurance against drops in export earnings, Stabex has no real corrective functions. It cannot provide answers to the structural or cyclical imbalance of ACP trade, any more than health insurance can cure the disease or accident insurance help avoid accidents. And to that extent,..the insurance cover is in many cases for the state and not the actual producers".[34] Regarding the ACP's insistence on a non-reciprocal free trade system, the Commission now argued that non-reciprocity "only constituted a possibility" and not "a trigger process of trade expansion." In their view this very much depended on national economic policies and "the ability to corner parts of the (world) market." One must ask how nations can adopt national policies under conditions where their economic management is taken over by international financial and regional financial institutions such as the Lomé Conventions? How are they able to 'corner' a market when the EEC itself blocks such efforts through protectionism, subsidies, and levies to cushion their own farmers? How indeed can they do it when EEC's transnational monopolies have the upper hand in monopoly pricing and undervaluing African products.

The "placing of man at the centre of development" as Lomé II pretended to argue for did not prevent "man" from being placed at the centre of the crisis, notwithstanding EEC's moralising. The EEC wanted to maintain "basic principles, approaches and methods" of Lomé III so as to "have change in continuity". The ACP, while paying tribute to the ideas of "co-operation" under the Conventions, was critical about the "gradual globalisation" of the Community's development policy. ACP countries complained about the attempts by the EEC to "disown them" under the GATT Uruguay Round in conceding preferences to other countries. Instead of moving forward to defend their sovereignty, ACP leaders instead now wept and sought solace in the warm womb of colonial and neo-colonial "development".

This then explains why the negotiations for Lomé IV were non-contentious since the African leaders -who were among the worst affected under Lomé Conventions- were now on their knees asking for all kinds of "support". The negotiations started with the European ministers describing their ACP counterpart's approach as being "positive", "constructive", "sound", and "moderate". The ACP team led by an African minister, described the EEC's stance as "positive" and "what we expected".[35] During the negotiations, the "presidential group" arrived at a new concept of "development" and this was defined as meaning "overall autonomous, self-sustaining progress." This was to be within the EEC-ACP "common heritage" of "inter-dependence, mutual interest, and respect for the sovereignty and social, economic and political choices of each party." These verbiage became increasingly self-effacing and meaningless.

The main "innovations" of the new Convention were said to be the inclusion of a new chapter (2 section 3) on structural adjustment and debt. Under Lomé IV, the African countries had pressed the EEC, to give them "assistance" to ameliorate the adverse social effects of the World Bank's structural adjustment programmes. A special provision was made to accommodate this appeal, also pressed for the inclusion of provisions for assistance into the Convention itself. This innovation provided for "economic rationalisation" policies to be applied by the ACP states. The EEC in turn would then co-ordinate with other "funder" for a "pragmatic, realistic, and differentiated approach to the problem of structural adjustment."[36]

The same chapter deals with the problem of debt. The Convention has provisions for converting "special loans", STABEX as well as sysbmin "aid", into outright grants. It also agrees to provide technical assistance to ACP states to help them manage the remaining debts. This means that the ACP states would no longer be required to repay these special loans.

The EEC effectively recognised the non-viability of African development. By implication it recognised a fact long known to African peasants: that cash crop production is a form of exploitation and subsidisation by peasant families to monopoly capitalist enterprises. The EEC noted that all previous STABEX funds had gone into state coffers iand not to the direct producers for whom they were originally intended. Their new position confirmed that debt relief would go into the neo-colonial coffers to prevent its collapse. It also meant that the peasants would continue to subsidize the EEC and state monopolies as required.

If the bureaucrats and politicians were pleased with this magnanimity on the part of Europe, they were even more impressed with the new concessions of STABEX and SYSMIN. Under the new Convention, the "revamped" provisions extended the coverage of the scheme to include a number of products: octopus, cuttlefish, cocoa products, and essential oils. The dependency thresholds were also lowered permitting a broader coverage. The fluctuation thresholds were also thrown out, making the system "more transparent." There were changes in the calculation of prices which further facilitated bureaucratic procedure. The SYSMIN was improved with a focus on viability of the mines rather than compensation. To seal the deal, the life of the Convention was extended to ten years from the previous five.

A further issue is the environmental one. Here too, the Lomé Convention had another "innovation". Under a new title of "Environment" (chapters 33-41), the Convention outlined a set of vague principles and declarations concerning environmental protection. It is well known that the African ecological crisis which has led to soil erosion and desertification is the result of cash cropping and the marginalisation of pastoralist peoples. The Convention nevertheless declares that the EEC will ensure that economic and social development is based on a "sustainable balance between economic objectives, management of natural resources and the enhancement of human resources." It is ironic that the EEC should make these empty promises when it's "aid" cannot even guarantee the economic existence of its poor producers through STABEX and other "innovations".

The EEC's concern with human rights and "respect for human dignity" also cannot be taken seriously, although declarations on the issue were included in the Convention, following years of wrangling between the ACP and the EEC. African countries used Europe's support for apartheid and the mistreatment ACP migrant workers and students in Europe as an argument against the EEC's interest in human rights, in ACP countries and in Africa in particular. In reality, however, multipartism has become the new clarion call for removing dictators who are no longer trusted or wanted, while simultaneously protecting others with new techniques. Furthermore, since the Gulf War, EEC has the upper hand in these matters.

Conclusion

The above analysis demonstrates that the Lomé Conventions have consolidated Europe's channels of economic exploitation and domination by ACP countries. The African continent has been the hardest hit and their subjugation has been clearest for all to see. The EEC has utilised the new relations established under multilateral imperialism in which the US has continued to dominate the world. Whilst Lomé III promised a 'new' grassroots approach to the problem of development, it is not advantageous for Europe to encourage self-reliant, endogenous, and human based development in Africa.

History shows that European powers, although weakened by the current US superpower arrangement has nevertheless exploited and dominated Africa with the Lomé Conventions. It is interesting that this same exploiter now holds itself up as a defender of 'the people' and of 'the least developed' countries and 'classes'! In fact, the European claim to this position clearly exposes the bankruptcy of the neo-colonial state and its representatives. These representatives come from the ranks of the African people and some even claim to be 'elected' by the masses.

However, most outright dictators use the mechanisms of international finance capital and the neo-colonial state to exploit and oppress ordinary people.

When these same exploiters go on their knees to ask for more money, they do so to feather their nests at the expense of the vast majority. In such a situation the neo-colonial state and its leaders experience a crisis of legitimacy. The fact that these countries cannot feed their populations represents a major crisis for these leaders who have relinquished the sovereignty of their own nations and people.

The EEC has used the food crisis to make a new and aggressive drive against the sovereignty and independence of the African people. Through its 'policy dialogue' Europe is attempting to administer the African affairs from Brussels. The crisis has demonstrated the limitations of political independence and the need for a second liberation struggle. Only then when this second liberation is won, together with the liberation of South Africa (Azania), can we really speak of African development.

Footnotes

1   D.W. Nabudere: "The Arusha Agreement Between the EEC and East Africa." - *East African Law Review*, Vol. 6 No.2 December, 1973
2   *The Stages of Economic Growth*, Cambridge, 1960.
3   *The Courier*: No. 31 Special Issue, March 1975, p.2.
4   See my " The Lome Convention and the Consolidation of Neo-colonalism" in: *Essays on the Theory and Practice of Imperialism*, 1978, Onyx Press.
5   Jim Fitzpatrick: "Trade in the Lome Convention" in *Lome Briefings* No. 9 of 1983.
6   E.A. Mulokozi, "ACP-EEC Cooperation: What Future": *Lome Briefings* No.7 of 1983.
7   Jim Fitzpatrick: op. cit.
8   *The Courier*, March 1975, p.25
9   Guy Martin "African-European Economic Relations under the Lome Conventions: Commodities and the Scheme of Stabilisation of Export Earnings in *African Studies Review* No. 3, Sept. 1984, p.49.
10   See for instance Adrian Hewitt: "Stabex: Time to Overhaul the Mechanics": *Lome Briefings*, No.6 of 1983.
11   *The Courier*, Dossier No.70, 1983, p.73.

12 *Courier* no.113- January-February, 1989,p.11
13 Quoted in Togba-Nah Tipoteh: "Lome III Which Way Africa Governments," *Lome Briefings*, No. 3 of 1983.
14 Mathew McQueen, "Lome: Rules of Origin, The Need for Reform," in *Lome Briefings* No.10 of 1983.
15 Ibid.
16 Ibid.
17 Klaus Meyer: *The Courier* No.61, May-June 1980, p.11.
18 *Ibid.*, p.11.
19 *Ibid.*
20 Jos van Genning and Pieter Meine van Dijk, "Food Strategies, NGOs and Lome III," *Lome Briefings*, No. 20, 1983.
21 Klau Meyer: op.cit
22 Jean Tanguy: "Pisani: A Grass-Root Convention,": *Lome Briefings* No. 5, 1983.
23 *Ibid : (Emphasis added).*
24 *The Courier* No.85 May-June 1985,p.12.
25 *The Courier* No. 83, Jan-Feb 1984, p.VIII.
26 *The Courier* No.31 of March-April, 1975, p.13.
27 *The Courier* No. 83 of Jan-Feb 1984, p.vii
28a Ibid. p.viii
28b Ibid.
29 *Ibid.*
30 *Ibid.*
31 Tony Hill, *The Courier*, No. 89, Jan-Feb 1985, p.5.
32 *The Courier*, No.120, March-April, 1990, p.27.
33 *Ibid.*
34 *The Courier*, No. 113, January-February, 1989, p.11.

——————— Chapter 11

LA CRISE DE LA MODERNISATION AGRICOLE LA PERSISTANCE DE LA QUESTION PAYSANNE ET DE L'INDUSTRIALISATION DE SOUTIEN A L'AGRICULTURE: OU EN EST LE DEBAT?

Bernard Founou-Tchuigoua

Si l'industrialisation et l'urbanisation maitrisées sont des indicateurs essentiels du développement socio-économique la révolution agricole en est une condition incontournable. Mais jusqu'ici, elle n'a été réalisée que dans un nombre limité de pays sur la planète, en Afrique moins qu'ailleurs. En fait tout se passe comme si le temps travaille contre les pays du tiers-monde dans ce domaine comme dans l'industrie.[1] Les transformations du système agro-alimentaire mondial constituent-elles des opportunités ou des obstacles? Une chose est claire: les pays capitalistes industriels menent des politiques agricoles efficaces, alors que celles des pays africains est chaotique. L'attention sera concentrée sur ce dernier aspect du problème. Pour ce faire, nous allons procéder à une brève clarification à conceptuelle et théorique (1) qui nous aidera poser le cadre général de la crise agricole en Afrique sub-saharienne (2) et celui des politiques néocoloniales (3) et populistes (4).

Du système agroalimentaire transnationalisé. Il faut sortir du formalisme théorique économique pour poser le problème des effets de la transnationalisation sur la crise agricole.

Le débat théorique sur l'agriculture, l'alimentation et le développement remonte pratiquement à la fondation de l'économie politique; les physiocrates accordaient une telle importance à l'agriculture qu'ils la mettait au centre de l'accumulation, une nation étant d'autant plus riche que le surplus généré par ce secteur était important. La théorie de la division du travail, d'A. Smith déplaça le débat faisant du travail appliqué méthodiquement à l'industrialisation et à l'agriculture la source de la richesse. Ricardo intégra l'agriculture dans l'accumulation comme secteur reservoir des biens salaires alimentaires; il tint pour négligeable son rôle dans la demande de produits industriels. En raison des rendements décroissants dans l'agriculture, la reserve de terres s'épuiserait en économie fermée, entrainant une élévation des salaires qui finirait par absorber tout le surplus industriel et conduirait donc à la stagnation et à la regression. Seul le couplage d'une économie industrièlle avec une économie à potentiel agricole éleve permet d'éviter cette issue catastrophique. Comme dans son système, l'industrie n'a pas pour fonction d'augmenter les rendements agricoles, il est évident qu'à terme, la reserve de main-d'oeuvre agricole étrangère pourrait aussi s'épuiser en raison des rendements décroissants. Il est très important de remarquer que Ricardo ne s'intéressait pas du tout au développement du pays agricole, partenaire du pays industriel dans le commerce international. Or il est légitime de supposer qu'en dyanamique, au bout d'une période plus ou moins longue, une industrialisation par substitution d'importation devient possible. Dans un cas comme dans l'autre, le progrès de productivité agricole n'est pas inclus dans la théorie.

Marx considère d'emblée que l'agriculture subit des progrès de productivité, quoiqu'à un rythme inférieur à celui de l'industrie. Le schéma de réproduction lui permet de montrer comment dans le capitalisme, une fois la révolution agricole réalisée, les développements de l'agriculture et de l'industrie sont indissociables. Il peut ainsi évacuer le problème de la surpopulation malthusienne en considérant que le capitalisme autocentré peut produire toujours assez d'aliments pour nourrir une population croissante. Le couplage avec une réserve agricole n'est donc pas une nécessité théorique. Plus précisément, une politique de développement qui s'appuie sur le schéma doit considérer la croissance démographique comme une donnée qui ne peut être modifiée que lentement. La théorie de l'échange inégal marxiste ne suppose pas une specialisation ricardienne, ni même néo-classique. En dynamique, la nation au départ agricole peut remplir les conditions de l'industrialisation, mais la théorie prétend que le rapport d'inégalité se maintiendra, l'échange inégal étant situé dans un contexte global qui en assure la reproduction. Elle montre qu'il y a transfert invisible du pays ratio productivité/salaire inférieur vers le pays à ratio supérieur.

C'est le théorème ricardien des coûts comparatifs qui a rationalisé la division internationale du travail jusqu'à sa formulation en termes de proportion de facteurs. Par contre, le caractère intensif de l'agriculture qu'implique le schéma de Marx a permis aux Etats du Centre de conceptualiser leur politique d'autosuffisance alimentaire en dynamique, non pas en laissant jouer "les lois du marché", mais en menant une politique systématique à multiples dimensions; car l'agroalimentaire a toujours été considéré par ces Etats comme un secteur stratégique. C'est que le schéma élaboré par Marx peut servir à rationaliser l'accumulation dans toute économie autocentrée, et (dans le cas qui nous préoccupe) dans l'agriculture "générant des changements techniques, qui sont nécessairement de la responsabilité de l'Etat". Mais surtout, il permet d'intégrer l'Etat dans l'analyse et par là de sortir de l'économisme et de montrer que la recherche de l'autosuffisance alimentaire obeit à une logique économique et politique profonde, contre laquelle vient buter dans les pays développés l'ideologie du néoliberalisme. Même si ce schéma ne permet pas d'intégrer directement des aspects du développement aussi importants que le renouvellement des ressources, et la lutte contre les tendances à la pollution, il n'en reste pas moins que même pour sauvegarder l'environnement, les révolutions agricole et industrielle sont nécessaires. L'expérience montre que ce sont les pays les plus industrialisés que disposent des meilleurs moyen pour diagnostiquer ces problèmes. C'est donc de ce schéma que nous pouvons partir pour affiner le concept de révolution agricole et donc de crise agricole; une agriculture étant en crise tant qu'elle n'a pas franchi le seuil qui par l'industrialisation la met à l'abri des aléas naturels.

Finalement, il nous permet de formuler convenablement le concept de révolution agricole dans le monde moderne. Le problème à l'ordre du jour est celui de la révolution agricole et du dédéveloppement rural. La révolution agricole n'est que la transition qui met fin à une situation où des crises agricoles et alimentaires peuvent se produire en raison de l'insuffisance des moyens materiels et organisationnels mis à la disposition du secteur. La securité alimentaire est alors assurée par la maîtrise technique et financière que la nation exerce sur son système agro-alimentaire. Cete révolution concerne, il faut y insister, toute l'agriculture et en particulier les cultures des produits de base. Cette acception suffit pour saisir la première révolution agricole capitaliste, dans la mesure ou elle n'impliquait pas nécessairement le développement rural et l'idée de la répartition équitable des produits alimentaires. Dans son acception moderne, quatre dimensions sont à combler: une augmentation de la productivité suffisant pour couvrir les besoins croissants et diversifies d'une population qui croit à 3% par an et s'urbanise à 5 - 6% par an; une base industrielle qui la soutienne; des alliances de pouvoir qui permettent une repartition équitable des produits entre groupes sociaux et individus; la sauvegarde du potentiel de production à long terme.[2]

Sans doute A. Lewis a été le premier à introduire l'agriculture dans une théorie de développement de l'après Deuxième Guerre Mondiale. Sa théorie de la croissance qui considère l'agriculture non capitaliste comme une reserve de main d'oeuvre illimitee a ouvert la voie à l'enumération des "fonctions" de l'agriculture dans un processus d'industrialisation. En particulier on a bati une pseudo-théorie de l'industrialisation par ponction sur l'agriculture. Pseudo théorie, parce qu'elle suppose que "l'epargne" prélevée sur l'agriculture ne peut être affectée qu'à l'industrie, bien qu'il soit évident qu'elle l'est souvent à des fins qui n'ont rien d'industrialisant; au contraire. Citons à cet effet l'exemple du Senegal. "Le développement rural, la production d'arachide, ont donc été ainsi utilisés pour des fins que s'assignait l'Etat. Les données de la Caisse de Péréquation et de stabilisation des Prix montrent que le solde net de la péréquation arachide/huile et des autres produits a été positif jusqu'en 1979 pour une somme globale de 49,4 milliards de FCFA. Ce qui veut dire que jusqu'alors, c'est le monde rural qui a subventionné les autres secteurs", car "Le surplus valorise de l'agriculture n'est pas réinvesti dans ce secteur. Les recettes exceptionnelles tirées des produits primaires, de l'exportation de l'arachide notamment, jusqu'au milieu des années 70, ont surtout été utilisées par l'Etat pour étendre le secteur parapublic, prendre des parts majoritaires dans plus de 30 societés et pour accroître ainsi l'emploi dans la fonction publique".

Entre 1975 et 1982 en pleine période de chute de la production agricole, l'effectif des fonctionnaires avait augmenter de 6% par an et la masse salariale du secteur parapublic de 78%. La théorie des fonctions n'est pas de Ricardo, car selon lui c'est une nation industrielle qui peut dépendre de l'extérieur pour son alimentation de base mais pas une nation agricole. La superiorité technologique et "l'intérêt des consommateurs", dans le pays de reserve sont une garantie que l'arme alimentaire ne pas être utilisée. Les prétendus disciples inversent les termes du problème lorsqu'ils disent qu'une nation agricole peut dépendre d'une nation industrielle pour son alimentation de base, en se spécialisant dans l'exportation de produites exotiques. Toujours est-il que cette interprétation de la division internationale du travail agricole a justifié des politiques agro-exportatrices, menant à la catastrope actuelle.

Pour avancer, il faut situer la question agricole dans le système capitaliste polarisé. L'agriculture mondiale est affectée par trois caractéristiques de base des agricultures les plus avancées des pays capitalistes industriels (PCI). D'abord la productivité globale y atteint un degré très élevé (souvent 50 fois plus qu'au Sud). L'accumulation agricole y est fondée sur la combinaison des marchandises pour obtenir des marchandises, tout comme dans l'industrie, dans la mesure ou un marché des titres fonciers fonctionne et ou le travailleur familial est traité du point comptable comme un salarié. Les marchandises ainsi produites sont avant tout des produits agricoles alimentaires de base directs ou indirects (s'ils entrent dans l'alimentation animale). Il s'agit donc surtout des céréales, des huiles et des sucres. Les produits destinés à l'exportation ou à satisfaire la demande de luxe n'en sont que les prolongements, même si dans certains cas les premiers peuvent jouer un rôle stratégique, notamment dans les rapports Nord-Sud et Ouest-Est. En somme les rapports organiques établis entre l'agriculture et l'industrie et la recherche agronomique depuis la révolution agricole du 18e siecle, se renforcent toujours plus.

Ensuite l'agriculture est dominée par le complexe de l'agrobusiness opérant à l'échelle du système mondial comme l'a montré Suzan George dans "Les stratégies de la faim". Les exploitations agricoles étant des entreprises capitalistes de petite dimension par rapport aux géants de l'agrobusiness leur sont soumises à travers une multitude de contrats concernant le financement, l'approvisionnement en semences et autres inputs, la commercialisation etc. Sans doute les profits que les firmes transnationales de l'agrobusiness en tirent dépassent-ils ceux qu'elles auraient obtenus en exploitant elles-mêmes les domaines agricoles, ce qui peut justifier l'idée que les exploitations familiales vont se perpétuer pour des raisons économiques. Mais les raisons économiques sont sans doute moins importantes que l'intérêt pour les nations de disposer d'une couche de "paysans", fut-elle très mince, afin d'assurer un certain équilibre psychologique collectif qui participe des mythes. Autrement dit dans les pays du centre les plus avancés la question paysanne a disparu à la fois sous les angles des rapports de production (la rente n'existe pratiquement plus), du poids démographique et du revenu; néanmoins - en raison des systèmes politiques qui font que la majorité gouvernementale ne dépasse l'opposition que de quelques pourcents, le poids électoral des agriculteurs est supériéur à la place de l'agriculture dans l'économie. D'où la nécessité structurelle des subventions agricoles.

Enfin, les politiques sont de plus en plus efficaces car les réactions de l'agriculture aux mesures d'encouragement ou de découragement de la production peuvent être anticipés et mésurées avec précision. On sait que dans la période postérieure à la Deuxième Guerre Mondiale, ces mesures étaient inscrites dans une forme d'accumulation dite fordiste d'augmentation parallèle de la productivité et des revenus des agriculteurs. On en connait les résultats. Depuis 1980, les USA ont encouragé la concentration des exploitations et ont obtenu des résultats importants accompagnés de faillites prévues. En Europe la politique fordiste n'est pas encore remise en question dans les faits.

Les stratégies de modernisation agricole mises en oeuvre en Afrique comme dans d'autres régions de la périphérie prennent plus ou moins comme référence l'agriculture du centre en ce qui concerne les performances techniques. Mais aucune n'est parvenue à réaliser cet objectif: même dans les cas les mieux réussis, le dualisme technologique persiste et la question paysanne n'est par resolue: c'est que les obstacles dus à la double polarisation externe et interne que caractérise le capitalisme periphérique se reproduisent dans l'agriculture. Un des mécanismes les plus puissant en est la diffusion des modèles alimentaires des centres par l'agrobusiness qui par des techniques de marketing de plus en plus sophistiquées impose également en amont des techniques agronomiques mises au point pour des conditions économiques, écologiques (notamment climatiques et pédologiques) spécifiques. Ces modèles peuvent s'adresser aux couches aisées de la population; mais la "macdonalisation" et la "cocacolisation" visent aussi une clientèle de pauvres. Cette diffusion entretient à la fois la nécessité d'exporter les produits temperés et d'encourager l'agriculture de subsitution d'importation (ASI). L'absence de priorité accordée à l'agriculture des produits alimentaires de base qui en résulte bloque à son tour une industrialisation soumise à l'impératif de la révolution agricole dans la mesure ou la demande de matériel agricole et d'inputs des secteurs dominants peut être très differenciée; la demande de consommation qui provient du surplus agricole approprié par l'Etat ou d'autres couches sociales donne lieu également à une demande très differenciée que justifie pas le développement des produits industriels de grande consommation.

Finalement, c'est la réproduction du dualisme malgré une certaine modernisation technique, plutôt chaotique, notamment dans le cas de la mécanisation et de l'immigration de grands périmètres.

C'est pourquoi la question paysanne reste entière autant sous l'angle des rapports de production, du revenu, de la démographie que de la politique. Si l'on excepte la Corée du sud et Taiwan, on ne trouve pas de pays en voie de développement capitaliste ou se dessine une réduction significative de la population agricole accompagnée d'un taux de croissance agricole nettement supérieur.

La pression sur la terre est un facteur puissant de l'expansion des rapports capitalites classiques dans l'agriculture. Ainsi près de 60% des ménages dans l'agriculture du tiers-monde sont des "quasi sans terre" et 13% des sans terre. Bien entendu les statuts de ce prolétariat qui forme plus de 70% des ménages sont très variables d'un pays à l'autre et souvent à l'intérieur d'un même pays.

Table II.1

Ménages sans terres ou quasi sans terre dans le tiers monde
(milliers et % du total)

Region	Total des ménages dans l'agriculture (millions)	Quasi sans terre (milliers)	%	Sans terre (milliers)	%
Total	232	36	59	31	13
Asie	162	94	58	24	15
Afrique	46	29	63	3	7
Amérique latine	24	13	54	4	17

Source: H. Jefrey Leonard and contribution: Environment and the Poor Development Strategies for a Common Agenda. Overseas Development, No. 11, 1989, p. 14.

Malgré l'ecléctisme qui régne dans les commentaires statistiques personne ne peut soutenir que depuis le début des années 1980 la pauvreté absolue et relative n'a pas augmenté dans le tiers-monde et notamment parmi les ménages agricoles. Ce qui fait par contre défaut ce sont des mouvements paysans puissants qui obligéraient les Etats et leur soient moins défavorables. En fait les Etats du tiers-monde, en réprimant les paysans, contribuent à perpétuer la question paysanne et agricole - prenons le cas de l'Afrique sub-saharienne.

L'agriculture africaine et surtout sub-saharienne est victime d'une expansion régressive de capitalisme polarisé. Expansion régressive dans la mesure où le prélèvement du surplus s'opère sans considèration de la conservation et de l'amélioration des rendements des ricardiens sur les deux indicateurs. Ainsi de 1965 à 1987, les taux annuels moyens d'expansion agricole les plus élevés d'Afrique sub-saharienne ont subi une évolution logistique (cf. Tableau II.2 ci-dessous).

Table II.2 - Afrique subsaharienne: les meilleurs taux de croissance annuel moyen du produit 1965 - 1987

1965-73	1973-80	1980-87
6,2	3,7	3,4
6,5	4,0	1,2
8,0	3,5	3,9
4,9	3,3	1,6
4,6	4,5	2,4
2,1	1,8	2,4

Source: Banque Mondiale, de la crise à la croissance durable, p. 264.

Il s'y ajoute un recul relatif très grave. En prenant pour base 1961-63 = 100, la perte de compétitivité est nette aussi bien pour les produits traditionnels d'exportation que pour les produits vivriers. Les seules exceptions notables concernent la canne à sucre, le thé et le coton (Tableau II.3). Remarquons en passant que la CEE est hostile à l'entrée en franchise du sucre de canne.

L'approche néolibérale de la crise concentre l'attention sur les facteurs locaux. En particulier, partant de l'hypothèse non fondée que tout état, indépendamment de sa base sociale à pour mission de créer un cadre favorable au développement, elle accuse surtout l'Etat africain de pêche d'incompétence technique. Il aurait accordé la priorité à l'industrialisation aux dépens de l'agriculture par sa politique macro-économique et micro-économique. Au niveau maroéconomique les politiques cambiaires, budgétaires et fiscales auraient pénalisé systématiquement l'agriculture. En particulier la surévaluation des monnaies aurait découragé le secteur agro exportateur, le secteur vivrier étant étouffé par les subventions aux produits importés. Au plan microéconomique, le biais anti-agricole des politiques économiques serait tout aussi évident: protection exagérée de l'industrie; trop grande ingérence de l'Etat dans les services d'approvisionnement et du crédit, dans la commercialisation et souvent dans la production.

Depuis le début des années 1980, chaque publication de la Banque Mondiale ou du FMI sur la crise africaine et ses alternatives abondent de preuves pour étayer cette thèse. Ces institutions n'ont d'ailleurs pas le monopole de la dénonciation de l'inefficacité des politiques en Afrique post-coloniale. Ainsi sur la Société Nationale de Développement rural" au Senegal, représentative pour l'ensemble de l'Afrique subsaharienne Ba et Kane écrivent: "la fourniture en temps voulu des semences, engrais, produits phytosanitaires, reste toujours peu satisfaisant. L'ONCAD qui en eut le monopole fut dissoute en 1980. La Sonar subit le même sort en 1985, et dans la campagne 1985-1986, on note des insuffisances dans l'approvisionnement, la quantité des facteurs de production mise à temps à la disposition des paysans. La fonction de diffusion technique et d'intensification de la production par le biais de la recherche et de la vulgarisation reste mal remplie. Les défauts (précités) de la recherche se retrouvent au niveau de la vulgarisation opérée par les sociéteés d'encadrement, une diffusion mécanique par des agents de vulgarisation ou d'encadrement insuffisamment formés pour travailler en association avec les paysans, ne tenant pas compte de leur savoir, de leurs initiatives pratiques, de leurs préoccupations (calendrier de travail, mode de vie). Les présentations des services des sociétés d'encadrement sont souvent aussi mal faites ou pas à temps - distribution d'intrants - et très onéreuse. Ce qui entraîne un endettement force des paysans et accroît les déficits des Agences de Développement Rural, eu égard aux faibles taux de récouvrement dus au faible pouvoir d'achat des paysans". Et ils ajoutent: "L'ONCAD*, à sa dissolution, la principale structure d'encadrement rural, employait quelque 5.000 agents. La SONAR*, 1.200 personnes; la SODEVA* a pu procéder à une déflation de 55% son personnel - 755 agents; La SOMIVAC*, de 38%; la SODAGRI* de 35%. Ces opérations n'ayant donné lieu à aucune incidence notable sur la production révèlent bien le caractère pléthorique du personnel utilisé dans les Agences de Développement Rural. Les Agences de Développement Rural absorbent presque 60% des subventions d'exploitation du gouvernement"[5]

Cette bureaucratie est dissoute depuis bientôt une dizaine d'années. En est-il résulté une augmentation de la production ou une accélération de l'intensification des techniques et un début de solution à la crise paysanne?

Le FMI et la Banque Mondiale veillent à l'application des programmes d'ajustement structurel agricole (PASA), promettent de les accompagner d'une aide à caractère social. Position démagogique, comme le montre le fait qu'en quatre ans le montant des subventions agricoles des USA et de la CEE à leur agriculture équivaut à l'encours de la dette extérieure de l'Afrique subsaharienne; que dans le cadre de la convention de Lomé III, la CEE à alloué moins de dix milliards de dollars en cinq ans, à l'aide au développement, tandis qu'elle en accorde 20 par an à ses agriculteurs, soit dix fois plus!

Revenous un peu plus longuement sur le problème crucial du surplus agricole et des prix. Les défenseurs de la transnationalisation considèrent la politique post-coloniale des prix agricoles comme le facteur par excellence de la crise politique défavorable aux prix des produits vivriers, à cause des subventions aux produits alimentaires de base importés et aux produits d'exportation par la surévalution des monnaies. Ils citent comme argument supplémentaire, la bureaucratisation et donc l'inefficacité des systèmes de commercialisation et de crédits agricoles; ils évoquent parfois, sans conviction l'effet négatif de l'aide alimentaire, mais évidemment pas celui de la politique agricole du centre qui pendant plus de trente ans maintenant a cherché à créer des excédents. Les "Nouvelles Politiques Agricoles" (NPA) qui inspirent ces analyses ont été mises en oeuvre dans la majorité des pays depuis le fameux rapport de la Banque Mondiale de 1981. Elles ont souvent été suivies d'un boom agricole éphémère ou catastrophique, le cas de la Côte d'Ivoire étant le plus spectaculaire. Dans ce pays l'augmentation des prix du cacao et du café au milieu de la décennie 1980 a entraîné une surproduction mondiale qui a accéléré la chute des cours. La fidélité sans faille du chef d'Etat ivoirien à ses alliances avec l'Europe de l'Ouest, les Etats-Unis et Israel, ses discours contre les spéculateurs n'ont pas évité l'effondrement des cours. Remarquons que l'augmentation de la production ivoirienne continue de s'operer selon le principe de la surexploitation des ressources.

La même mésaventure est en train de se produire au Sahel avec les produits vivriers. Grâce à la bonne pluviométrie et sans doute aux Programmes Nationaux Alimentaires, la récolte céréalière a été abondante dans l'Ouest Sahelien en 1989 (8,2 millions de production) au point de couvrir toute la demande en termes de calories. Et pourtant, les pays du Sahel vont importer en 1989/1990 environ 1,1 million de tonnes de céréales... essentiellement du rix et du blé dont 20% d'aide alimentaire, pendant que dans un pays comme le Mali, faute de vendre à un prix rémunérateur, les associations villageoises doivent stocker la nouvelle récolte dans des greniers encombrés par la récolte précédente, soit environ 420.000 tonnes [6]. C'est qu'en réalité les politiques agricoles des "Programmes d'ajustement structurel" s'inscrivent toujours dans la ligne de la croissance régressive et donc éphémère.

Un autre point de controverse est celui de la formation des prix agricoles. L'orthodoxide libérale considère que la dérogation au principe de la concurrence pure et parfaite est la cause ultime des échecs des politiques agricoles. Elle oublie que le prix contient en général une rente que les acteurs autres que les producteurs veulent s'approprier. Pour refuter cette thèse, envisageons successivement le cas de la formation des prix agricoles intérieurs et celui des prix extérieurs.

Pour la formation des prix intérieurs, une comparaison avec l'Amérique latine permet de comprendre en quoi les déterminants socio-politique sont plus importants que les "mecanismes" du marche. Il s'agit de savoir pourquoi les capitalistes agraires sud-américains obtiennent des prix plus rénumérateurs que le petit paysan africain soumis à une rente fiscal isée très forte (voir tableau II.4 ci-après).

L'évolution des prix intérieurs africains est caractérisée par une stabilité relative, alors que l'Amérique latine est victime d'hyperinflation. Le tableaux met en évidence qu'entre 1980 et 1986, le taux d'inflation annuel du Nigeria (10%) a été quinze fois inférieur à celui du Bresil trente deux fois inférieur à celui de l'Argentine, deux fois inférieur à celui de la Grèce et a été comparable à celui de l'Espagne; celui du Zaire (54%) a été inférieur à celui du Mexique. En un mot, les maxima africains semblent assez proches des minima lationo-americains. Pourquoi cette différence?

On peut d'abord penser aux différences dans les gestions monétaires et financieres; la gestion africaine serait plus orthodoxe. De fait, on constate dans l'ensemble des taux d'inflatión officiels monétaires plus bas les pays membres de zones monétaires qui subissent une discipline monétaire extérieure, que dans les pays à monnaie indépendante. Mais il faut ajouter que même dans ce dernier cas, l'hyperinflation de type latino-américain s'explique par des facteurs non économiques: désorganisation complète (Zaire); situation de guerre civile (Soudan, Somalie, Mozambique); guerre extérieure (Tanzanie contre l'Ouganda). On peut aussi penser qu'en Afrique l'hyperinflation est contenue par le recours aux subvaluation des monnaies) des biens de consommation et des biens d'équipement importés. Mais à notre avis, deux facteurs fondamentaux entrent en jeu, la structure et les relations de pouvoir d'une part, l'aide de l'autre.

En Amérique latine, les propriétaires fonciers ont une influence considérable sur les décisions governementales en matière de fixation des prix. Ils arrivent à obtenir le protectionnisme agricole et ne tolèrent donc pas la subvention important pour les produits alimentaires. En fait, ils sont à même de s'opposer au contrôle des prix agricoles. En raison d'une prolétarisation et d'une syndicalisation anciennes, les ouvriers et les classes moyennes ont réussi à imposer une indexation plus ou moins officielle des salaires sur l'indice des prix. Dans ces conditions, c'est principalement la masse des travailleurs du secteur informel urbain, les petits paysans, les ouvriers agricoles, etc... qui sont les victimes directs de l'hyperinflation.

En Afrique, par contre les paysans sont totalement désorganisés et opprimés et, sauf dans quelques pays comme le Zimbabwe, il n'y a pas de capitalistes agraires ni des grands propriétaires capables d'imposer l'élimination des subventions d'importation. Le syndicat des travailleurs du secteur moderne urbain souvent unique n'est en général qu'une branche du parti au pouvoir et n'est pas très revendicatif. La masse non salariée du secteur informel est toujours prête pour une émeute de la faim et oblige le gouvernement à maintenir les subventions des prix des produits alimentaires.

Mais d'où viennent en définitive les moyens de subventionner et pourquoi? L'Afrique est l'une des parties du monde qui bénéficie le plus de "transfert de ressources sans contre-parties visibles", autrement dit pour l'essentiel de ce qu'il est convenu d'appeler l'aide publique au développement et les aides d'urgences. Ainsi, en 1987, l'ADP représentait 25,5 $ par habitant contre 8,6 $ par habitant pour l'Amérique et 8,3% du PNB contre 0,4% pour les Caraïbes. Il faut remarquer qu'une partie parfois très importante de cette aide provient des pays arabes[7].

Un autre indicateur de l'importance de cette aide est la structure et le niveau de l'endettement. Durant les années 1970, écrit la Banque Mondiale, "les gouvernements ont contracté des emprunts à l'étranger afin de maintenir les revenus et les investissements. La dette à long terme de l'Afrique s'est multipliée par dix depuis 1970 et égale actuellement le PNB; cette région est la plus fortement endettée du monde (la dette de l'Amérique latine ne représente quant à elle qu'environ 60% de son PNB). Les obligations au titre du service de la dette, en 1988 - qui correspondait à 47% des recettes d'exportation - n'ont été honorées que pour moins de la moitié. On a négocié plus de cent rééchelonnements et, malgré cela, les arrières continuent de s'accumuler."[8]

La part des prêts publics (étatiques ou multilatéraux) est très élevée en Afrique subsaharienne. Or il s'agit généralement de prêts comprenant un élément de don très important.

Dans ce contexte, la politique orthodoxe de stabilisation des prix ne peut qu'appliquer la règle d'or du libéralisme, c'est-à-dire cesser de prêter aux conditions de faveur et pratique la "vérité des prix" révélée par le marché. Mettre fin à l'aide serait sans doute contraindre les classes dirigeantes à assumer leurs responsabilities; mais les conflits d'intérêts entre pays développés et entre ceux-ci et les détenteurs de pétrodollars empêchent d'envisager cette solution portant logique avec la philosophie du libéralisme. Au contraire, l'aide à l'Afrique subsaharienne est très insitutionalisée par de liens spéciaux avec la CEE, le Commonwealth, la France et la Francophonie, l'organisation des Etats Islamiques, les agences spéciales des Nations Unies, etc. Or l'aide est la principale source de la corruption que annihile toute possibilité de développement; elle crée le cercle de l'endettement: par exemple si le prix d'un chantier routier de 100 millions de dollars même finance entièrement par l'extérieur est artificiellement gonfle de 100%, le pays semble avoir reçu 100 millions alors qu'il en a reçu 50 et la moitié de l'aide est restee dans le pays de financement ou dans le pays de l'entrepreneur... or le calcul joue toujours dans le même sens; l'aide est toujours surevaluee.[9] Cette "générosité" générale à l'égard du continent s'explique sans doute par la place qu'il tient dans certains enjeux stratégiques.

Qu'en est-il des prix des produits agricoles exportes? Nous avons dit que la maximisation des recettes d'exportation est l'un des objectifs majeurs des stratégies de la croissance. Or le poids des pays africains dans la fixation des prix de ces produits est très limité alors que les prix de la plupart des produits exportés tropicaux contiennent une rente. C'est ce qui ressort nettement de l'étude du cas du cacao. En nous basant sur les données de la Banque Mondiale[10] nous avons évalué à 8,5 milliards de dollars le montant du différentiel entre le prix du beurre du cacao et le cours du cacao brut à la bourse de Newyork entre 1976 et 1985. Le ratio moyen du prix du kilogamme de cacao sur celui du beurre de cacao a été de 53%! Or pratiquement tout le beurre de cacao est exporté par des grandes firmes multinationales. La différence entre le prix FOB du café, du thé ou du tabac et leur prix de détail ou de leurs produits "transformés" dans les pays du centre est aussi important malgré la profonde biasse tendantielle des cours.

Manifestement, si les exportateurs africains arrivaient à capter une partie de cette rente, elle pourrait leur permettre d'améliorer leurs balances des paiements courants et donc de réduire le poids de la crise de l'endettement. Est-ce possible? La voie de la cartellisation qui permet de saisir la rente à l'état pur est fermée puisque les pays du centre ont pu s'y opposer efficacement par la substitution des "organisations internationales, des pays exportateurs et acheteurs de telle ou telle catégorie de produits; ou encore des Fonds de régulations ou de compensation partielle comme le STABEX. L'expérience montre que l'utilité de ces formules est extrêmement limitée pour les pays producteurs. La captation indirecte de la rente peut passer par l'imbrication des firmes de pays exportateurs dans la filière du produit exporté. Mais une imbrication commerciale ou industrielle suppose l'autonomie financière et technologique; faute de quoi, les accords de "coopération" passés avec les sociétés transnationales qui dominent les filières du commerce des industries alimentaires entraînent des pertes qui alourdissent plutôt les dettes. Ce qui ne veut pas dire que la marge de manoeuvre soit nulle, mais qu'elle est extrêmement étroite et qu'elle ne peut pas servir de substitut à une politique de révolution agricole. D'ailleurs quelle société peut être forte sur le marche extérieur si elle n'a pas d'assises nationales solides? Sur ce plan là aussi les pays du quart monde sont nettement moins nantis que ceux de la périphérie dans la mesure ou leurs marchés internes très étroits et parfois inexistants pour les produits qu'ils exportent.

En fait l'importance de la détérioration des prix est souvent exagérée dans la crise de développement; des prix internationaux favourables n'entraînent pas automatiquement la maîtrise du surplus et son affec-tation à une industrialisation maîtrisée; ils ne mettent à l'abri ni de la corruption, ni de l'endettement qui en découle pour une part essentielle. Plus incompatibles avec le modèle sont l'accélération de la croissance démographique et urbaine et les revendications liées au contexte de l'indépendance. Avant 1960, le taux de croissance de la population dépassait rarement 2% en Afrique au Sud du Sahara. Le rythme s'est accéléré considérablement au point que la population a plus que doublé depuis l'indépendance et pourrait encore doubler avant vingt ans, faisant du Nigeria en termes de population l'equivalent des Etats-Unis actuels! La population urbaine est passée de 14% à 27% entre 1965 et 1967; en 1960, 1% seulement de la population urbaine vivait dans les villes de 500.000 millions d'habitants ou plus, contre 36% en 1987 (Nigeria exclu). Or cette population croissant et en voie d'urbanisation quoique de moins en moins productive, est de plus en plus exigente en revenu, en éducation, en soins de santé, en logements, etc. Une partie de l'élite révendiqué le développement autocentré, démocratique et socialiste. Aucun système de garantie des prix ne peut permettre de faire face aux pressions qui en résultent. C'est la révolution économique et elle seule qui est le véritable remède.

En l'absence de cette révolution, une économie qui ne dispose pas de réserves pétrolières illimitées comme l'Arabie Saoudite ou le Koweit ne peut pas fonctionner sans que les importations représentent au moins 20% du PIB. Comme elle ne génère pas des devices en quantité croissante, il n'y a pas d'autres alternatives à l'intérieur du système que le recours à l'endettement extérieur, lequel peut retarder la crise, mais pas la résoudre. Les programmes d'austérité sont totalement inopérants, car ils réposent sur les hypothèses fausses que les populations peuvent les accepter avant que leurs intérêts ne soient reflétés dans le pouvoir et avant que l'objectif majeur de l'industrialisation ne soit affirmé et mis en oeuvre. Voyons à présent quelques expériences nationales en insistant sur les rapports entre l'agriculture et l'industrie, la question paysanne et l'Etat, les revenus et les rapports sociaux.

La crise des agricultures ouvertes ou néocoloniales. L'analyse des rapports entre l'agriculture et l'industrie s'appuiera surtout sur les cas de la Côte d'Ivoire et du Kenya, celle des rapports agriculture/Etat sur la Mauritanie et le Kenya, et enfin le problème de la paupérisation paysanne sera traité en référence à la Tunisie, au Senegal, au Kenya.

Dans ces expériences la volonté d'échapper à l'entreprise de l'agrobusiness mondial a été minime. En sorte que les rentes industrielles situées en amont ou en aval de l'agriculture sont toujours sous contrôle étrange du point de vue du capital ou de la technologie. Les liaisons techniques en aval paraissent parfois significatives, mais le secteur vivrier n'est intéressé que dans quelques cas: sucre, riz (et parfois maïs), l'huile n'étant traitée industriellement au profit des populations pauvres que très rarement. La recherche en industrie alimentaire est souvent orientée vers la production de substitution alimentataire. Il n'est donc pas étonnant que la modernisation agricole au lieu d'amorcer l'intestification conduise plutôt à des catastrophes écologiques.

En Côte d'Ivoire [11] la modernisation agro-exportatrice appuyée sur le café et le cacao ne décolla qu'après la Deuxième Guerre Mondiale et se deploya dans la première décennie de l'indépendance. Les tentatives de diversification notamment par le développement de la palmeraie, de la cotonneraie et de l'ananas échouerent. En sorte que trois produits dominent toujours le secteur des exportations agricoles: le café, le cacao et le bois.

Par contre, la croissance de ces produits fut fantastique à tel point que les défenseurs de la soumission à la transnationalisation ont fabriqué l'expression de "miracle ivoirien", en oubliant que la péripherie est remplie de cimétières de miracles sans lendemain, comme l'a écrit S. Amin dans "L'Afrique de l'Ouest bloquée".

Tableau II.5

Volution de la production du cacao en Côte d'Ivoire

Surfaces plantees Rendements		Surface en production		Production ivoirienne/ Mondiale	
1.000 ha	kg/ha	1.000 T	%	1.000 T	%
562	708	261	185	1.410	13,1
897	552	557	308	1.508	20,4
1.163	589	721	425	1.672	25,4
-	-	-	630	2.106	30

Source: D'après Marchés Tropicaux et Méditerranéens, No. 1893, 19 fevrier 1982 et No. 2217, 6 mai 1988

Or cette croissance était fondée sur des bases très fragiles et en particulier sur les hypothèses fausses que les cours des matières premières resteraient soutenus malgré la concurrence des produits de substitution, la concurrence d'autres pays du tiers-monde, le protectionnisme des PCI même malgré la crise économique mondiale; et que la mécanisation du défrichement forestier et le raccourcissement de la durée des jachères non compensé par l'usage d'engrais n'entraîneraient pas inexorablement la chute tendancielle des rendements. Or, comme il fallait s'y attendre l'expansion de la production sur un mode particulièrement extensif a été accompagnée de la diminution des rendements à l'ha; en 1980-1981, ils étaient à 80% du niveau de 1970-1971. C'est que de même qu'un paysan peut vendre le bois issu du défrichement d'une jachère à un prix très bas, parce que pour lui ce bois n'a pratiquement pas de valeur par rapport au produit agricole que la défriche va porter, de même la classe dirigeante ivoirienne vit dans le défrichement de la forêt, une source de revenu complémentaire des recettes issue de la vente des produits agricoles. Or ce qui est concevable au paysan pris individuellement ne l'est pas à l'échelle d'une communauté villageoise qui grandit et a plus forte raison d'une nation dont l'avenir réside dans l'intensification agricole. Dans ce pays l'innovation technologique a consisté pour l'essentiel à mécaniser la défriche forestière et la production dans quelques complexes agro-industriels, la recherche agronomique et l'investissement continuant à être orientés en faveur du secteur agro-exportateur. Le seul secteur d'agriculure de base qui a bénéficié de l'attention est celui du riz. L'industrie locale a joué un rôle mineur dans cette tentative de modernisation. L'unité de production la plus importante dans ce contexte a une capacité de production d'engrais de 170.000 t par an. Et elle est en crise depuis que l'Etat a réduit la subvention et les prix des produits d'exportation: sa production est tombée de 100.000 t en 1981 à 50.000 t en 1984. L'industrialisation agro-exportatrice, inscrite plus dans la politique commerciale qu'industrielle reste limitée pour l'essentiel au conditionnement et à la production de biens intermédiaires: emballages des bananes, extraction de l'huile de palme, égrénage du coton, broyage des fèves de cacao pour en obtenir la mousse, débitage des grumes de bois. Si le taux de transformation paraît significatif pour le bois et le cacao c'est qu'en réalité il s'agit de biens intermédiaires. Pour le café en poudre dont le marché est local ou sous-régional, 5% seulement des produits sont transformés en Côte d'Ivoire (Cf. tableau).

Tableau II.6

Transformation du café, du cacao et du bois de 1980 à 1983 en %

Quantité			Valeur		
1980	1982	1983	1980	1982	1983
5	5	5	5	5	5
26	23	26	26	23	26
36,6	44	44	18	29,1	21,75

Source: Traore, op. cit., pp. 17-18

Somme toute la modernisation chaotique et catastrophique de l'agriculture ivoirienne s'inscrit dans la logique de la soumission passive à la transnationalisation. Elle est gréffé sur l'agrobusiness mondial au plan des équipements comme du financement. Ali Traore cite à cet égard l'exemple du Projet palmier cocotier lancé en 1963. L'investissement de 83 milliards CFA fut financé à 78% par des fonds extérieurs, les principaux bailleurs étant la Banque Mondiale (12,8%), le Fonds Européen de Développement (9,8%), la Banque Européenne d'Investissement (6,8%), la Caisse de Coopération Economique (5%), etc. La Banque mondiale qui critique aujourd'hui l'Etat ivoirien joua le rôle de catalyseur dans la réalisation de ce projet qui a contribué à la catastrophe financière que connaît le pays: en 1981-1982, son chiffre d'affaires ne fut que de 30 milliards.

Au Kenya[12] la modernisation agricole sur le modèle dualiste était evidemment plus avancee qu'en Côte d'Ivoire parce que ce pays avait connu une colonisation de peuplement. Le niveau de l'investissement agricole etait donc très eleve (14% de l'investissement total en 1964). Une grande partie etait d'ailleurs consacrée à la mécanisation: il y avait alors 6.442 tracteurs dans le pays contre 161 au Ghana et 78 en Côte d'Ivoire; 28 fois plus au'au Nigeria qui en avait 231. Cependant la crise de la mécanisation allait commencer pratiquement des l'independance. L'agriculture des colons utilisait aussi un volume d'inputs industriels important. Le mouvement a continué en proportion de la valeur du produit agricole jusqu'au début des années 1980. En 1973 et 1983, les parts de l'énergie commerciale et des produits chimiques dans les inputs furent respectivement de 14,8% et 18,7%; 17% et 17,7%. Par contre celles de l'utilisation des engrais était tombée dans le même temps de 23% à 16,8%. Donc comme en Côte d'Ivoire l'utilisation des engrais diminua parallèment à la durée du temps de la jachère! En outre il a fallu laisser en friche une partie des terres cultivables à cause des parcs nationaux. Il n'est pas étonnant que dans ces conditions les rendements aient diminué notamment dans le secteur agro vivrier; plutôt faibles pour le maïs, 1.450 kg/ha en 1969-1971), ils étaient tombés à 1.300 kg/ha (-9%) en 1979/1981. En aval de la production agricole on retrouve une structure comparable à celle de la Côte d'Ivoire. Qu'en est-il de la question paysanne et de l'Etat?

Concernant la question paysanne sous l'angle des revenus et des rapports sociaux nous avons montré que la paupérisation touche la majorité des ménages agricoles. Ainsi, en Tunisie, "la paysannerie a été maintenue dans une situation de pauvrété parfois dramatique et est dans l'incapacité de dégager l'épargne nécessaire à la préservation et à l'amélioration des moyens de production. En effet, l'enquête nationale sur le budget des ménages de 1980 révéla que plus de la moitié de la population des campagnes vit en dessous de seuil de pauvrété et que sur une population de 1.865.000 personnes vivant en-dessous du seuil de pauvrété, quatre sur cinq résident en milieu rural"[13]. Dans ce pays, comme dans beaucoup d'autres, les ménages agricoles pauvres souffrent plus de la détérioration des termes de l'échange interne que les koulaks.

Or ce phénomène a affecté pratiquement tous les petits agriculteurs en Afrique d'économie ouverte. En Tunisie les paysans pauvres produisent surtout des céréales, blé dur, blé tendre, orge; l'orge se contentant des conditions climatiques et pédologiques les moins propices à l'agriculture en sec. Dans ce pays, les prix du quintal des trois produits ne représentaient en 1980 que respectivement 53%, 65% et 78% de ce qu'ils étaient en 1961. Au Kenya, sur la base de 1982 = 100, les termes de l'échange étaient défavorables de 1964 à 1984, sauf en 1976-1977 années du boom des prix du café. En Côte d'Ivoire les prix au producteur du cacao et du café ont chuté de 50% en 1989. En Mauritanie comme dans les autres pays du sahel, le cycle de sécheresse des années 1970 précipita la paupérisation des éleveurs déjà inscrite dans la surexploitation de la nature caractéristique du capitalisme colonial, notamment quand il s'agit de l'économie de traite. Il en est résulté une détérioration des termes de l'échange interne très préjudiciable aux éleveurs, dont certains sont devenus des salariés au service de proprietaires absentéistes, commerçants ou fonctionnaires qui ont des relations moins affectives et plus "cash oriented" avec les animaux. Ould Cheikh a décrit avec précision la formation de cet élevage secondaire.

Les menages "agricoles sans terre", c'est-à-dire pour l'essentiel des ouvriers agricoles et des travailleurs agricoles à temps partiels sont vraiment les grandes vicitimes de la surexploitation. En Afrique les statistiques des salaires agricoles sont rares. Citons néanmoins le cas de la Côte d'Ivoire, pays ou la main-d'oeuvre migrante joue un rôle crucial dans la café-culture et la cacaoculture. Malgré l'amélioration des termes de l'échange revenus de l'agriculture entre 1970 et 1978, les salariés agricoles qui formaient 82% des effectifs ne percevaient que 5% des salariés, tandis que les "salariés" non africains surpayés avec 1,2% des effectifs, se taillaient 28% du total.

Rappelons que paupérisation rime souvent avec rente transférée à l'étranger. Sur les cent soixante douze milliards de F CFA transférés du Senegal sous forme de profit pour cinq années (1977; 1979; 1981; 1983; 1984), une partie importante provenait de l'agriculture comme pendant la colonisation. [14] En Tunisie, le volume du surplus prélevé sur les grands produits de grande consommation (céréales et olives) représenta 135% de l'investissement agricole net en 1980. [15]

Il est devenu courant de dénoncer l'exploitation de la paysannerie en Afrique subsaharienne. La Banque Mondiale qui ne soutient pourtant que les projets agricoles visant à détruire les rapports communautaires pour les remplacer en principe par les rapports capitalistes, écrit des textes démagogiques sur l'efficacité du petit paysan. Mieux, dans un de ses multiples rapports, elle avance timidement l'idée que le fait pour les gouvernements de la crise. Mais le concept de démocratie auquel la banque se réfère est celui du monde anglo-saxon qui attribue à la democratie un rôle essentiellement stabilisateur, alors que l'Afrique a besoin d'une démocratie qui fasse accéder réellement le peuple à l'exercice du pouvoir.

Ici il nous faut, à l'aide du cas mauritanien et Kenyan rappeler comment l'Etat contribue à la reproduction de la paupérisation paysanne.

L'analyse du cas mauritanien permet de montrer comment les rapports "précoloniaux" peuvent retarder l'émancipation de la paysannerie. L'Etat se présente comme une fédération des tribus aux sommets desquels il y avait des nomades pasteurs exerçant le pouvoir sur des agriculteurs noirs, esclaves ou anciens esclaves, mais intégrés verticalement. Il semble que le cycle de sécheresse qui a sevi au sahel au long de la décennie 1970, en décimant les troupeaux et en obligeant les nomades à entrer dans le circuit monétaire pour assurer leur subsistance a avantagé les anciens esclaves et ceux qui n'ont été affranchis qu'au début des années 1980. Mais les anciens maîtres d'esclaves devenus responsables politiques entendent conserver toute leur clientèle tribale de nobles et roturiers, et les Noirs sont toujours au bas de l'échelle sociale dans la tribu. L'effort des intellectuels noirs de substituer les relations de clientélisme racial à celui du clientélisme tribal est ainsi fondé sur une compréhension insuffisante de la réalité mauritanienne. Laissons la parole à Ould Cheikh: "le transfert massif des structures hiérarchiques de la société pastorale précoloniale dans l'ordre éthnique mauritanien actuel (marabouts et guerrires occupant les emplois bureaucratiques et commerciaux, les hratins* et esclaves remplissant les tâches plus pénibles et les moins bien rémunérées: manoeuvres, employés de maison, etc.) contribue à péréniser, voire à immortaliser, dans l'esprit aussi bien de ceux qui le subissent que de ceux qui en profitent, un ordre social dont le contenu brutalement hiérarchique (ponction tributaire, travail non rémunéré, châtiment corporel...) cède progressivement le pas à une pratique clientélaire et pseudo-philanthropique ou les maîtres d'hier devenaient les inévitables intermédiaires bureaucratiques d'aujourd'hui (pour toutes démarches administratives, pour trouver un emploi sur un marché de travail particulièrement étroit...) se posent en protecteurs quand ce n'est pas en victimes d'une clientèle qu'en ville il faut parfois loger et nourrir... La perpétuation du modèle politique tribal à travers ses prolongements clientélaires explique aussi, en partie, l'ambiguité de l'expression politique du mouvement d'émancipation des "hratins". Cette ambiguité trahit à la fois la prégnance du modèle en question selon la logique de la dominance de l'idéologie de la classe dominante et de l'hétérogénéité sociologique d'un mouvement à base rurale et "tribale" "dirigé" par un encadrement urban issu de la sphère moyenne de la bureaucratie et aspirant à convertir en notabilisme clientélaire une "représentativité" qui ne saurait autrement prendre pleinement effet. La "voie" tribale, fondant son prestige et sa légitimité sur une (re) construction généalogique excluatit les esclaves et hratins, n'étant pas praticable pour ces derniers, il restait à l'horizon des identifications communautaires disponibles la "voie" ethnique. D'autant plus tentante qu'elle permettait à leurs "representants" de jouer des rivalités ethniques ambiantes - une des marques fondamentales du paysage politique mauritanien - en s'y insérant tout en (re) valorisant une origine ethnique (les hratins et esclaves sont de souche negro-africaine) qui était dans l'ordre tribal une marque permanente de leur infériorité. On a vu ainsi au lendemain du coup d'Etat de juillet 1978 des tracts exprimant dans le sens d'un appel au partage du pouvoir sur une base ethnique, les revendications des "hratins" assimilés à une "ethnie"[16].

Dans ces conditions la révolution agricole pourra d'autant moins se faire, que la division entre pasteurs et cultivateurs continue d'être empreinter de préjugés qui rendent difficile le libre exercice des professions nécessaires à toute révolution économique. Pour tirer profit des possibilités de révolutionner l'agriculture qu'offre le barage de Manantali (60.000 ha irrigables), il faudrait régler les problèmes socio-politiques, dans un sens qui contraindrait l'Etat et la classe dirigeante à moins compter sur la rente minière et l'aide extérieure et plus sur la mobilisation de ressources intérieures et des emprunts extérieurs bien gérés.

Au Kenya, à l'apogée de l'economie coloniale (de peuplement), les terres de colonisation plus de 10 millions d'ha, dont 7,3 millions seulement mises en exploitation, comme terres de cultures ou terres d'élevage; 4.000 colons se les partageaient. En 1948, le pays comptait 30.000 colons européens environ 100.000 immigrants d'origine indienne ou pakistanaise et 5 millions d'Africains dont 95% vivaient dans les "réserves"; 30% du revenu national étaient imputés aux Africains qui formaient plus de 90% de la population. Sous le contrôle de la métropole, les colons (settlers) et la bureaucratie administrative exerçaient le monopole du commandement dans l'économie, secondes lorsque nécessaire par des Indiens et des Pakistanais. Deux catégorie d'Africains souffraient particulièrement de cette situation. D'un côté ceux qui contestaient la légitimité de l'occupation des terres par les colons et posaient le problème de la restitution. Il s'agissait alors essentiellement des groupes appauvris et prolétarisé par la décomposition des sociétés africaines précoloniales. De l'autre côté, les groupes qui disposaient d'assez de terre pour produire pour le marché local ou pour l'exportation, mais qui se heurtaient au monopole légal accordé aux settlers. Du premier groupe sortit le nouveau mouvement *mau mau*, la plus grande révolte armée paysanne de la région (1952), dans la décennie de la Conférence de Bandung. Elle donna le départ à une série de réformes agricoles qui allaient se poursuivre apres l'accession du pays à l'indépendance en 1964. Non seulement, l'interdiction de l'agriculture commerciale par les Africains fut levée, mais une politique d'aide systématique à l'insertion dans ce secteur fut mise en oeuvre, notamment à travers les réinstallations de paysans modernes sur des terres des zone de colonisation (settlement areas). Mais la structure fondamentale demeure: le pouvoir économique et politique est monopolisé par une minorité qui a réussi à exclure le monde paysan de l'exercice du pouvoir malgré le fait qu'à travers la révolte *mau mau* il joua un rôle crucial dans la radicalisation des revendications nationalistes et s'attendait de ce fait à un véritable développement alternatif en rupture avec le modèle colonial.

Les pays à pouvoir populiste ont-ils fait mieux? En Tanzanie, la production et les rendements ont augmenté plus dans le sécteur des biens de consommation de base et des biens à marché urbain dans le secteur d'exportation. Cette évolution, observée entre 1976 et 1983, n'est pas attribuable à la volonté du gouvernement d'accorder la priorité à la production vivrière. Mapulo[17] insiste sur le fait que c'est la résistance paysanne à la surexploitation manifestée depuis la colonisation qui est à son origine. Par là il réintroduit l'idée que l'héritage précolonial est suffisamment puissant pour s'opposer à une modernisation qui reposerait sur le principe de l'extraction du surplus. Dans des pays comme la Tanzanie qui n'a jamais rien connu qui ressemble de près ou de loin au féodalisme, et ou il y a disponibilité de terres inhabitées et non cultivées, ce processus ne peut être que long et difficile. La paysannerie peut aisément se replier sur une économie de subsistance. Dès lors il devient nécessaire par un contrôle multiforme de vider la propriété paysanne sur la terre de son contenu d'abord en l'obligeant à fournir du surplus en nature ou en travail et de creer par la force si nécessaire des besoins monétaires. Mais le repli sur l'autosuffisance est-il encore possible? La thèse qui attribue la crise agricole au succès de la stratégie de repli ignore la distinction entre petites et grandes exploitations agricoles et le caractère irréversible de la dynamique des besoins monétaires introduits depuis plusieurs siècles. En effet les exploitations sans ressources suffisantes en main d'oeuvre familiale et par conséquent en terres, sont les premières à reagir à la baisse persistance des prix par la réduction du surplus agricole commercialisé. Mais comme leurs besoins monétaires augmentent sans cesse, les familles sont contraintes d'organiser la vent de la force de travail localement, ailleurs dans le pays ou même à l'extérieur. Si ces possibilités disparaîssent c'est la famine.

Pour les grandes exploitations en main d'oeuvre et en terre et à fortiori en matériel agricole moderne, le retrait du marché n'est jamais envisagé, précisément parce qu'elles sont autosuffisantes et en facteurs de production et en produits alimentaires, ce qui leur permet de continuer à produire pour le marché même lorsque tendance à la baisse des prix agricoles persiste, notamment lorsqu'elles peuvent mener des activités de commerce ou de transport. Il est par contre patent que les "chefs" des familles, petites ou grandes, n'ont pas une approche productiviste caractéristique des capitalistes agraires classiques. Généralement, ils intégrent la monétarisation de la consommation et du surplus (quand il y en a) dans un cycle de réproduction simple avec la prétention de conserver les structures sociales des modes de production communautaires ou tributaires suivant le cas, mais dans le cadre d'alliances sociales-locales, internes et externes dominées par le capitalisme mondial qui bloquent la formation d'une classe d'entrepreneurs agricoles publics ou privés. C'est donc une erreur théorique et politique fondée sur une observation superficielle que d'attribuer l'échec agricole à la résistance paysanne comme le confirme le cas algérien ou la problématique du repli paysan n'a plus de sens.

Il mérite d'être analysé avec beaucoup d'attention de par son importance historique et la qualité des études qui lui sont consacrées. Contrairement à ce qui s'est passé dans un pays de capitalisme agraire colonial comme le Kenya où le pouvoir colonial avait organisé lui-même la transition et noué des alliances de classes précises, avant l'accession du pays à l'indépendance, la transition a été violente. Les colons agraires ont du abandonner leur domaine au lieu de les vendre et le secteur agricole public s'est constitué très rapidement (secteur socialiste). La classe dirigeante elle-même étant nationaliste, un Etat relativement fort, c'est-à-dire contrôlant réellement des secteurs économiques importants et dynamiques a bati une administration, moins compradore qu'au Kenya. D'où une certaine efficacité de la politique économique, malgré les contradictions.

L'agriculture algérienne a été mise d'abord au service de l'Algérie. La colonisation avait spécialisé le pays dans l'exportation des vins produits sur les meilleures terres avec la main-d'oeuvre agricole la plus qualifiée et avec les techniques de gestion le plus évoluées. La réaffectation la plus spectaculaire a concerné précisément le vignoble dont la superficie est passé de 500.000 hectares en 1962 a 233.000 hectares en 1975-1976, soit une diminution de 53,4%. Cette réorientatioin, l'une des plus radicales de l'histoire de la décolonisation agricole, s'explique sans doute, moins par l'aversion contre le vin dans un pays musulman, ou par la volonté de réduire la dépendance, que par les difficultés de trouver des débouches [18] et surtout par la possibilité de substituer les recettes d'exportation des produits agricoles en général. Ainsi, de 1972 à 1977, la rubrique produits alimentaires, boissons et tabac à baissé en quantités de 900.000 tonnes à 580.000 tonnes et en valeur courante de 664 millions de dinars à 550 millions. Alors qu'en 1970, les produits agricoles procuraient encore 20,5% et les hydrocarbures 70,5% des recettes d'exportation, les pourcentages étaient respectivement de 2,45% et 96% en 1978".[19]

Pour autant, la priorité accordée au secteur d'alimentation populaire n'a pas reçu toute l'attention méritée. En raison des revenus élevés issus du pétrole et des tendances spontanées à une rédistribution des revenus favorable aux catégories à alimentation riche en protéines animales, en légumes frais et en fruits (imitation de l'Europe), le secteur de l'ASi a connu une croissance plus forte que celui de la consommation populaire. Avec la nouvelle politique agricole, "les exploitants privés ont davantage porté l'accent sur les cultures maraîchères (+ 45%), les fourrages: (+ 35%) et l'orge (+ 36,7%) destinés à l'alimentation animale et la production de viande. Les grandes entreprises d'Etat, les domaines agricoles socialistes, ont accru les superficies en légumes secs, en blés, en cultures fourragères pour la production laitière. La politique appliqué au secteur d'Etat tente ainsi de corriger les effets du marché et du système des prix qui favorisent davantage les productions de légumes, de viande, que celles des légumes secs, céréales ou du lait". Par contre, les rendements à l'hectare sont restés très médiocres, en particulier dans la céréaliculture, ou ils restent inférieurs en moyenne à 7 quintaux (contre 40 q au centre), entraînant une production qui ne dépasse guère 1,8 millions de tonnes depuis le début du XXe siècle. (1985 fut une année exceptionnelle avec un rendement de 109/Ha et une production de 3 millions de tonnes)

Pourtant le modèle de développement algérien était en principe autocentré, l'agriculture étant à la fois un marché pour les biens d'équipement et biens intermédiaires d'origine industrielle et un fournisseur de produits pour le secteur agro-alimentaire. L'importance des crédits alloués aux équipements, les efforts consentis pour la formation et recherche agricoles ont été remarquables. Mais contrairement aux prévisions, la croissance de la mécanisation a été liée davantage aux subventions des importations qu'à l'utilisation du matériel agricole produit localement et à l'amélioration de la capacité d'absorption des techniques modernes. Il s'est agi d'une mécanisation sans véritable amorce de révolution agricole, parce que trop déterminée par la rente pétrolière et non par un effort patient d'industrialisation maîtrisée.

Tableau II.7

Rapport du ble et des engrais

Prix du blé au producteur	Prix des engrais au producteur	Rapport prix céréales-engrais	Rapport à l'ha
67,70	55,2	1,15	5,8
125,00	55,2	2,26	6,4
200,0	69,0	2,90	6,90

Source: Ait Amara, op. cit., p. 59

La décennie 1973-83 connut une forte croissance de l'emploi des biens de production industriels par l'agriculture; des subventions consenties pour le machinisme agricole, les produits chimiques, le matériel d'irrigation. L'Etat a en particulier, par le système des prix relatifs des céréales et des engrais, tenté d'accroître la demande d'engrais et de produits phytosanitaires. Comme l'indique le tableau II.7, le rapport blé/engrais est passé de 1,15 en 1974 à 2,90 en 1985.

Mais l'investissement n'a pas été accompagné d'une politique de recherche et de formation efficace. Ait Amara, soutient que la recherche a été pénalisée d'un double point de vue; que la prise en compte des conditions locales n'a pas reçu la priorité requise et que l'organisation du système mis en place a été défectueuse.

Dans les régions semi-arides, les conditions de sol et de pluviométrie rendent toute adaptation très difficile et la consommation de technologie importée s'est révélée d'une très faible efficacité productive. Par contre elle a conduit à elargi la dépendance à l'egard des industrialisés subordonnant de plus en plus la production agricole à des importations croissantes et coûteuses de techniques souvent inadaptées.

L'ajustement à cette situation a consisté à mettre en place des instituts de développement (onze) gérant des programmes par grands groupes de spéculations, et à démanteler le système de recherche agricole mis en place durant la période coloniale, mieux articulé aux ressources locales. En 1980, l'Institut National de la recherche Agronomique (INRA), ne comptait plus, dans une quinzaine de stations de recherche, qu'une vingtaine d'ingénieurs et trente techniciens couvrant en principe tous les domaines de la recherche agricole. Le plus important des Instituts de développement, celui pour les cultures céréalières, légumes secs et fourrage, cultures qui concernent 87% de la S.A.U. totale ne dispose pour six stations de recherche expérimentale que de dix sept ingénieurs et cinquante techniciens.

Dans le domaine de la formation agronomique, un effort considérable a été fourni. De 1973 à 1983, quelques 4.800 ingénieurs d'application et 1.000 ingénieurs d'Etat ont terminé leur cycle de formation dans les différentes écoles d'agriculture. Cependant, malgré l'accroissement des effectifs formés, l'impact du système d'enseignement sur le changement technique et social de l'agriculture a été peu sensible. Le système d'enseignement agricole est démeuré doublement extérieur à la société rurale par le recrutement de sa population et par l'implantation des écoles, elles-mêmes situées en milieu urban. C'est ainsi que le recrutement favorise non les fils de paysans ou ceux destinés à s'établir comme agriculteurs mais les enfants de citadins, aspirant à la fonction publique. La paysannerie est exclue de la formation spécialisée et encore plus de la formation générale. Par ailleurs, la quasi totalité des produits de l'enseignement est absorbée par les services de l'Etat ou des organismes para-publics de l'agriculture.

La question paysanne est restée sans solution satisfaisante du point de vue économique, sociologique et politique, voire idéologique. On sait que l'accaparement des meilleures terres par la colonisation est l'une des causes essentielles de la forme très violente qu'a prise la lutte de libération nationale en Algérie. La colonisation de peuplement à capitalisme agraire s'était traduite par la formation de grands domaines mis en valeur avec des techniques modernes liées étroitement à la métropole, le micro-fundisme et l'élevage à reproduction régressive, l'un dans les régions montagneuses l'autre dans les hauts plateaux secs. Expropriation, croissance démographique et absence d'industrialisation avaient entraîné la formation d'une masse toujours croissante d'ouvriers agricoles, de paysans pauvres micro-fundistes ou sans terres qui grossissaient les bidonvilles. Les pauvres, en fait le peuple, prirent une part essentielle à la guerre de libération nationale et attendaient naturellement de l'indépendance une réforme araine et une politique de l'emploi et des revenus en leur faveur.

Le problème de la réforme agraire reçut un début de solution des 1963 par la nationalisation des terres des colons de facto organisées en fermes d'etat, mais de jure autogérées par les travailleurs permanents. Au début de la décennie 1970, un secteur coopératif, issu de la limitation de la superficie de la propriété privée par famille fut constitué, mais la masse des sans terre ne diminua pas sensiblement.

Fait original, sur le plan du revenu, les agriculteurs n'ont pas été victimes du transfert massif du surplus. L'Etat leur a fait bénéficié du partage de la rente pétrolière: entre 1974 et 1980, le prix du kg de blé à la production passa de 67,70 dinars à 125 dinars, tandis que le prix du kg d'engrais au producteur était fixé à 55,2 DA. Plus généralement l'agriculture et le milieu rural ont bénéficié d'investissements importants. Les grands barrages ont été construits et le parc du matériel agricole (matériel de traction, matériel de récolte, matériel aratoire, moto pompe) a augmenté considérablement en une décennie: en 1983, le nombre de tracteurs était (49.000 unités) le double de celui du Maroc (24.000) et dépassait celui de Egypte (41.000). Que l'investissement ait été en général inefficient[20] ne doit pas occulter le fait que de 1964 à 1980, le taux de l'investissement agricole (en pourcentage du PIB) n'est descendu au-dessous de 10% que durant les trois dernières années. C'est absolument remarquable selon les normes africaines. Et ce d'autant qu'il était complémentaire d'un autre à caractère industriel et social en milieu rural.

Les investissement d'infrastructures agricoles très intensifs en capital, de surcroît importé, ont créé des emplois qui temporairement du mois ont plus que compense la diminution d'emploi liee à la mécanisation. Mais l'inefficacité de l'investissement notamment dans l'irrigation n'a pas permis de maintenir un volume d'emploi agricole suffisant pour absorber l'offre. Les deux débouches essentiels ont les services et les bâtiments, le plus souvent à temps partiel en milieu rural; l'émigration notamment vers la France ou selon le recensement français de 1975, il y avait 308.375 actifs algériens représentant 13% de la population occupée en Algérie".[21] Le travail à temps partiel et l'émigration sont le fait de la paysannerie prolétarisée vivant sur les 70% des exploitations de moins de 10 ha à culture sèche. Cette paysannerie mois différenciée que dans les pays voisins comporté néanmoins une couche de paysans aisés qui possède des tracteurs et une autre qui doit louer le matériel de culture ou la main d'oeuvre. Le problème des alliances avec la couche dirigeante dans ce contexe peut être analysé ainsi: jusqu'aux alentours de 1980, le pouvoir était idéologiquement opposé à la koulatisation et cherchait l'alliance des couches moyennes et des salariés permanents. Depuis, la priorité étant donnée à l'efficacité c'est la couche supérieure qui a les faveurs du pouvoir.

La crise et l'ajustement. Au début des années 1980, la combinaison des facteurs "extérieurs" et "internes", économiques et non économiques créa une situation de crise. La chute des recettes pétroliers entraîna un processus d'endettement de plus en plus insupportable pour un pays ou le sentiment nationaliste est très fort. EN 1970, l'encours de la dette était de 941 millions de dollars, représentant 19,4% du PNB. Le service de la dette extérieure absorbait seulement 0,9% du PNB et 3,9% des recettes d"exportation. En 1985, ces chiffres étaient respectivement de 13,660 millions, 24% du PNB pour l'encours; de 8,1 et 33,3% pour le service des années fastes, l'Algérie peut faire encore face à son service de la dette, malgré la détérioration de la balance des paiements, mais au prix de la perte de la maîtrise sur les conditions de l'accumulation et même des rapports politiques avec la paysannerie qui reste un des piliers du pouvoir. Or la situation de l'emploi s'est gravement détériorée et le chômage s'est accru dans des proportions considerables, du fait de l'auto-"ajustement structurel" qu'impose la crise de la dette. D'ici la fin de la décennie il est probable qu'il atteindra le taux de 20% de la population active. Les freins apportés, après le début des années 1980, à l'extension du secteur industriel contraignent désormais l'agriculture à garder tout ou partie des fractions additionnelles de la population active rural qui ne trouveront pas à s'employer en dehors de l'agriculture et en peuvent plus émigier. En somme, un retour à la situation qui prévalait durant la décennie 1960 avant le démarrage des plans d'industrialisation"[22] est à craindre. La libéralisation des prix risque de profiter davantage aux intermédiaires et aux grands propriétaires qu'aux paysans. La privatisation larvée à travers la décentralisation de la gestion agricole qui fait des travailleurs des domaines d'Etat et des coopératives des proprietaires à vie, stimulera certes l'offre de produits, mais ne résoudra que très partiellement la question paysanne au centre de laquelle se trouve toujours le problème d'un emploi rémunératetur. L'aggravation de la crise est à craindre car l'investissement rural non agricole a diminué constamment et la désaffection de la petite paysannerie à l'egard de l'Etat risque de s'accentuer.

Au total après environ quatre vingts ans de colonisation et trente ans d'indépendance, la révolution agricole n'est pas engagée en Afrique. Les deux obstacles principaux en sont le développement inégal et les rapports de pouvoir dans les différents pays. Le développement inégal se manifeste depuis la Deuxième Guerre Mondiale principalement par des politiques de subventions agricoles qui permettent à la périphérie d'acheter les céréales à un prix très inférieur aux coûts de production réels locaux. Ainsi le développement de secteur vivrier se trouve bloqué faute de débouches. En termes économistes, subventionner massivement la production au Nord conduit à subventionner la consommation au Sud et notamment en Afrique. Les aides extérieures directes à l'agriculture africaine concernent plus le secteur d'exportation que le secteur vivrier. L'Etat local s'appuyant avant tout sur les classes moyennes, les politiques des prix et du crédit favorisent davantage l'agriculture de substitution d'importation que l'agriculture vivrière dont les prix de produits sont maintenus très bas à la consommation non pas à cause des subventions comme dans les centres, mais du rapport de pouvoir très défavorable au paysan qui permet de lui extorquer du surplus même s'il reste très pauvre. Ce biais contre l'agro-vivrier a plusieurs conséquences; d'abord il est immédiatement cause de la dépendance alimentaire, même dans des pays réputés agricoles mais sans politique d'industrialisation, a plus forte raison dans ceux qui comme l'Algérie ont lancé des grands programmes d'industrialisation; puisque dans ce cas, à l'effet de la croissance du revenu s'ajoute celui de la population et de l'urbanisation. Ensuite il prolétarise la paysannerie et la différencie au profit des couches qui peuvent selon des techniques archaïques produire pour une clientèle de luxe; c'est particulièrement le cas pour l'élevage. Le reste de la petite paysannerie est parfois obligé d'émigrer vers l'Europe ou vers d'autres pays du Sud considérés comme "prospéres". C'est ainsi qu'un courant migratoire vers certains pays pétroliers a pris une grande ampleur au cours de la décennie 1970 et s'est accentué avec la crise des années 1980. Enfin dans beaucoup de pays, le surplus agricole autrefois pontionné par l'Etat diminue rapidement suite à la baisse des rendements et des cours mondiaux des "produits tropicaux". Les politiques d'ajustement en cours consistent à libérer les prix et à supprimer les subventions des intrants qui étaient au fait plus comptables que réelle puisqu'en général il y avait un transfert du surplus de l'agriculture. A court terme ces politiques peuvent entraîner une augmentation de l'offre même de produits agricoles, sur la base de techniques extensives. L'adoption des techniques intensives et la transformation des rapports d'équilibre en faveur de la paysannerie moyenne et petite suppose une politique agricole qui laisse peu de place aux prix mondiaux qui sont fixés par les productivités et les politiques des pays centraux. Elle sera le résultat des luttes populaires contre les Etats qui pratiquent la repression à l'égard de la paysannerie.

Références

1   Hamid Ait Amara et Bernard Founou Tchuigoua : la crise agricole africaine dans ses rapports avec l'Etat, l'industrialisation et la paysannerie. (sous la direction de) voir bibliographie.
2   Samir Amin, id Preface
3   Baba Ba, Pape Soz, Sidi Kane : L'Etat et le développement rural du Senegal de 1960 a 1985, sauf indications contraires les citations renvoient à cette contribution.
4   Lettre de Solagrale:Supplement No. 32 Mars-Avril 1990.
5   Charbel Zarour et Bernard Founou Tchnigoua in Samir Amin (sous la direction de), la coopération arabo-africaine pour quelle insertion dans l'économie mondiale? No. Special Africa Development vol. No. 2-3 1988.
6   Banque Mondiale, Afrique subsaharienne de la crise à la croissance stable, 1988.
7   Marchés tropicaux 19-01-1990.
8   World Bank commodity price trends 1988-89 ed.
9   Ali Traore : Bilan et perspectives des développements agricole et industriel en Cote d'Ivoire et leurs rapports mutuels in Hamid Ait Amara et Bernard Founou-Tchuigoua (sous la direction de) o.c.
10 W. Oluoch Kossura Relations entre l'agriculture et l'industries au Kenya. id.
11 Mahmud Ben Romdhane : l'Etat, la paysannerie et la dépendance alimentaire en Tunisie, in ait Amara et Founou-Tchuigoua (sous la direction de) o.c.
12 Baba Ba, et autres o.c.
14 Abdel W. Ould Cheikh : Nomadisme et capitalisme peripherique en Mauritanie, in Ait Amara et Founou-Tchuigoua (sous la directioin de).
15 Henry Mapolu : Impérialisme, Etat et paysannerie en Tanzanie, in H. Ait Amara and B. Founou-Tchuigoua, (sous la direction de) o.c.
16 Bedrani : L'agriculture algérienne depuis 1966, Office de Publication Universitaire, Alger 1987.
17 Hamid Ait Amara : Le développement autocentré et les relations agriculture-industrie. Le cas algérien in H. Ait Amara et B. Founou)

o.c. sauf indication contraire, les citations sans référence suivante sont tirées de ce texte.

18 Abdelatiff Benanchenhou : Planification et développement en Algérie 1962-1980. Office de Publication universitaire Alger 1982.

19 B. Founou Tchuigoua : Leçons de l'echec des tentatives de maîtrise agricole sans deconnexion : Algérie, Tanzanie, in Ait Amara et Founou-Tchuigoua o.c.

20 Hamid Ait Amara : le développement autocentré o.c.

───────────────────────────────Chapter 12

LA CRISE SOMALIENNE ACTUELLE
SA NATURE ET SES RAISONS

Eglal Mahmoud Raafat

Le 28 janvier 1991, le régime de Siad Barre s'est effondré à la suite d'une guerre civile sanglante, obligeant le président déchu à pendre la fuite au sud du pays. Immédiatement, le Congrès de la Somalie unifiée - une des organisations de l'opposition - a nommé Ali Mahdi Chef d'Etat et a formé un gouvernement provisoire ayant en tête Omar Orta Ghaleb. Ces événements ont eu lieu aprés une guerre civile prolongée qui a débuté vers la fin des années soixante-dix au nord et qui s'est étendue à l'ensemble du territorie jusqu'au point que le gouvernement de Siad Barre ne contrôlait plus - vers la fin -que la captiale et ses alentours. Les combats de Mogadiscio ont alors éclaté à la fin du mois de décembre 1990. Ils ont menés jusqu'au bout par les troupes militaires de la Somalie unifiée.

L'importance de l'étude de cette récente crise somalienne émane de son caractére particulier: comment expliquer ces violentes hostilités entre les enfants d'un seul peuple, marqué par rapport aux autres populations africaines, par une rare unité sociale, à savoir l'unité de race, de religion, de langue et d'histoire. Partant, cette étude met l'accent sur l'analyse de la nature de la crise et sur l'examen des raisons qui ont transformé une rébellion au nord de la Somalie en un mouvement populaire égendu qui s'est déchaîné dans tout le pays, se rapprochant ainsi de la révolte populaire puis en une guerre civile sanglante entre les factions de l'opposition et le Congrès de la Somalie unifiée.

D'autre part, cette étude a rencontrée quelques difficultés ci-après résumées:

1. L'actualité du sujet est à l'origine de la rareté des études sérieuses effectuées à cet effet, surtout ce que nous en recevons en Egypte. C'est la raison pour laquelle l'examen s'est appuyé - dans la partie concernant les récents événements - sur deux études essentielles : la première a été publiée en 1990 par Dr. Ahmed Samatar, professeur somalien enseignant les sciences politiques à l'université Lawrence à New York. La deuxième a été publiée en 1991 par Helmi Chaarawi, un des spécialistes égyptiens dans les affaires africaines ainsi que le Directeur de centre de recherche arabe. En outre, il s'est référé aux informations recueillies dans les circulaires; les journaux arabes et étrangers, les rapports de l'Organisation pour les droits de l'homme au Caire et dans données publiées par le Front national somalien. La recherche s'est également appuyée sur les informations obtenus du Conseiller de l'ambassade de la Somalie au Caire, Mohamad Ali Sarare et d'un des égyptiens travaillant en Somalie et revenu dans la capitale égyptienne à la suite des récents événements de Mogadiscio. Il s'agit de l'ingénieur Ataf Abdel Razek au Centre de recherches du Conseil consultatif (Choura).

2. La faiblesse du gouvernement actuel dont la légitimité n'a pas encore été établie. Au niveau intérieur, un certain nombre d'autres fronts s'oppose à la constitution de ce gouvernement, dont: le Front démocratique de salut somalien, le Mouvement patriotique somalien et le Mouvement national somalien. Au plan extérieur, aucun pays arabe, africain ou étranger n'a reconnu, officiellement, jusqu'à maintenant, ce gouvernement. De surcroît, les conditions de vie sont très mauvaises. Elles ont même atteint la limite de la famine et des épidémies. De telles conditions conjuguées créent l'instabilité qui, à son tour, aboutit à des changements imprévus. Ce qui rend difficile la possibilité de prévoir les forces politiques agissantes dans l'avenir de la Somalie.

3. L'évolution rapide et continue des événements entrave la suivi et l'analyse. Par conséquent, l'étude s'est arrêtée à la fin du mois d'avril 1991.

4. Le chercheur a identifié neuf fronts d'opposition seulement. Il s'agit des factions les plus importantes dans l'action politique. En effet, ce

n'est pas un inventaire complet de l'opposition somalienne vu que les informations et les documents concernant la crise ne sont pas disponibles et vu que de nouvelles organisations et alliances sont créées sans cesse, rendant difficile la tâche de leur suivi.

L'étude est donc divisée en trois parties:

I - Nature de l'opposition au régime de Siad Barré

- les factions de l'opposition
- les objectifs des factions de l'opposition
- la nature de ces factions

II - Les raisons intérieures qui ont provoqué la crise somalienne:

- divisions tribales
- régime totalitaire de Siad Barré
- détérioration de l'économie somalienne

III - Climat international et crise somalienne

- Politique de détente internationale et crise somalienne
- Guerre de Golfe et crise somalienne

Conclusion: les résultats de l'étude.

Nature de l'opposition Somalienne au Régime de Siad Barre

Présentation des factions de l'opposition

Le recensement de l'opposition somalienne est, dans cette conjoncture agitée, une tâche extrêmement difficile. Les forces politiques sur le scène, dans le pays, sont de nature complexe. Ce qui ne permet pas leur classification en organisations indépendantes. A titre d'exemple, certaines conditions ont été à l'origine de la fusion de deux fronts de l'opposition en une seule organisation réunissant tous les Darods, sans, toutefois supprimer les deux fronts initiaux. D'autre part, un nouveau groupe, appelé l'Alliance somalienne, a été créé. Il comprend aussi des personnalitiés des autres formations sans que cela ne soit la fin de leur ancienne appartenance.

Sur la scène politique somalienne, les mouvements et les fronts forment ainsi des coalitions ou se séparent en fonction de la conjoncture en état de changement politiques et militaires les plus importantes en suivant la chronologie de leur création:

Front démocratitque de salut somalien [1]

Ce front a été créé en 1979 à la suite d'un coup d'état militaire manqué d'Abdallah Youssef, fils des tribus de Darods. Ce font comprend des personnalités du nord et du sud. Mais le clan de Majertin consitue son fondement tribal. Il s'agit d'une tribu qui vit à l'est, au nord et au sud. L'orientation de la pensée de cette formation suit la ligne radical.[2] Son siège est à Rome. Le front est conduit par Moussa Islah Fareh.[3]

Mouvement national somalien [4]

Ce mouvement a été établi en 1981[5]. Il est fondé essentiellement sur les tribus d'Issaq au nord. L'opposition effective à Siad Barré en est partie au nord avant même que le front ne soit officiellement constitué. Cela a en lieu vers la fin des années soixante-dix. Aprés sa formation, le mouvement a depuis 1983, lancé des attaques contre Hergeisa et Berbera. Il comprend une élite d'hommes politiques cultivés, de commercants et surtout de dirigeants de l'ancienne bourgeoisie lésés par la phase socialiste. D'autre part, cette faction a abrité et soutenu un million de réfugiés fuyant la Somalie Ouest vers l'intérieur lors de la guerre entre la Somalie et l'Ethiopie.[6]

Au départ, ce mouvement était basé en Ethiopie. Mais le gouvernment de ce pays lui a demandé de quitter à la suite de la signature du Traité de non-agression avec la Somalie en 1988. Ainsi, il s'est établi au nord de la Somalie [7.] Mais ses dirigeants ont continué à se déplacer entre Addis-Abéba et Londres.

Mouvement patriotique somalien [8]

Ce mouvement est composé de deux tribus, l'Ogaden et Majertein à l'Ouest et au sud du pays, notamment dans la vielle de Kismayo et ses alentours. Il comprend certaines personnalités qui ont travaillé avec Siad Barré puis se sont révoltés contre lui. Du point de vue poids politique et militaire, il est moins important que les deux fronts précédents [9]. A noter que les tribus de l'Ogaden et de Majertein ont des relations de parenté avec la tribu de Siad Barré, Marehan. Il s'agit dans l'ensemble de branches des Darods. C'est pourquoi, Siad Barré a essayé - au début de la crise avec l'opposition - d'exploiter leurs différends avec les autres tribus et clans afin que ces tribus le rejoignent dans les combats qu'il menait contre les nordistes. Ahmad Omar Habis[10] se trouve à la tête de ce mouvement.

Mouvement islamique somalien

Le rôle des imams des mosquées s'est accru car ils sont devenus en quelque sorte une source importante d'information: les mosquées étaient les seuls lieux sur lesquels aucun contrôle gouvernmental n'était exercé. Ce groupe a commencé par condamner la détérioration de la situation dans le pays à la suite des hausses de prix et de la repression gouvernmentale accrue. Il s'est heurté au gouvernement après l'assasinat de l'envoyé papal : en 1989 et après que le gouvernement l'ait accusé de ce meutre. Les hostilités se sont terminées par la liquidation compléte du mouvement islamique soit en arrêtant ses dirigeants ou en les exécutant.[11]

Front de la Somalie Unifiée [12]

Ce front est apparu au nord du pays dans la région frontaliére avec Dijibouti. Il est soutenu sur le plan tribal par le clan Mamache qui se trouve entre les deux états et auquel appartient le Président de Dijibouti Hassan Goulet. D'ailleurs, le gouvernment de Djibouti a appuyé cette formation naissante. Ce qui a amené le Mouvement national somalien à protester et à considérer cette position comme une ingérence inacceptable dans les affaires somaliennes de la part du gouvernement de Djibouti. Toutefois, cette formation ne présente pas une grande importance sur la scène politique somalienne. Il semble qu'elle est née des circonstances qui prévalent sur les frontières entre les deux pays. Le chef de ce front est Miyad Nour[13].

Congrès de la Somalie Unifiée [14]

Ce front est issu du rassemblement de divers groupes de l'opposition somalienne et il a été créé à Rome en 1989. Il réunit quelques anciens hommes politiques, tels que Amou Sobil, jadis ministre, avant la révolution de 1969 ainsi que quelques officiers et hommes politiques qui ont servi pendant l'ère de Siad Barré mais qui ont refusé son hégémonie et son pouvoir unique, tels que le général Mohamad Fareh. Il regroupe également des personnalités sudistes comme le général Mohamed Abdi et des personnalités qui se sont dégagés du Mouvement national somalien à l'instar du colonel Ahmed Mir [15.] Ainsi, le Congrès de la Somalie unifiée donne l'impression d'un rassemblement patriotique de perssonnalités politiques de différentes tendances. Toutefois; le fondement tribal essentiel de ce front est constitué des clans des Haziye au centre du pays, dont Ali Mahdi, le Chef d'Etat qctuel. Ces tribus sont peu nombreuses comparées à celles d'Issaq et de Darods. Néanmois, elles se sont manifestées en taut que force militaire importante lors des combats de Mogadiscio qu'elles ont menés jusq'au bout. C'est pourquoi, elles ont considéré de leur driot de former l'actuel gouvernement de ses membres ainsi que de quelques autres personnalitées qui se sont alliées à ces gouvernements comme Omar Arta Ghaleb, le premier ministre, du nord et des tribus des Issaqs[16]. D'ailleurs, celui-ci était membre au Mouvement national somalien.

Quant à la formation politique et économique de l'actuel chef d'Etat, il s'agit d'un ancien parlementaire qui a occupé le poste de ministre dans le dernier gouvenement de Siad Barré. De même, il a signé le communiqué de Mogadiscio. Il est un des grandes hommes d'affaires et il a financé les récents combats de Mogadiscio[17]. Néanmois, sa désignation à la tête du pays a été la volonté individuelle des dirigeants du Congrés de la Somalie unifiée. Il n'y pas eu de consensus avec les autres détachements de l'opposition - ni même au sein de son propre front sa désignation comme président. Son rival aux postes de chef d'Etat et de président du front est le général Fareh Idid[18], réfugie en Ethiopie et revenu en Somalie quatre jours avant le début des combats[19]. Probablement, la bonne relation entretenu par Idid avec l'Ethiopie a été à l'origine de son éloignement lors de la désignation du président surtout pendant cette période critique. On craignait de provoquer les sentiments des somaliens qui considérent encore l'Ethiopie avec réserve, surtout en ce qui concerne le Mouvement national somalien appartenant aux tribus de l'Ogaden.

Le Groupe du communiqué de Mogadiscio Manifesto

Le communiqué deMogadiscio a été annoncé le 15 mai 1990. Il

rassemblait un certain nombre d'anciens hommes politiques estimé être de 114 personnes, telles que Adam Osman et Mohammad Saîd Samanter, parmi ceux qui veulent revenir au précédent équilibre tribal et au libéralisme des partis[20]. En effet, le Manifesto est considéré le seul groupe de l'opposition attirant la grande majorité de l'élite des tribus somalienne et ayant eu une position modérée à l'égard de la réforme tentée par Siad Barré au cours de la derniére année de son régime. Ce groupe a accepté de prendre part aux élections promises par Siad Barré après son adoption de la constitution du 12 octobre 1990 autorisant le multipartisme[21]. Toutefois, ce groupe s'est écroulé avec la dissidence de ses membres qui sont allés rejoindre d'autres fronts suivant leurs appartenances tribales.

Front national Somalien [22]

Ce front a vu le jour après la chute de Siad Barré. Il est un rassemblement les tribus des Darobs (Marihan, Ogaden, Majertein). Il est préside par Ahmad Omar Habeis[23]. La fuite de Siad Barré et de ses collaborateurs vers le sud pour se réfugier dans leurs clans a été la raison de l'apparition de cette formation. Il semble en fait que l'ancien président somalien ait réussi à exploiter les conflits existants entre les détachements de l'opposition pour en séparer les Darods et les attirer à ses côtés dans le combat pour la reprise du pouvoir. Il compte à cet effet, d'une part, sur le chauvinisme tribal et, d'autre part, sur la crainte que ressentement les Darods de perdre les priviléges politiques et économiques acquis lors de l'ancien régime, surtout les Marehan. Cependant, le Front national somalien a nié - dans un communiqué - son alliance avec Siad Barré et a ajouté que les fronts des Darods (S.S.D.F. et S.P.M.) ont été les premiers à mener l'opposition armée contre Siad Barré en dépit de son appartenance aux Marehans, une des branches des Darods. La raison en a été ses insuffisances graves qui ont nui au pays. Quant à son opposition au Congrés de la Somalie unifiée, il a mentionné d'autres motifs [24]:

• Les tribus des Darods sont les plus grandes en Somalie et elles sont les plus étendues. Par conséquent, elles représenteraient la majorité du peuple somalien et ne devraient pas être écartées du pouvoir.
• Les Darods ont une longue histoire dans le Mouvement national somalien. De leurs rangs, sont sorties des personnalités importantes qui ont contribué à la lutte pour l'independance et d'unité. On en cite Mohamad Abdallah Hassan, un leader nationaliste somalien de

l'Ogaden. Il a combattu, au début de ce siécle, les anglais pendant vingt ans. Nous mentionnons également Yassin Osmane qui a institué la parti de l'Unité de la jeunesse somalienne avant l'indépendance et dont les branches ont couvert tout le pays. C'est pourquoi, les Darods ont le droit de participer au gouvernment du pays.

• Le Congrés de la Somalie unifiée est l'un des derniers fronts à déclarer son opposition armée à Siad Barré et n'a réalisé de victoires concrètes qu'à partir de 1990. Dès lors, il n'a pas le droit de présider les autres factions de l'opposition qui ont fait la guerre, pour plus de dix ans, au régime.

• Les membres du Congrès de la Somalie unifiée commettent d'horribles massacres contre les Darods pour des raisons purement tribales indépendamment de leurs positions patriotiques.

• Quelques - uns des membres du nouveau régime sont les mêmes hommes politiques qui ont travaillé avec Siad Barré. Le Congrès unifié les a fait participer justement parce qu'ils appartiennent aux tribus de Haziye indépendamment de leurs positions négatives précédentes. Par conséquent les choix dans le nouveau gouvernement sont plus de nature tribale qu'objectifs.[25] A titre d'exemple Hussain Kalmeh Afrah, le lieutenant Mohamad Cheikh Osman, le général Mohamad Nour Galal, Ahmad Jelioo et Abdullah Ahmad Adou.

L'Alliance Somalienne

Cette nouvelle organisation politique est apparue à la suite de la chutte de Siad Barré. Elle regroupe des personnalités d'autres fronts (SNF, SNM, SSDF). Au sujet des objectifs de cette formation, Mohamed Hassan Mahmoud, membre du Comité politique[26] dit : "L'alliance vise à réunir les idées et les efforts nationanux éparpillés et à ancrer les principes du rapprochement et de l'entente entre les différents fronts au service d'un noyau pour la grande alliance somalienne en vue de rémédier à la situation de division de la patrie".

Quant au support populaire à cette nouvelle organisation, Mohamad Hassan Mahmoud ajoute: "...les partisans de l'Alliance sont présents au Sud de le Somalie et au Nord, ils représentent la majorité du peuple somalien et veulent sauvegarder l'unité du territoire somalien". Nous n'avons recu aucune information sur l'efficacité de cette nouvelle alliance sur la scène politique et militaire somalienne.

Objectifs des factions de l'opposition

Les factions de l'opposition les plus importantes précitées conviennent de deux objectifs en particulier:

1. la déliverance du régime de Siad BARRE
2. le rétablissement du multipartisme aboli après la révolution d'octobre 1969. A part ces deux objectifs, les déclarations des responsables dans les différentes factions de l'opposition n'indiquent aucun autre objectif au plan national.

Au niveau tribal, quelques fronts ont exprimé des buts particuliers. Le Mouvement national somalien a exprimé le désir d'une certaine autonomie au nord. Cette position du SUM ne reflèterait pas un désir de séparation mais plutôt une tentative de pression sur le prochain gouvernement - à la rédaction de la nouvelle Constitution - afin d'obtenir plus de grains pour les "nordistes" [27]. Quant au Congrès de la Somalie Unifiée, son but serait de reprendre la force économique qui distinguait la Tribu des Hawiyé avant que Siad Barré et son clan ne saisissent seuls tous les privilèges du pouvoir politique. Cette force économique reposait sur le commerce du bétail avec l'Arabie Saoudite et les pays du Golfe. Le rêve d'annexer la Somalie Ouest à la République de la Somalie reste une visée que tiennent à coeur les tribus de l'Ogaden qui sont le fondement du Mouvement patriotique somalienne. [28] Revenant aux objectifs nationaux des factions de l'opposition, il semble que la ligne bilatérale, traduite par le désir collectif d'établir le multipartisme, ne se limite pas à la réorganisation des institutions politiques mais s'applique aussi à la politique économique prévue pour le nouveau gouvernement somalien. La composition sociale bourgeoise et l'arrière-plan commercial capitaliste de plusieurs leaders des factions de l'opposition y compris l'actuel chef d'Etat, confirment le virage à droite du nouveau régime. La déclaration de M. Abdou Osmane, le représentant du Congrès de la Somalie unifiée au continent asiatique, mettrait en avant la forme politique et économique du nouveau régime somalien: "La Somalie a déjà fait l'expérience du socialisme marxisme puis du capitalisme occidental ensuite de tribalisme sous-développé. Tous ces systèmes ont échoué et n'ont pu réalisé le progrès dans le pays. C'est pourquoi les responsables ont choisi l'application du système islamique."[29]

Le responsable somalien n'a pas précisé les détails de ce régime choisi. Toutefois, il ne s'agirait en réalité que de deux éventualités: l'intention, dans cette déclaration, est d'attirer l'Arabie Saoudite afin qu'elle satisfasse la demande du gouvernement somalien en matière d'aides financières et alimentaires de grand volume ou que le responsable somalien exprimait effectivement une nouvelle méthodologie intégrée pour le nouveau régime fondée sur la Charia (la loi) islamique. Dans les deux cas, la ligne conservatrice ressort.

D'autre part, les relations extérieures des factions de l'opposition démontrent cette orientation. Nous constatons qur les états qui tentent la conciliation entre Siad Barre et l'opposition ainsi qu'entre les factions hostiles sont les Etat-Unis, l'Egypte, le Royaume d'Arabie Saoudite et le Koweit [30]. Cependant; il y a une exception à cette règle. Il s'agit de la relation éthiopien. Ce rapprochement ne signifie pas néssairement, toutefois, l'identité de la pensée et de la ligne de conduite. Ce rapprochment indique, en revanche, que les conditions de voisinage et le besoin que ressent l'opposition, surtout au nord, de disposer d'un abri proche à partir duquel elle peut attaquer le régime de Siad Barre. A cette époque, il était dans l'intérêt de l'Ethiopie d'aider à l'effondrement du régime somalien qui préconisait l'idée de la récupération de la Somalie occidentale et qui oeuvrait pour mettre en oeuvre. Sans oublier la précédente relation de certaines de ces factions avec la Libye et l'Irak. Mais cette orientation radicale n'est pas apparue dans les récents événements en Somalie.

Nature des Factions de l'Opposition

L'analyse de la genèse et des visées des différentes factions somaliennes ainsi que de leur action sur la scène politique et militaire jusqu'à présent prouve que cette opposition est de nature tribale prévalent sur toute autre tendance nationale. Cette opposition aurait pourtant pu être le noyau d'une opposition démocratique patriotique éclairée. Elle ne s'est unie que pour faire chuter le régime de Siad Barre. Quand cela a été réalisée, elle est tombée dans ses dissensions sans rechercher à réaliser le deuxième objectif, c'est-à-dire le multipartisme. Il semble qu'un tel concept chez ces groupes diffèrent en son essence du concept libéral: le désir du pluralisme par l'opposition n'est que transitoire et prend fin du moment ou l'un d'eux met la main sur le pouvoir. Quant au principe de la participation à l'administration politique, l'essence même de la démocratie politique, il chavire encore, paraît-il. La preuve en est la guerre civile redevenue violente et sanglante après la chute de Siad Barre. Mais, cette fois-ci entre un des détachements qui a pris le pouvoir et les autres. A noter que les fronts demeurés à l'opposition commencent à se reconstituer sur une base plus tribale évidente. Le Front national somalien regroupant tous les membres des Darods, avec leurs précédents différents détachements, a été créé contre les tribus des Hawiyé au pouvoir.

D'autre part, la nature tribale de l'opposition somalienne a aboutit à des résultats graves qui influent extrêmement sur l'intérêt général somalien, surtout sur l'unité du territore somalien. La nette division entre les différentes factions a été la cause de l'ajournement de la Conférence de conciliation nationale. [31] Cet ajournement a créé une réalité dangereuse, à savoir la naissance de trois gouvernements représentant trois tribus principales se partageant la Somalie [32]:

*   un gouvernement d'Issaqs au nord ayant en tête Abdul Rahman For Tor et dont la capitale est Hargeisa
*   un gouvernement de Hawiyé au centre présidé par Ali Mahdi Mohamad et dont la capitale est Mogadiscio
*   un gouvernement de Darods au sud, conduit par l'ancien président Siad Barre et dont la capitale est Kismayo [33]

La nature tribale de l'opposition indique la présence d'un mal social dangereux dont souffre le peuple somalien comme tous les pays africains sub-sahariens, à savoir la composition structurelle fondée sur les divisions sociales verticales. Cette forme tribale de l'opposition est considérée la conséquence politique directe de cette composition structurelle particulière produisant nécessairement d'autres aspects sociaux négatifs influant sur la crise actuelle.

D'autre part, la nature tribale de l'opposition ne signifie pas que les raisons de son déchaînement se limitent aux motifs sociaux. Il faut plutôt chercher du côté des autres conjonctures politiques et économiques qui ont influencé, apparemment, le déroulement de la crise et le climat international qui l'a entourée. Partant, le chapitre suivant de la recherche sera consacré à l'examen des éléments intérieurs et extérieurs ayant créé cette situation explosive en Somalie.

Les raisons intérieures qui ont provoquées la crise

On peut résumer les plus importantes dans trois facteurs suivants:

*   la composition structurelle de la société somalienne
*   l'absolutisme de Siad Barre
*   la détérioration de la situation économique.

La composition structurelle de la société somalienne

La Somalie est presque le seul pays africain situé au sud du grand Sahara qui jouit d'une unité raciale presque totale. 90% à peu près de la population appartiennent à la descendance somalienne, une branche spéciale de la race caucasienne [34]. On la retrouve aussi à Djibouti (les Affars, en Erythrée, en Ethiopie (les Orsomos) et au nord du Kenya (NED) [35] (Borane et Jala). Tandis que les 5% qui restent sont répartis entre les descendances: les ponis, pêcheurs vivant dans la vallée des riviéres chbili et Hobla et parlant swahili ainsi que les bagonis, vivant, jusqu'en 1975, dans les îles bagouns en face de la ville de Burao puis déplacés par le gouvernement somalien à la ville de Kisimayo [36].

Cette unité de race n'a pas empêchée le peuple somalien de se séparer en trois tribus principales, à savoir les Darods, les Irirs, les Subs divisés, à leur tour, en plusieurs clans [37] dont les Mayerten et Ogaden appartenant aux Darods et vivant au nord-est du pays, à l'Ouest et au sud jusqu'a la province (NED), les Darods sont les plus grandes tribus en nombre et les plus étendus dans la pays. Les Irirs comprennent les tribus de Hawiyé au sud de la Somalie et autour de la capitale Mogadiscio ainsi qu'autour de la riviére Chbili et dans la province (NED), les Issaqs vivant au nord de la Somalie et en Ethiopie et les Dirs au nord-ouest du pays, à l'est de l'Ethiopie et dans la ville de Heiar ainsi qu'à Djibouti. Quant aux Sabs, ils comprennent les Rahwein et les Digils, moins nombreux que les précédents. Leur importance provient de leur présence dans la partie fertile située entre les deux riviéres Chbili et Joba.[38]

Ces différentes tribus somaliennes sont unies par les mêmes coutumes reconnues par tous, appelées XEER. Malgré cela, cette société est caractérisée par de nombreux conflits intérieurs entre clans et tribus. Le professeur Lezis estime que la crise actuelle devrait être examinée de cette perspective. Les dissensions tribales n'ont pas pris fin avec l'édification de l'Etat moderne après l'independance. C'est pourquoi le nationalisme somalien est considéré fragile non valable, jusqu'à présent, pour l'instauration de la structure sociale de l'Etat moderne.[39]

Quant au Prof. Ahmed Samatar, il va plus loin en considérant que la crise somalienne est née:[40]

- de la coexistence de deux modèles sociaux différents: l'ancien modéle fondé sur la tribu comme division sociale, sur le pâturage et le troc comme modéle de production et le modéle moderne qui repose sur la collectivité urbaine et le systéme intégré dans le marché mondial.

* des problèmes associés à la création d'un nouvel état politique étendu.

En analysant les pensées des deux professeurs Lewis et Samatar, nous constatons un dénominateur commun. Il s'agit du fait que la composition structurelle somalienne est encore tribale en dépit de l'unité de race, de religion, et d'histoire commune. Cette composition structuelle influe sur la société somalienne, que ce soit par ses divisions verticales et par sa friction entravante avec le moderne. Partant, l'importance de reconnaître l'existence des divisions tribales dans le pays comme une réalité grave devrait absolument être pris en considération lors de la planification d'une nouvelle constitution pour le pays. Parmi les défauts principaux de l'ancien régime de Siad Barre, sa négation continue de ces répartitions et de leur influence sur la vie sociale et politique somalienne. Il prétendait que le régime politique formé d'un parti unique a fusionné tous ces conflits vingt ans après le coup-d'état de 1961, les différends tribaux ont éclaté avec une rare violence annonçant ainsi sa présence et son influence permanente sur les différents aspects de la vie dans la société somalienne. A noter que Siad Barre même a gardé, dans son for intérieur, cette mentalité tribale qui est réapparue lorsqu'il a fait face au risque d'un coup-d'état contre lui à partir de la fin des années soixante-dix.

L'absolutisme de Siad Barre

Siad Barre a accédé au pouvoir en Somalie à la suite d'un coup-d'état qui a eu lieu en 1969 et conduit par un groupe de jeunes somaliens radicaux ayant fait des études en Egypte de Nasser et dans les pays socialistes.

Ce groupe de jeunes officiers ont vu dans Siad Barre la personne qui convient à la direction de l'état, pour plusieurs raisons: [41]

* facteur d'âge: Siad Barre était le plus âgé des membres du Conseil de la révolution
* formation militaire stricte: il a étudié la police en Italie à l'ère fasciste et il est ensuite entré à l'armée somalienne
* appartenance tribale: Siad Barre appartient à la tribu Marehan, qui est un petit clan au sud et dont la position sociale et économique est limitée. Cela éloigne du nouveau régime le soupcon de l'hégémonie du Sud sur le nord car cette accusation créait toujours des problèmes entre le Nord et le Sud le lendemain de l'unité et de l'indépendance du pays.

Les prémices de l'absolutisme du régime de Siad Barre sont apparus dès le départ par trois mesures prises en trois phases:

1. Siad Barre a dissous tous les partis politiques somaliens à la suite de son accès au pouvoir et il a continué a diriger le pays à travers le Conseil de la révolution jusqu'en 1976
2. Siad Barre a créé en 1976 le système du parti unique. Il a donc institué le parti socialiste révolutionnaire somalien et lui a transféré le pouvoir de Conseil de la révolution. Un des plus graves défauts du système du parti unique, celui de la non-application des deux volets du principe de la centralisation socialiste sur lequel est fondé ce système. Le côté démocratique s'en évanouit pendant que le part de la centralisation se développe en donnant à l'action politique la couleur dictatoriale.
3. Siad Barre a élaboré une nouvelle Constitution pour le pays en 1979 dans laquelle il concentre les pouvoirs de l'Etat dans les mains du Président de la République.

Lorsque des tentatives de coups d'etat contre le régime de Siad Barre ont commencé à se succéder et quelques factions de l'opposition ont commencé par la suite à se former, Siad Barre a procédé à l'application d'une politique tribale évidente. Il a chargé les membres de sa tribu de postes politiques importants dans le pays. Puis, ces sections ont été progressivement rétrécies jusqu'à ce que les postes dirigeants importants aient été monopolisés par les membres de sa famille. De la sorte, il n'a plus eu recours aux membres des autres tribus dont des personnalités ayant une compétence et une expérience précédentes.[42] Cet absolutisme est dangereux dans des sociétés tribales qui souffrent de divisions sociales verticales outre les dissensions de classes ou de catégories. Leur présence crée des divergences d'intérête et d'objectifs, qui se concrétisent nécessairement dans des formes politiques légales se chargeant de la critique adressée à la politique générale du gouvernement et de la présentation des propositions qui servent les intérêts nationaux du pays. L'alternative - à savoir l'hégémonie individuelle, partisane ou tribale - crée indisposablement une coupure entre le gouvernant et les masses allant en s'accusant et donnant naissance à des mouvements politiques secrets et à des factions militaires opposées. C'est ce qui s'est exactement passé en Somalie. L'absolutisme du pouvoir n'a pas seulement mené à une crise sociale et politique mais a aussi abouti à une forte crise économique.

Cependant, l'objectivité nous commande de mentionner que la

dictature de Siad Barre n'était pas, dans l'ensemble de ses conséquences, négative. Le précédent chef d'Etat a, surtout au cours des dix premières années, fait des réalisations importantes et difficiles exigeant, pour leur accomplissement, un pouvoir central fort. Au plan national, Siad Barre a oeuvré pour écrire la langue somalienne et a appliqué la politique de l'alphabétisation en cette langue; ce qui a longuement contribué au développement politique et à la réanimation du patrimoine historique et littéraire somalien. De même, Siad Barre croyait à l' idée de l'Unité de la Grande Somalie considérée, par les citoyens de ce pays, une foi à laquelle ils ne renoncent jamais. Il a oeuvré pour la réalisation dans la province occidentale jusqu'à l'échec essuyé par la Somalie devant l'Ethiopie en 1977 à cause de l'apporté par l'Union soviétique au Gouvernement de Hella Maryam. Le traité de non-agression conclu entre la Somalie et l'Ethiopie n'était qu'un moyen de protection pour les régimes des deux présidents et n'a pas influé sur l'idée de l'unité de la Grande Somalie. En outre, il a fait efforts sérieux pour libérer l'économie nationale, en nationalisant quelques industries et entreprises étrangères et il a mis sur pied des plans quinquennaux successifs pour lancer la roue de développement.   Quant au plan extérieur, Siad Barre s'est déploye pour que la Somalie adhère à la Ligue arabe en dépit des nombreuses difficultés rencontrées à l'intérieur et à l'extérieur.

Détérioration de la situation économique

Le professeur Said Samatar analyse la début de la détérioration qui a touché la société somalienne en disant [43] : l'environnement pastoral traditionnel de la Somalie se distingue par la production collective et par le troc entre les différents clans et tribus. Mais, le colonialisme européen, lorsqu'il a dominé la pays, a introduit ce milieu pastoral dans le cercle de la production pour le marché. Un nouveau modèle de production a ainsi été créé. La coexistence des deux modèles, ancien et moderne, a donné jour à deux classes distinctes: la classe des pasteurs producteurs et celle des marchands entreprenant la commericalisation du bétail à l'intérieur et à l'étranger. Les intérêts de l'administration coloniale et des commerçants ont coincidé pour priver la classe des bergers de l'excédent de la production et ce par l'intermédiaire du troc inéquitable du bétail et des produits de consommation finis. Bien que la bétail constitue 80% des exportations de la Somalie, le pasteur producteur n'en obtienne que la bénéfice modeste.

Plusieurs autres facteurs se sont conjugués pour réduire le revenu national somalien:

- La sécheresse qui s'est abattue sur l'Afrique de l'est, surtout dans la corne africaine, sous forme de vagues successives qui ont débuté pendant les premiers temps des années soixante-dix et qui durent jusqu'à présent.
- La concurrence entre l'Australie et la Somalie dans la domaine de l'exportation du bétail au marché saoudien qui absorbait environ 90% de la production somalienne.
- La baisse du prix du pétrole au début des années quatre-vingt jusqu'au commencement de la crise du Golfe, le 2 août 1990.
- La crise économique au Royaume d'Arabie Saoudite, dans les Emirats et au Koweit due à la guerre du golfe a négativement influé sur l'absorption par le marché arabe de la production somalienne en se reflétant sur les revenus des pasteurs producteurs et des commerçants.
- L'épuisement des capacités du pays dans sa guerre contre l'Ethiopie pour récupérer la Somalie occidentale.

Tous ces facteurs, réunis, ont gonflé l'endettement public le faissant passer à 3 milliards de dollars. [44] L'intervention des institutions financières internationales - la Banque mondiale et le Fonds monétaire international - s'ensuivit pour changer la structure économique de la Somalie. Le gouvernement de Siad Barre n'a pu surmonter ces problèmes. Il s'est mis alors d'accord avec le FMI en 1985 et le gouvernement a été obligé de réorienter sa politique capitaliste. Le modèle tribal ancien s'est ainsi effondré avant que le système économique moderne ne s'aguerrisse. La conséquence en a été l'échec du système économique somalien et, partant, l'échec du régime de Siad Barre. [45]

Climat international et la crise somalienne
Politique d'entente internationale et crise somalienne

La politique de la Perestroïka annoncée par Gorbachev en 1985 est édifiée sur l'entente internationale et sur la règlement des conflits par la voie pacifique. Il semble que l'Union soviétique était propulsée dans cette direction par les problèmes économiques intérieurs qui ne cessent de croître et qui rendent l'aide octroyée aux régimes socialistes dans les pays du Tiers-Monde une charge financiére et militaire ne pouvant être prise dans de telles conditions intérieures nouvelles. La conséquence en a été le retrait de l'Union soviétique de certaines zones stratégiques dans le monde, appliquant ainsi la nouvelle politique d'entente. De ces régions, la corne de l'Afrique, où elle se concentrait depuis le début des années soixante en Somalie puis en Ethiopie. Ce retrait a abouti à plusieurs changements dans les régions, dont les plus importants sont:

(a) Le retrait de l'Union soviétique de la Corne de l'Afrique a laissé le champ libre aux Etats-Unis d'Amérique et a réduit l'importance de cette région dans la concurrence stratégique entre les deux pôles. Pourtant, l'objectif des Etats-Unis dans cette région est passé de la concurrence à l'Union soviétique à la recherche de l'instauration de la sécurité et de la mise à fin des conflits entre les pays de la région pour servir les intérêts americains.

(b) Les EtatsUnis sont devenus l'unique source de financement pour la région et, par conséquent, il lui est devenu facile d'y étendre son hégémonie. Cela ressort des positions suivantes:
  • les Etats-Unis ont exercé une position sur la Somalie par l'intermédiaire du FMI en exploitant le fort besoin du pays d'obtenir des crédits afin de le pousser vers l'ouverture capitaliste. Pourtant, une telle ouverture présente un grand risque pour une société qui oscille encore entre les systèmes sociaux traditionnels et la structure de l'état moderne, comme nous l'avons déjà relevé;
  • les Etats-Unis ont demandé à Siad Barre de renoncer à la dictature et d'adopter un régime plus démocratique;
  • les Etat-Unis et l'Italie ont interdit les assistances militaires et financières accordées au gouvernement somalien sous le prétexte qu'il nuit aux droits de l'Homme. [46]
Cette nouvelle conjoncture internationale a aggravé la détérioration de la situation intérieure en Somalie qui recevait, depuis une certaine période, des aides matérielles et en nature de l'Italie, de la Grande-Bretagne et de l'Ethiopie. Vu cette situation intérieure désastreuse, Siad Barre a fait quelques tentatives pour s'allier l'opposition et calmer le front intérieur. Il a fait des promesses pour une plus grande démocratie en commencant par la publication de la nouvelle Constitution en Octobre 1990 fondée sur le multipartisme ensuite en invitant à des élections libres au niveau de la République. Finalement, il a tenté de rencontrer l'opposition dans le cadre du Congrès de concilation patriotique. Toutes ces tentatives ont été vouées à l'échec.

Toutefois, les efforts déployés par Siad Barre ont tardé à venir. La Somalie était déjà disposée au soulèvement populaire qui n'accepteriat pas moins de l'effondrement de Siad Barre. Les conséquences directes et indirectes de la politique de la Prestroïka ont ainsi été à l'origine de la chute du gouvernement de Siad Barre et de la préparation du peuple somalien à accueillir la contagion de la démocratie libérale venant de l'Europe de l'Est.

A noter à cet érgard la réalité à expliquer la position des Etats-Unis d'Amérique du front intérieur somalien. L'Appel au respect des droits de l'Homme, l'exigence d'instaurer un régime démocratique et la pression exercée par les moyens économiques précités n'expriment pas, à l'avis de l'auter de l'étude, une position morale de la part des Etats-Unis défendant la légitimité et les droits de l'Homme. Les Etats-Unis édifie ses positions internationales sur une base d'intérêts évidente. Les Etats-Unis ne sont pas les seuls à suivre ce système d'intérêts dans la politique internationale. Mais ils sont les seuls probablement - dans cette phase historique avec toutes ses données économiques et politiques - à disposer d'une immense capacité à activer les mouvements dans le monde pour aller dans le sens de leurs objectifs. Nombre de fois, les Etats-Unis ont soutenu et soutiennent encore des régimes absolus et terroristes. A titre d'example, Israël, l'Afrique du Sud et les régimes conservateurs du Golfe. Ils interviennent même parfois contre la démocratie dans certains cas comme ils tentent de la faire à présent en faisant pression sur le roi Hussein en Jordanie afin qu'il réduit le rôle du courant islamique que la récente vague de démocratie a fait apparaître sur la scène politique jordanienne. Cette contradiction dans les positions des Etat-Unis ne peut être expliquée que par le désir ancréé d'atteindre l'intérêt américain mais avec des moyens qui varient selon les situations.

Guerre du Golfe et crise somalienne

La crise du Golfe a mis en avant le rôle des Etats-Unis d'Amérique dans le nouvel ordre international. Ils sont devenus la seule superpuissance agissante dans le monde. On peut par conséquent se demander: quel est le rôle joué par les Etat-Unis d'Amérique dans l'actuelle crise somalienne, surtout que la région de la Corne d'Afrique n'est pas loin de la région du Golfe qui constitue aujourd'hui le foyer d'intérêt des Etats-Unis et des pays européens?

1. La région de la Corne de l'Afrique contrôle avec ses trois états: la Somalie, Djibouti et Ethiopie à l'entrée du Golfe d'Aden et de la mer

rouge, la voie maritime naturelle pour le transport du pétrole du golfe en Europe et aux Etats-Unis. De là vient l'importance de l'instauration de la sécurité dans cette région.

2. La Somalie, avec ses côtes qui s'étendent sur l'Ocean indien et sur le golfe d'Aden, représente une profondeur stratégique importante pour l'Egypte et le Soudan. D'autre part, l'Egypte est un des trois pricipaux ététs [47] sur lesquels repose toute stratégie pour le Moyen-Orient. Par conséquent, il devient important pour les Etat-Unis d'étendre son hégémonie sur l'orientation politique du gouvernement égyptien en planifiant un nouvel ordre qui servirait ses intérêts au Moyen-Orient. Cette hégémonie ne s'arrête pas à la politique intérieure du pays concerné mais comprend les pays voisins où il y a la profondeur stratégique et les sources d'énergie.

3. Pourtant, l'Ethiopie représente une grande importance pour les Etats-Unis. Elle posséde les sources du nil bleu qui alimente 80% des besoins en eau de l'Egypte. L'Ethiopie devient de la sorte une carte gagnante dans la main des Etats-Unis avec laquelle ils fait pression sur l'Egypte et la cernant du Sud. A noter que les Etats-Unis avaient fait en 1956 des études pour l'édification de barrages sur les affluents du Nil bleu et sur le lac Tana. Ce fut à la suite de la transaction tchèque d'armes à l'Egypte. Il semble que cette action était dirigée contre le régime Nasser qui commencait alors à se tourner vers le bloc de l'Est. Israël entreprend, depuis des années, la mise en oeuvre de quelques-une de ces études afin de s'étendre dans les projets agricoles et les projets concernant l'énergie. Cela influe évidemment sur la quote-part de l'Egypte dans les eaux du Nil.[48]

4. L'Ethiopie représente également une région convenable pour l'intervention au sud du Soudan. Or, le sud du Soudan est considéré comme un maillon important dans la ceinture de séparation créée par le colonialisme britannique et français et qui a commencé à partir du sud de la Mauritanie à l'ouest jusqu'au sud du Soudan à l'est. Le colonialisme a exploité à cet effet plusieurs facteurs dont les plus importants sont l'existence du Grand Sahara Africain comme obstacle nuturel entre les deux parties de l'Afrique et la différence entre les races sur les deux côtés. La politique coloniale veillait toujours à créer et à confirmer les frictions dans ces régions entre arabes du nord et les autres races at ethnies au sud du Sahara. Le problème du sud du Soudan est, partiellement, une conséquence directe à cette ancienne politique

coloniale et une poursuite de ses objectifs dans cette région. C'est pourquoi nous trouvons Israël et quelques pays occidentaux offrant, en entente avec le gouvernement éthiopien, des assistances militaires et financières aux soudanais du sud afin de garder ces troubles comme carte gagnante avec laquelle ils font pression sur le soudan et sur l'Egypte.

5. L'Ethiopie représente, à travers le territoire érythréen, une position stratégique importante pour Israël sur la mer rouge face au Royaume de l'Arabie Saoudite et du Yemen. Il s'agit de la seule ouverture, hormis Eilat, qui permet à Israël d'avoir une présence civile et militaire en mer rouge, tous les autres pays bordant cette mer étant des états arabes musulmans. Il devient donc important pour les Etats-Unis d'étendre tout d'abord son hégémonie sur le région de la Corne africaine ensuite d'aider à régler ses conflits intérieurs en sorte d'instaurer la sécurité dans cette région sensible. Toutefois, l'importance stratégique de lEthiopie, les bonnes relations qui l'ont toujours lié aux Etats-Unis et le poids démographiques, politiques et économique qui marque l'Ethiopie par rapport à la Somalie et à Djibouti, rendent, dans l'ensemble, nécessaire, du point de vue américain; le maintien de l'Ethiopie forte et unie dans tout règlement des conflits de la région. Partant, les fronts erythréens doivent renoncer à leur volonté d'indépendance et la Somalie doit abandonner sa réclamation de l'Ogaden. Deux impératifs suivent cet objectif:

(a) la suspension des aides financières et militaires octroyées aux fronts erythréens. Dans la conjoncture de la crise du golfe, cet objectif est devenu facile: les Etats-Unis ont complètement dominé le Royaume d'Arabie Saoudite et l'Irak a été complètement détruit. Ainsi, l'action de ces deux états arabes qui offraient de vastes assistances aux fronts érythréens a été paralysée. Quant à l'Egypte, le refuge de toujours pour les fronts de libération en Afrique, ses capacités ont été limitées dans ce domaine en entrant explicitement dans le cadre de la stratégie américaine au Moyen-Orient et en raison de son désir permanent de neutraliser l'Ethiopie qui peut exercer sur elle des pressions par l'intermédiaire de sa politique en matière d'eau. Ne reste que le Soudan et la Libye. En plus de sa conjoncture intérieure désastreuse, le Soudan a toujours besoin de négocier avec l'Ethiopie et de mettre comme condition à la suspension de son aide aux erythréens l'arrêt par l'Ethiopie d'offrir abri et assistance aux soudanais du sud. Quant à la libye, elle demeure le seul pays arabe musulman dont la conjoncture permet probablement l'octroi d'assistance aux fronts erythréens combattants.

Le fait que les Etats-Unis ne désirent pas l'indépendance de l'Erythrée ressort nettement des suggestions présentés lors des négociations qui ont eu lieu entre le Front populaire erythréen et le gouvernement éthiopien à Atlanta puis à Naïrobi. Ils ont présenté deux solutions pour mettre fin à ce conflit: une union fédérale ou confédérale avec l'Ethiopie ou un régime pluraliste en Ethiopie auquel participeraient, à pied d'égalité avec les autres ethnies, les érythréens. [49]

(b)   Changer Siad Barre est devenu peu valable pour la phase actuelle. En fait, son régime a été caractérisé par plusieurs principes ne servant pas les intérêts americains, à savoir: l'unité somalienne, le socialisme et la dictature.   Jusqu'à présent, il apparaît que la majorité des dirigeants des forces politiques agissantes aujourd'hui en Somalie - surtout les factions du nord et du centre - sont liées au gouvernement éthiopien par de solides relations.   D'autre part, l'ancienne classe de la bourgeoisie [50] - constituée de commercants et d'hommes d'affaires - qui trouve que ses intérêts commerciaux sont avec les Etats-Unis - les pays occidentaux et l'Egypte domine les fronts somaliens.   Nous avons en effet senti ce rapprochement dans les tournées effectuées par M. Omar Orta Ghaleb, le premier ministre provisoire de la Somalie dans les pays arabes alliés aux Etats-Unis en Ethiopie. [51] Les forces politiques actuelles en Somalien, ou du moins certaines d'entre elles, sont disposées à s'entendre avec les Etats-Unis d'Amérique et à conclure un accord avec l'Ethiopie sur les frontières litigieuses. Par conséquent; la solution du problème de l'Ogaden dans l'intérêt de l'Ethiopie devient une probabilité dans les prochains règlements dans la Corne africaine.

Conclusion

De l'étude de l'opposition somalien, des motifs de son apparition et du climat international qui l'a accompagnée, nous dégageons quelques réalités importantes qui déterminent la crise somalienne et la place qu'elle occupe dans le cadre des événements dans le monde:

1. La crise somalienne a pris forme en passant par trois phases:

- Elle a commencé par des réclamations régionales exprimant des objectifs tribaux limités: réclamer aux "nordistes" une équité dans la répartition du pouvoir entre eux et les "sudistes", demander à l'occident d'intensifier les aides dans la guerre de l'Ogaden, etc.
- Elle s'est transformée en un soulèvement populaire qui s'est généralisé dans le pays et qui a atteint le niveau national. Il s'agit d'un refus de la dictature et d'un ardent désir d'instaurer la démocratie.
- Après la chute de Siad Barré, l'opposition s'est achoppée à la part concernant la réalisation de la démocratie et a glissé dans une guerre civile intense dont l'objet était la concurrence pour le pouvoir. Il semble que l'intérêt que portaient les différents détachements à la démocratie pluraliste visait l'accès et non la participation au pouvoir. Cela ressort clairement de l'existence de trois gouvernements, chacun représentant une tribu donnée et dominant une partie du pays.

2. Cet achoppement au cours de la dernière phase de la lutte indique une réalité importante, à savoir l'incapacité des gouvernements somaliens qui se sont succédés d'édifier des institutions politiques, trente ans après l'indépendance, qui s'ancreraient avec le temps pour constituer l'infrastructure de la société somalienne afin de la protéger de l'écroulement à la suite des crises. Ses régimes ont continué à être axés sur l'individu unique, le leader ou le chef d'Etat. Si cette personne centrale disparaît, le régime politique s'affranche et toute la société se déchire.

3. Les différends entre les facteurs de l'opposition n'expriment pas des différences intellectuelles ou méthodologiques. En revanche, ils reflètent essentiellement la lutte pour le pouvoir politique. En dépit du consensus entre eux sur la ligne libérale à suivre, soit au plan politique ou au plan économique, la lutte sanglante et violente se poursuit autour de qui des détachements dirigent la Somalie.

4. Il est difficile d'évaluer les forces politiques agissantes en Somalie. D'une part, ces forces ne proposent aucun programme politique ou économique clair sur lequel reposerait la politique future du Pays. En dépit de ses graves aspects négatifs, le régime de Siad Barré était, par contre, fondé sur quelques principes évidents par lesquels il a gouverné le pays pendant presque vingt ans. Au plan national, Siad Barre avait

foi dans l'unité de la grande Somalie. Au niveau politique; il a adopté le système du parti unique. A l'échelle économique, il a appliqué la ligne socialiste et la nationalisation. Siad Barré n'a changé cette politique qu'au cours des dernières années lors de l'aggravation de la crise.

D'autre part, les prémices de l'application démocratique ne sont pas encore apparus chez le gouvernement actuel du Congrès de la Somalie. Pourtant, c'était ce qui le distinguait du régime de Siad Barre. Ainsi, les combats violents se poursuivent vu que le Congrès somalien vise à détruire les autres détachements et à les dominer entièrement.

5. L'opposition n'a pas présenté, jusqu'à présent, un régime national pouvant remplacer celui de Siad Barré. Par conséquent, l'équation politique suivante se présente: un régime dictatorial violent pouvant réprimer les tendances tribales graves qui penacent l'unité de l'Etat ou le pluralisme; la division et le cahos politique. Cette équation a trait au problèmes de la démocratie dans le Tiers-Monde, en particulier en Afrique où il y a des divisions sociales nombreuses et diverses.

6. Le réglement de la crise somalienne est lié au nouvel ordre international et au sysème de sécurité que planifient les Etats-Unis au Moyen-Orient. Il ne sera pas permis à cette crise de produire un régime national opposé à cette planification indépendamment de l'intérêt national somalien. C'est pourquoi l'éventualité de l'intégration de la Somalie dans la stratégie américaine de la région dans la prochaine période est possible sur la scène internationale. Il ne s'agit pas ici de la Somalie seulement mais du reste des pays de la Corne africaine.

Pour terminer, nous pouvons dire que la crise somalienne a été induite par de nombreux facteurs qui ne sont pas étrangers aux pays africains. Ces facteurs sont fondés sur la nature de la société tribale, sur la structure économique des pays en développement et sur le retard politique représenté par la mainmise du leader ou de son clan sur le pouvoir. Ajoutons à cela, l'élément de l'ingérence étrangère dans les affaires intérieures des pays africains car cette ingérence vise toujours la réalisation des intérêts des grandes puissances. Il arrive que l'intérêt étranger et celui national conviennent de la chute d'un certain régime, comme en Somalie. Mais cette communauté d'intérêts ne représente qu'une étape suivie par la lutte Nord-Sud: de la part des grandes puissances, il s'agit d'obtenir de plus grands gains et de la part des pays, il s'agit d'une lutte pour la survie.

Références

1. Front démocratique de salut somalien: Somali Salvation Democaric Front (S.S.D.F.).
2. Fathi Hassan Atoua "Les récents troubles en Somalie et l'avenir de la stabilité politique", Politique Internationale, Numéro 98, Le Caire, Al Ahram, octobre 1989, pp. 158-161, 169.
3. Helmi Chaaraoui "Somalie..vers où? Tribalisme ou nationalisme?...recherche non publiée, 1991, p. 12.
4. Mouvement national somalien: Somali National Movement (SVM)
5. Entretien personnel avec M. Mohamad Ali Serar; le conseiller à l'ambassade de la Somalie au Caire, le 24/4/1991.
6. Helmi Chaarawoui, op.cit., p. 12.
7. Fathi Hassan Atoua, op. cit. p. 159.
8. Mouvement patriotique somalien: Somali Patriotic Movement (SPM).
9. Helmi Chaarawoui, op.cit., p. 12.
10. Journal Al Chark Al Awsat, numéro paru le 29/1/1991.
11. Fathi Hassan Atoua, op. cit. p. 159.
12. Front de la Somalie unifiée: United Somali Front (USF).
13. Journal Al Hyatt, numéro paru le 5/3/1991.
14. Congrès de la Somalie unifiée: United Somali Congress (USC).
15. Helmi Chaarawoui, op.cit., p. 12.
16. Journal Al Hyatt, numéro paru le 3/3/1991.
17. Journal Al Chark Al Awsat, numéro paru le 31/1/1991.
18. Journal Al Hyatt, numéro paru le 29 et le 31 /1/1991.
19. H. Chaarawoui, op.cit., p. 13.
20. H. Chaarawoui, op.cit., p. 13.
21. Journal Al Hyatt, numéro paru le10/11/90 et 29/1/91.
22. Somali National Front (SNF).
23. Entretien personnel avec M. M. A. Sarar, Conseiller, ambassade de la Somalie au Caire, 24/4/91. Journal Al Chark Al Awsat, 29/3/1991.
24. S.N.F. rapport sur la Somalie ... à qui veut savoir, 91, pp. 3-4.
25. Ibid, p.7.
26. Journal Al Hyatt, numéro du 20/3/91.
27. Le Monde, Paris: 27/2/91.
28. Journal Al Hyatt, numéro du 29/1/91.
29. Journal Al Chark Al Awsat, numéro du 4/2/1991.
30. Journal Al Ahram, No. du 20/11/90.
31. Le Front national somalien et le Mouvement national somalien conviennent avec d'autres factions sur plusieurs conditions à la

tenue de cette Conférence: Cessez-le feu dans la capitale Mogadiscio et en dehors; Tenue de la conférence générale en dehors de la Somalie en raison de l'absence de la sécurité dans la capitale; le parti du Congrès de la Somalie unifiée assiste à la conférence en tant que faction en tant que gouvernement. Le Congrès de la Somalie unifiée n'accepte évidemment pas ces conditions.

32. Journal Al Hyatt, No. du 16/3/91.
33. Les informations sur la présidence de Siad Barre du gouvernement Darods sont contradictoires. Il y a ceux qui l'affirment tandis que les renseignements donnés par le Front National somalien nient toute coopération avec Siad Barre et assure son opposition à l'ancien chef d'Etat de la Somalie en raison de ses graves insuffisances.
34. La race caucasienne vit à l'ouest de l'Asie, et constitue la plupart des habitants du continent européen, et de lapartie nord et nord-est de l'Afrique.
35. N.F.D. = Northern Frontier District.
36. Philippe Decraene, L'Expérience socialiste somalienne, Paris, Berger-Leurault, 1977, p. 20.
37. Voir les cartes tribales de la Somalie dans les annexes de la recherche.
38. I.M. Lewis, A modern history of Somalia, London and New York. Longman, 1980. pp. 6-9.
39. I.M. Lewis, "The Ogaden and the fragility of Somali Nationalism", Madrid: international conference on the conflict in the Horn of Africa, 1989. pp. 11-12, cité dans Ahmed Samatar, "Internal struggles in Somalia, London, Cairo: International Institute of Strategic Studies, Centre for political research and studies, 1990, p. 9.
40. Ibid, p. 11.
41. Helmi Chaarawi, réf. précité, p. 11.
42. Journal Al Ahram, du 20/11/90.
43. Ahmed Samatar, op.cit. pp. 13-17.
44. Helmi Chaarawi, réf. précité, p. 11.
45. Ahmed Samatar, op.cit. pp. 13-17.
46. Bulletins publiés par l'Organisation arabe pour les droits de l'Homme, Le Caire, 1990 et 1991.
47. Les deux autres Etats sont la Turquie et l'Iran.
48. Dr. Abdel Azim Anis, "L'eau ... et la politique", la crise de l'eau du Nil, Le Caire: Centre de recherches arabes, pp. 114-117, p. 116.

49. Tarek Hassan Abou Senna, "Les récents évolutions dans la Corne africaine", Politique Internationale, le numéro centenaire, avril, Le Caire, Al Ahram, 1990, pp. 220-226.
50. Le Chef d'Etat somalien actuel est un homme d'affaires connu.
51. L'actuel premier ministre M. Omar Orta Ghaleb annoncé que le gouvernement actuel oeuvre pour instaurer de bonnes relations avec tous les pays, surtour les pays voisins, l'Ethiopie, le Kenya, Djibouti. Voir le journal Al Hyatt du 27/3/91.

List of Participants

ALGERIA

1. Nacer Bourenane
    4Ai Mohamadia B7 No. 137
    16130 E.H.
    Algiers, Algeria

BOTSWANA

2. Mike Mothobi
    SAPES TRUST
    P. O. Box 401
    Gaborone, Botswana

3. Mogopodi H. Lekorwe
    University of Botswana
    P/Bag 0022
    Gaborone, Botswana

4. Molomo Mpho
    University of Botswana
    P/Bag 0022
    Gaborone, Botswana

5. Balefi Tsie
    P/Bag 0022
    Gaborone, Botswana

6. Bojosi Otlhogile
    University of Botswana
    P/Bag 0022
    Gaborone, Botswana

7. Jonathan M. Kaunda
    University of Botswana
    Dept. of Pol. & Admin. Studies
    P/Bag 0022
    Gaborone, Botswana

8. Mogopodi Lekorwe
    University of Botswana
    P/Bag 0022
    Gaborone, Botswana

DENMARK

9. Dani Nabudere
    P.O. Box MP 201, Mount
    Pleasant, Zimbabwe

EGYPT

10. Eglal Raafat
    Centre for Political Science
    5, rue Kambiz
    Doki, Quizeh, Egypt

11. Helmi Sharawy
    9 Al Muntasir Street
    Agouza - CAIRO,Egypt

12. Fawzy Mansour
    29 Rifaa Street
    Dokki, CAIRO 12311,Egypt

ETHIOPIA

13. Berhanu Dinka
    Finance Section, E.C.A.
    P. O. Box 3005
    Addis Ababa, Ethiopia

FRANCE

14. Amadou Tankoano
    15, Rue du Chateau
    Boite 16
    06300 - Nice, France

GHANA

15. Kwame Ninsin
    Dept. of Pol. Science
    University of Ghana
    P. O. Box 64
    Legon, Ghana

16. Amos Anyimadu
    Dept. of Political Science
    University of Ghana
    Legon, Ghana

KENYA

17. Olewe Nyunya
    University of Nairobi
    P. O. Box 30197
    Nairobi, Kenya

18. Bishop Henry Okullu
    Diocese of Maseno South
    P. O. Box 380 or 114
    Kisumu, Kenya

19. P. Anyang' Nyong'o
    African Association of Political
    Science
    P. O. Box 14798
    Nairobi, Kenya

LESOTHO

20. Khabele Matlosa
    Nul, ISAS Roma 180
    Lesotho

21. Motsama Mochebelele
    P O Roma 180
    National University of Lesotho
    Lesotho

22. Frank Baffoe
    P. O. Box 7590
    Maseru 100, Lesotho

MOZAMBIQUE

23. Vieira Sergio
    Centro de Estudos Africanos
    Universidad Eduardo Mondlane
    Maputo, Mozambique

24. Lutucuta Paula
    Institute Supercion de
    Relacaes Internaciomais
    Julius Nyerere Avenue
    1109 Maputo, Mozambique

25. Miguel De Brito-ISRI
    1109 Julius Nyerere Avenue
    Maputo, Mozambique

26. Eugenio Macamo
    Faculty of Economics
    Eduardo Mondlane University
    P. O. Box 257, Maputo
    Mozambique

27. Bethuel Setai
    P. O. Box 783
    Maputo, Mozambique

28. Agostinho Zacarias
    Director, Institute of Interna-
    tional Relations
    Maputo, Mozambique

NAMIBIA

29. William A. Lindeke
    Dept. of Political Studies
    University of Namibia
    Private Bag 13301
    Windhoek, Namibia 9000

30. Sackey Schikwambi
    Ministry of Foreign Affairs
    P/Bag 13347
    Windhoek, Namibia

31. Benzo Marenga
    University of Namibia
    P/Bag 13301
    Windhoek 9000, Namibia

32. Uatirouje M. Katjirua
    P/Bag 13301
    University of Namibia
    Windhoek 9000, Namibia

33. Gibbs Mumbula
    P/Bag 13237
    Windhoek 9000, Namibia

34. S. Mapenzi
     Ministry of Foreign Affairs
     P/Bag 13347
     Windhoek, Namibia

35. Winnie Wanzala
     P/Bag 13301
     Windhoek 9000, Namibia

36. Charles Muliokela
     Fof 8495
     Katutura, Windhoek

37. Alistair Tjahere
     Posbus 48
     Windhoek, Namibia

38. Sandra Williams
     Box 10905
     Windhoek, Namibia

39. Israel T. Shikongo
     University of Namibia
     P/Bag 13301
     Windhoek, Namibia

40. John Kodisang
     P. O. Box 23687
     Windhoek 9000, Namibia

41. Eslon Karirue Siririka
     P. O. Box 60815
     Katutura, Namibia 9000

42. Maureen M. Hinda
     Box 3839
     Windhoek, Namibia

43. Gerhard Totemeyer
     University of Namibia
     P/Bag 13301
     Windhoek, Namibia

44. Fred Koita
     University of Namibia
     P/Bag 13301
     Windhoek, Namibia

45. Freddy Lawrence
     P. O. Box 10823
     Khomasdal
     Namibia

46. Mam Biram Joof
     UNESCO
     Sanlam Centre
     Windhoek, Namibia

47. Ion Porojan
     Embassy of Romania
     3 Hamerkop Street
     Windhoek, Namibia

48. Beata Magano Muteka
     P. O. Box 22013
     Windhoek
     Rep. of Namibia 9000

49. Paul Kalenga
     P. O. Box 22013
     Windhoek, Namibia

50. Fanuel Tjingaete
     CDM
     Box 1906
     Windhoek, Namibia

51. A.Z. Shipanga
     P. O. Box 21579
     Windhoek, Namibia

52. Arnold M. Mtopa
     Commonwealth Secretariat
     Box 13345
     Windhoek, Namibia

53. Fanuel Tjingaete
     CDM
     Box 1906
     Windhoek, Namibia

54. A.Z. Shipanga
     P. O. Box 21579
     Windhoek, Namibia

55. Arnold M. Mtopa
     Commonwealth Secretariat
     Box 13345
     Windhoek, Namibia

56. Vuyani Singondo
     P/Bag 13301
     Academy
     Windhoek, Namibia

57. Marenga Skue G.
Box 751
Windhoek 9000, Namibia

58. Romeo Pedlo
P. O. Box 3330, Rehoboth
Namibia, 90, Namibia

59. Siona Luipert
P. O. Box 7005
Windhoek 9000, Namibia

60. Nicholas Zaranyika
P/Bag 13301
Academy Windhoek
Namibia

61. Paska Patrick Mofokeng
Academy
P/Bag 13301
Windhoek, Namibia

62. Isack Zenaune Kavari
Box 60586
Katutura, Namibia

63. Andrew Mothiba
University of Namibia
P/Bag 13301
Windhoek, Namibia

64. Ben Karamata Rikondja
Ministry of Foreign Affairs
Windhoek, Namibia

65. Andries S. Aspara
P. O. Box 7273
P. O. Katutura
Namibia

66. Rowena Moutloatse
P/Bag 13238
Windhoek 9000, Namibia

67. E.G. Kaiyamo
MFA, OAU-Desk
Box 7022
Windhoek, Rep. of Namibia

68. Simon Moeketsi
P. O. Box 21900
Windhoek, Namibia

69. Kenneth Abrahams
P. O. Box 21075
Windhoek, Namibia

70. Pius Dunaiski
Director of Information
Ministry of Foreign Affairs
Namibia

71. Mnci Vuyani
R 326
Academy of University of
Namibia
Windhoek, Namibia

72. Kavari Vijura
Eof 1334
Sunridge, Windhoek
Namibia

73. Roberty N. Mapenzi
University of Namibia
P/Bag 13301
Windhoek, Namibia

74. Kaomo-Vijanda Tjombe
Namibia Today
P. O. Box 24669
Windhoek, Namibia

75. Nama Goabab
Namibia Economic Policy
Research Unit
P. O. Box 40219
Ausspanplatz
Windhoek, Namibia

76. Tor Sellstron
NEPRU, P. O. Box 40219
Auspannplatz - Windhoek
Namibia

77. Bryan-Bethuel N. Katjimune
P. O. Box 22381
Windhoek, Namibia

78. Kahh Bantu Uariua
P. O. Box 20067
Windhoek, Namibia

79. Kasungo Elvis Masule
University of Namibia
P/Bag 13301
Windhoek, Namibia

80. George Simataa
P. O. Box 2231
Windhoek 9000, Namibia

81. Immanuel Iyambo
P/Bag 13301
Windhoek, Namibia

82. Dorothy Fransman
P. O. Box 22463
Windhoek, Namibia

83. Nambata Ulenga
P. O. Box 1566
Windhoek 9000, Namibia

84. Y. O. Obanewo
Nigeria High Commission
4 Omurnmba Road
Windhoek 9000, Namibia

85. Daluxolo Mrwata
P/Bag 13301
Windhoek, Namibia

86. Claudius Hengari-Kandjou
P. O. Box 21230
Windhoek, Namibia

87. H. L. Ndimwedi
P. O. Box 7320
P/Bag 13301
Windhoek 900, Namibia

88. Aina E. Iiyambo
Ministry of Foreign Affairs
P/Bag 13347
Windhoek, Namibia

89. Harryson-Gerson Kapanda
P. O. Box 751
Windhoek, Namibia

90. Suneline Dreyer
Box 1237
Windhoek, Namibia

91. Philip Lilungwe
P/Bag 13237
Windhoek, Namibia

92. George Eiseb
N.I.S.E.R.
P/Bag 13301
Windhoek 9000, Namibia

93. Sello Moeketsi
Dept. of Economics
University of Namibia
P/Bag 13301
Windhoek, Namibia

94. Saul T. Kahuika
P/Bag 2032
Okahandja, Namibia

NIGERIA

95. Adele Jinadu
Dept. of Political Science
Lagos State University
P.M.B. 1078, Apapa, Badagry
Expressway,
LAGOS, Nigeria

SENEGAL

96. Bernard Founou Tchiogua
Third World Forum
B.P. 3301
DAKAR, Senegal

97. A. Bathily
Dept. of History
University Cheikh
Anta Diop
DAKAR, Senegal

98. Samir Amin
Third World Forum
DAKAR, Senegal

99. Thandika Mkandawire
Executive Secretary
CODESRIA
B.P. 3304
DAKAR, Senegal

SOUTH AFRICA

100. James Adera Ogude
      African Literature Dept.
      University of Witswatersrand
      P. O. Box 2050
      Wits, Johannesburg
      South Africa

101. Ben Turok
      Institute for African Alterna-
      tives
      41 De Korte St. Braamfontain
      2001
      Johannesburg, South Africa

102. Frank R. Molobi
      P. O. Box 242
      Noordwyk, Midrand 1685
      South Africa

103. Hendrik J. Kotze
      Dept. of Political Science
      University of Stellenbosch
      7600 Stellenbosch
      South Africa

104. Adv. E. Dikeane Moseneke
      Pan Africanist Congress
      1008 Momentum Centre
      343 Pretonous Str.
      PRETORIA, South Africa

105. Moeletsi Mbeki
      Box 1019
      Johannesburg 2000
      South Africa

106. Nefolovhodwe Pandelani
      Box 81, Roodeport
      South Africa 1725

107. Mojanku Gumbi
      P. O. Box 5217
      Johannesburg 2000
      South Africa

108. Yvonne Chengwe
      Private Bag 5501
      Oshakati 9000
      South Africa

SWAZILAND

109. B.A.B. Sikhondze
      Umsera, P/Bag Kwaluseni
      Swaziland

110. Bongani Nsibande
      University of Swaziland
      P/Bag No. 4
      Kwaluseni, Swaziland

111. Nomthetho Simelane
      University of Swazilane
      P/Bag, Kwaluseni
      Swaziland

112. Bonginkosi Sikhondye
      University of Swaziland
      P/Bag Kwaluseni
      Swaziland

TANZANIA

113. Haroub Othman
      Institute of Development
      Studies
      University of Dar-es-Salaam
      P. O. Box 35169
      Dar-es-Salaam, Tanzania

U.K.

114. Abdulrahman Mohammed Babu
      257 Mt. Pleasant Road
      London No. 17 6 HD
      U.K.

U.S.A.

115. Nzongola Ntalaja
      Howard University
      College of Liberal Arts
      Department of African Studies
      Washington, D.C. 20059
      U.S.A.

ZAMBIA

116. Gilbert Mudenda
      University of Zambia
      Box 30752
      LUSAKA, Zambia

117.   Donald Chanda
        ADS Department
        University of Zambia
        P. O. Box 32379
        LUSAKA, Zambia

118.   Bertha Z. Osei-Hwedie
        PAS Department
        University of Zambia
        P. O. Box 32379
        Lusaka, Zambia

ZIMBABWE

119.   Ibbo Mandaza
        SAPES TRUST
        P. O. Box MP 111
        Mount Pleasant
        4 Dreary Avenue
        Harare, Zimbabwe

120.   Allast Mwanza
        SAPES TRUST
        P. O. Box MP 111
        Harare, Zimbabwe

121.   Grace T. Mutandwa
        33 Richwell Gardens
        St. Andrews Park
        Harare, Zimbabwe

122.   Mosibudi Mangena
        Box 4017
        Harare, Zimbabwe

123.   Tania Dos Remedios
        P. O. Box 771
        14 Guest Avenue
        Harare, Zimbabwe

124.   Lloyd Sachikonye
        Zimbabwe Institute
        of Dev. Studies
        Box 880
        Harare, Zimbabwe

125.   J. Makumbe
        University of Zimbabwe
        Box MP 167
        Mount Pleasant
        Harare, Zimbabwe

126.   Mapopa Chipeta
        SAPES TRUST
        Box MP 111
        Harare, Zimbabwe

127.   Patrick Tigere
        2095-6th Road
        Glen View 1-Harare
        Zimbabwe

128.   Donald P. Chimanikire
        Zimbabwe Institute of Dev.
        Studies
        P. O. Box 880
        Harare, Zimbabwe

129.   L. Kazembe
        SAPES TRUST
        P. O. Box MP 111
        Mount Pleasant
        4 Dreary Avenue
        Harare, Zimbabwe

Bibliographical References

Abdel W. O. Cheikh : Nomadisme et capitalisme peripherique en Mauritanie

Abott, G. C. 1984. "Debt and the Poorest Developing Countries" Development Policy Review 2.2

Adebayo Adedeji. 1990. "The African Challenges in the 1990's" in *The Indian Journal of Social Science*, Vol. 3, no. 2, Sage Publication.

Adrian, Hastings. 1979. A History of African Christianity, Cambridge University Press, pp.187

Africa Recovery. 1988. June: 23

African Centre for Monetary Studies, 1980. Monetary Theory and Policy in Africa Symposium.

African Press Service. 1981. 25 May.

Ait Amara, Hamid A : Le developpement autocentre et les relations agricultur-industrie. Cas de l'Algerie.

Ali Traore : Bilan et perspectives des developpements agricole et industriel de la Côte d'Ivoire et de leurs rapports mutuels.

Amin, G. A. 1980. The Modernization of Poverty [A Study in the Political Economy of Growth in Nine Arab Countries] Leiden: E.J. Brill

Amin, S.1960.*The Stages of Economic Growth*, Cambridge.

——1987. 'Preface: The State and the Question of "Development" 'in: P. A. Nyong'o ed. *Popular Struggles for Democracy in Africa* London/New Jersey: Zed Books

—— 1989. Preface les rapports entre la revolution agricole et l'industrialisation dans le developpement africain". Version anglaise : Agriculture : critical choices,Zed Books.

—— 1990. 'The Agricultural Revolution and Industrialization' in: H.
—— A. Amara and B. Founou-Tchuigoua eds African Agriculture: The Critical Choices London/New Jersey: Zed Books. *Class and Nation*, New York: Monthly Review Press, New York.

Anis, Dr. Abdel Azim , "L'eau ... et la politique", la crise de l'eau du Nil, Le Cairemm: Centre de recherches arabes, pp. 114-117, p. 116.

Baba Ba, Pape Sow, Sidi Kane : l'Etat et le developpement rural du Senegal 1960-1985.

Bagchi, E. 1982. The Political Economy of Underdevelopment
Cambridge University Press

Balton, D. 1985. Nationalization - A Road to Socialism? The Lessons
of Tanzania London: Zed Press

Banque Mondiale. 1988. Afrique subsaharienne de la crise a la
criossance stable.

Baran, P. 1957. The Political Economy of Growth Monthly Review
Press.

Bedrani. 1987. : L'agriculture algerienne depuis 1966, Office de
Publication Universitaire, Alger.

Benachenhou, Abdelatiff. 1982. : Plantification et developpement en
Algerie 1962-1980. Office de Publication unverisitaire Alger.

Bhatt, V. V. 1974. 'The Sterility of Equilibrium Economics: An
Aspect of the Sociology of Science' in: A Mitra ed. Economic
Theory and Planning Bombay: Oxford University Press

Bible, The. Book of Amos, Chapter 3 verse 8.

Bicanic, R. 1972. Turning Points in Economic Development The
Hague: Mouton.

Boahen,A. Adu. 1985. "Colonialism in Africa: Its Impact and Significance," in A. Adu Boahen, *Africa Under Colonial Domination:
General History of Africa,* Vol VII Heieneman and Unesco, 1985.

Bonhoeffer, Dietrich , Letters and Papers, as above, p. 382

Bourenane,N. "The impact of bi-lateral and multi-lateral aid on African
Agriculture" (Ed. CODESRIA).

—— 1984.A Socio-economic analysis of hunger and food self-sufficiency
in Africa", CODESRIA / UNESCO.

—— 1985."The instruments of economic measure: inappropriate tools in
measuring the crisis" in *Revue Politique Aujourd'hui,*Paris.

—— 1988. "The Food Crisis in Africa", ACARSTOOD ECA, 1988,

—— 1988. N"The State and the Promotion of Entrepreneurs in Africa",
AAS.

Brandt et.al., 1986. States and African Agriculture in: *IDS (Sussex)
Bulletin* 17(1).

Brandt, H. et. al. 1985. Structural Distortions and Adjustment
Programmes in the Poor countries of Africa Berlin: German
Development Institute

Bruton, H. J. 1983. "Egypt's Development in the Seventies" Economic Development and Cultural Change 31.4

Chaaraoui, Helmi. 1991. "Somalie..vers où? Tribalisme ou
nationalisme?...recherche non publiée, p. 12.

Charbel Zarour et Bernard Founou Tchuigoua. 1988. in Samir Amin,

La coopération arabo-africaine pour quelle insertion dans l'economie mondiale? Nᵒ. Special *Africa Development* vol. No. 2-3.

Cheikh, Abdel W. O. : Nomadisme et capitalisme peripherique en Mquritanie, in Ait Amit et Founou-Tchuigoua.

Cheru, F. 1989. *The Silent Revolution in Africa* London: Zed Books

Cole, K. 1984. "Review" F. Perroux A New Concept of Development. *Journal of Development Studies* 20.3

Coleman, J. S. 1977. 'The Concept of Political Penetration' in: L. Cliffe et.al. eds *Government and Rural Development in Africa* The Hague: Martinus Nijhoff

Cooper, R. N. and E. M. Truman. 1977. "An Analysis of the Role of International Capital Markets in *Providing Funds to Developing Countries* Center Paper no.70, Yale University

Cowen, M. 1977. "Some Problems of Capital and Class in Kenya" Occasional Paper no.26, Nairobi: IDS

Daily Nation.1981. Nairobi, 22 January.

Davis, R.H. "Agriculture, Food and the Colonial Period" Art Hansen and Della McMillan(ed.)

Decraene, Philippe , L'Expérience socialiste somalienne, Paris, Berger-38.

Desta, A. 1988. "Africa's External Debt and Perspective" *Journal of African Studies* 15.1 - 2

dos Santos, President Jose Eduardo , Speech of 25 October, 1990, published in the *Southern Africa Political and Economic Monthly (SAPEM)*, Vol.4, No.2, November, 1990.

ECA. 1983. ECA and Africa's Development 1983 - 2000: A Preliminary Perspective Study. Addis Ababa

—— 1989. Statistics and Policies Preliminary Observations on the World Bank Report 'Africa's Adjustment and Growth in the 1980s' Addis Ababa

Fanon, F. 1965. *The Wretched of the Earth.* London: Macgibbon & Kee

Fathi Hassan Atoua "Les récents troubles en Somalie et l'avenir de la stabilité politique", Politique Internationale, Numéro 98, Le Caire, Al Ahram, octobre 1989, pp. 158-161, 169.

Faudez, J. and S. Picciotto eds. 1978. The Nationalization of Multinational Firms in *Peripheral Economies.* London and Basingstoke: Macmillan Press

Fitzpatrick, Jim "Trade in the Lome Convention" in *Lome Briefings* No. 9 of 1983.

Founou-Tchuigoua, Bernard. 1989. : Lecons de l'echec des tentatives

de maitrise agricole sans deconnexion : Algerie, Tanzanie, in Ait
Amara et Founou-Tchuigoua *L'agriculture africaine en crise, dans
ses rapports avec l'Etat, l'industrialisation et la paysannerie,*
l'Hamattan.

——1981. *Fondements de l'économie de traite au Senegal,* Paris Silex.

—— Crise de l'ideologie collective de l'autosuffisance alimentaire.
Lecons de l'echec des tentatives de maitrise agricole sans
deconnexion : Algerie et Tanzanie

Friedrickse, Julie . 1991. *The Unbreakable Thread: Non-Racialism in
South Africa,* Ravan Press, 1990. Reviewed by Patrick Laurence,
"No, the Nats Did Not 'Live With' Black Consciousness", *The
Star,* Johannesburg, 30 January.

Furtado, C. 1965. "Political Obstacles to Economic Growth in Brazil"
International Affairs 41.2

——1978. "Accumulation and Creavity" CEPAL Review Second
Half

Gakou Lamine. 1984. : La crise de l'agriculture africaine, Paris Silex.

Gulhati R. and Sekkar. 1981. "Industrial Strategy for Late Starters:
The Experience of Kenya, Tanzania and Zambia,"Washington
D.C.: World bank staff working paper No. 457.

Hamid Ait Amara et Bernard Founou-Tchuigoua. 1989.
L'agriculture africaine en crise, dans ses rapports avec l'Etat,
l'industrialisation et la paysannerie, l'Hamattan.

Helleiner, G. K. 1989. "Lessons for Sub-Saharan Africa from Latin
American Experience?" *African Development Review* 1.1

Mapolu , Henry : Imperialsime, Etat et paysannerie en Tanzanie

Hewitt, Adrian. 1983. : "Stabex: Time to Overhaul the Mechanics":
Lome Briefings, No.6.

Hill, Tony. 1985. *The Courier,* No. 89, Jan-Feb., p.5.

Hoffman, Stanley. 1981. *Duties Beyond Borders,* Syracuse University
Press, Syracuse, pp.22/28.

Hugon, Philippe. 1988. "What economic future for Africa?" in
Afrique Contemporaine, no 146, Paris.

Hymer, S. H. 1970. "Capital and Capitalists" Centre Paper no. 148,
Yale University.

Hyne, Jeff. 1990. "Africa in the international system: problems and
prospects" (review article) in *Africa: Journal of the international
African Institute* 60(3). London.

International Herald Tribune. 1990. 24 April.

John V, Christianity and Politics in Africa

Jos van Genning and Pieter Meine van Dijk. 1983. "Food Strategies,

NGOs and Lome III," *Lome Briefings*, No. 20.

Journal Al Ahram, No. du 20/11/90.

Journal Al Chark Al Awsat, numéro du 29/1/1991, 31/1/1991, 4/2/ 1991, et 29/3/91.

Journal Al Hyatt, numéro du 10/11/90, 29 et 31/1/1991, 3, 5, 16 et 20/3/91.

Kalecki, M. 1966. "Observation on Social and Economic Aspects of 'Intermediate Regimes'" Coexistance 4.

Kaunda, Kenneth D. , *A Humanist in Africa*, p.100

Kennedy, P. 1977. "African Businessmen and Foreign Capital: Collaboration or Conflict?" *African Affairs* 76.30

Kenya Sessional Paper No. 10. p.41

Keynes, J. M. 1965. The General Theory of Employment, Interest and Money New York, Harcourt: Bruce and World Inc. First Harbinger Edition.

Killick, S. 1987. "No Simple Solutions for Africa's Problems" Development and Cooperation no.5

Killick, T. 1983. "Development Planning in Africa: Experiences, Weaknesses and Prescriptions" *Development Policy Review* 1.1

Kossura , W. Oluoch : Relations entre l'agriculture et l'industrialisation au Kenya.

Lapido , Rigobert Oladiran : Cultures industrielles et d'exportation au Nigeria et en Cote d'Ivoire depuis 1960

Le Monde, Paris: 27/2/91.

Lele, U. 1975. *The Design of Rural Development: Lessons From Africa* Baltimore: Johns Hopkins University Press.

Lenin, V.I. , "Bourgeoisie and Proletarian Democracy" in *On Soviet Socialist Democracy*, Progress Publishers, 1980, p.61.

Leonard, H. Jefrey . 1989. Environment and the Poor Development Strategies for a Common Agenda. Overseas Development, No. 11, p. 14.

Lessa, C. 1979. "Economic Policy: Science or Ideology" CEPAL Review no. 7 April.

Lettre de Solagrale: Supplement No. 32 Mars-Avril 1990.

Lewis, I.M. , A modern history of Somalia, London and New York. Longman, 1980. pp. 6-9.

___1989. "The Ogaden and the fragility of Somali Nationalism", Madrid: international conference on the conflict in the Horn of Africa, pp. 11-12, cité dans Ahmed Samatar, *Internal struggles in Somalia*, London, Cairo: International Institute of Strategic Studies, Centre for political research and studies, 1990, p. 9.

Maer, Karl. 1990. "Outmanoeuvring RENAMO: The Motives Behind Mozambique's New Constitution" the *Southern Africa Political Monthly (SAPEM)*, Vol. 4, No. 5, February.

Mahjoub, A. ed. 1990. Adjustment or Delinking?: The African Experience London/New Jersey: Zed Books.

Mahmud B. Romdhane : l'Etat, la paysannerie et la dependance alimentaire en Tunisie

Mahmud Ben Romdhane. 1989. l'Etat, la paysannerie et la dependance alimentaire en Tunisie, in ait Amara et Founou-Tchuigoua *L'agriculture africaine en crise, dans ses rapports avec l'Etat, l'industrialisation et la paysannerie,* l'Hamattan.

Mandaza, Ibbo. 1988. "Introduction: The Political Economy of Transition" in Ibbo Mandaza (ed.), *Zimbabwe: The Political Economy of Transition, 1980-1986,* CODESRIA.

—— 1990."Election Results a Barometer to Assess First Decade of Independence and Consider Future Prospects," *The Financial Gazette,* 12 April.

Mapolu , Henry. 1989. Imperialisme, Etat et paysannerie en Tanzanie, in H. Ait Amara and B. Founou-Tchuigoua, *L'agriculture africaine en crise, dans ses rapports avec l'Etat, l'industrialisation et la paysannerie,* l'Hamattan.

Marches Tropicaux et Mediterraneens. 1988. No. 1893, 19 fevrier 1982 et No. 2217, 6 mai.

Martin, Guy. 1984. "African-European Economic Relations under the Lome Conventions: Commodities and the Scheme of Stabilisation of Export Earnings in *African Studies Review* No. 3, Sept. p.49.

Mazrui , A. and M. Tidy. 1984. *Nationalism and New States in Africa,* Heinemann, p.285

McQueen, Mathew. 1983. "Lome : Rules of Origin, The Need for Reform," in *Lome Briefings* No.10.

Meyer, Klaus : *The Courier* No.61, May-June 1980, p.11.

Michelena, J. A. S. 1971. "State Formation and National Building in Latin America" International Social Science Journal XXIII.3

Mulokozi, E.A.. 1983. "ACP-EEC Cooperation: What Future": *Lome Briefings* No.7.

Nabudere, D.W. 1973. : "The Arusha Agreement Between the EEC and East Africa." - *East African Law Review,* Vol. 6 No.2 December.

——1978. The Lome Convention and the Consolidation of Neo-colonalism" in: *Essays on the Theory and Practice of Imperialism,* Onyx Press.

Ndiaye, B. 1989. "Foreword" *African Development Review* 1.1

Ngindu Mushete, in Christianity in Independent Africa, as above, p.238

Nyerere, J. *Uhuru Na Moja: Freedom and Unity,* Oxford University Press, 1967.

——1968. *Ujamaa: Essays on Socialism,* OUP.

OAU. 1986. "Africa's Submission to the Special Session of the UN General Assembly on Africa's Economic and Social Crisis" 15th Extra-Ordinary Session of the OAU Council of Ministers, Addis Ababa: OAU/ECM/2XV/Rev 2

OECD, 1980. Development Cooperation, 1980 Review Paris

Perroux, F. 1983. A New Concept of Development London/Paris: Croom Helm/UNESCO

Pickett, J. 1989. "Reflections on the Market and the State in Sub-Saharan Africa" *African Development Review* 1.1

Pinches, C. R. 1978. "Economic Development: The Need for an Alternative" Economic Development and Cultural Change 26.1

Prewitt, K. 1972. "The Functional Justification of Inequality and the Ndegwa Report: Shaping an Ideology", paper presented at EASSC, Nairobi

Richards, L. 1977. "The Context of Foreign Aid: Modern Imperialism" Review of Radical Political Economy 9.4

Rigobert Oladiran Lapido. 1960. : Cultures industrielles et d'exportation au Nigeria et en Côte d'Ivoire depuis.

Rodney, W. 1976. *How Europe Underdeveloped Africa* Dar es Salaam and London: Tanzania Publishing House and Boy Le L'Overture Publications

Rostow, W.W. 1960.*The Stages of Economic Growth,* New York.

Sachikonye, Lloyd M. 1990."Worker Mobilisation Since Independence", *Southern Africa Political and Economic Monthly (SAPEM),* Vol.3, No.7, April.

Sender, J. and S. Smith. 1986. *The Development of Capitalism in Africa* London and New York: Methuen

Senna, Tarek Hassan Abou. 1990."Les récents évolutions dans la Corne africaine", Politique Internationale, le numéro centenaire, avril, Le Caire, Al Ahram, pp. 220-226.

Shaaeldin, E. 1989. "Book Review" G.M. Meier and W. Steel eds *Industrial Adjustment in Sub-Saharan Africa* New York: Oxford University Press.

Shah, A.A. 1964. "Socio-Economic Structure and Economic Development: An Essay on Theory and History" Enquiry 1.1

Shivji, I. G. 1990. 'Tanzania: The Debate in Delinking' in: Mahjoub Adjustment or Delinking. *The African Experience London*. New Jersey: Zed Books.

Sibanda, Arnold. 1990. "The Economy Since Independence", *The Southern Africa Political and Economic Monthly (SAPEM)*, Vol.3, No.7, April.

Slovo, J. , 1990. *Has Socialism Failed?*, Inkululeko Publications, London, p.8.

——1969. "On the Non-Capitalist Road to Socialism", *Marxism Today*.

Tanguy, Jean : "Pisani: A Grass-Root Convention,": *Lome Briefings* No. 5, 1983.

Thandika Mkandawire, "De-industrialisation in Africa, Africa development.

——1989. "Political Independence and Agrarian Transformation in Africa", CODESRIA (Mimeo).

The Courier. 1975. No.31 of March-April, pp. 2,13, 25.

—— 1983. Dossier No.70, p.73.

—— 1984. No. 83 of Jan-Feb, p.vii

—— 1985. No.85 May-June,p.12.

—— 1989. no.113– January-February,p.11

—— 1990. No.120, March-April, p.27.

Togba-Nah Tipoteh: "Lome III Which Way Africa Governments," *Lome Briefings*, No. 3 of 1983.

Traore, Ali : Bilan et perspectives des developpements agricole et industriel en Cote d'Ivoire et leurs rapports mutuels in Hamid Ait Amara et Bernard Founou-Tchuigoua *L'agriculture africaine en crise, dans ses rapports avec l'Etat, l'industrialisation et la paysannerie*, l'Hamattan 1989.

Turok , Ben "Zambia's System of State Capitalism" Africa Development

UN. 1984. "Committee for Development Planning Statement", New York

Unity in Action Among Liberation Movements", the *Southern Africa Political and Economic Monthly (SAPEM)*, Vol.4, No.1, October, 1990.

W. Ouoch Kossura : Relations entre l'agriculture et l'industrialisation au Kenya

Walton, C. 1984. "Lessons From East African Agriculture - Review of the Design of Bank Agricultural Projects in the Region over 1972 - 82 Shows Mixed Results" Finance and Development 21.1

Wassink, D. 1978. "Economic Development with Unlimited Finances: Foreign Exchange Surplus in OPEC Countries" *Rivista Internazionale di Scienze Economiche e Commerciali* XXV

Weeks, J. 1973. "Uneven Sectoral Development and the Role of the State" IDS (Sussex) Bulletin 5.2 -3

Wheeler, Joseph "Subsaharan African Thirty Years From Now", *Observateur de l'OCDE*, no 143, November 1986.

World Bank commodity price trends 1988-89 ed.

World Bank, 1981. Accelerated Development in Sub-Saharan Africa: An Agenda For Action Report no.338, Washington, D.C. [The "Berg" Report]

World Bank, 1984. Towards Sustained Development in Sub-Saharan Africa: A Joint Program of Action Washington, D.C. The "Please" Report.

World Bank, 1989. *Sub-Saharan Africa: From Crisis to Sustainable Growth Washington*, D.C.

Zattler, J. 1989. "The Effects of Structural Adjustment Programmes" Intereconomics Nov. - Dec.

Ziemann, W. and M. Lanzendorfer. 1977. 'The State in Peripheral Societies' in: R. Miliband and J. Seville eds. *The Socialist Register.*

Zimbabwe's First Decade: What of the Next?", Editorial in *"Southern Africa Political and Economic Monthly (SAPEM)*, Vol.3, No.7, April, 1990

Index